ROBERT ROGERS, *Ranger*

MAJOR ROBERT ROGERS,

Commander in Chief of the INDIANS *in the Back Settlements of* AMERICA.

Publish'd as the Act directs Oct.r 1 1776 by Thos Hart London.

ROBERT ROGERS,
Ranger

THE RISE *AND* FALL
OF AN AMERICAN ICON

MARTIN KLOTZ

WESTHOLME
Yardley

Facing title page: "Major Robert Rogers," by Thomas Hart, London, 1776.
This iconic portrait of Rogers is not drawn from life and is generally regarded as
fanciful. There are no known portraits of Rogers taken from life. (*Anne S. K. Brown
Military Collection, Brown University Library*)

Westholme Publishing, LLC
904 Edgewood Road
Yardley, Pennsylvania 19067
Visit our Web site at www.westholmepublishing.com

ISBN: 978-1-59416-429-3

Also available as an eBook.

Printed in the United States of America.

CONTENTS

ILLUSTRATIONS

Maps

Halftones

An unnumbered gallery follows page 80

William Shirley

Frederick Haldimand

William Johnson

Thomas Gage

Lord Loudoun

Marquis de Montcalm

Johnathan Carver

Charles Townshend

Israel Putnam

George Augustus Howe

Jeffery Amherst

William Howe

A Perspective View of the Battle fought near Lake George on the 8th of Sepr. 1755

AUTHOR'S NOTE

AT the time of the French and Indian War, all Europeans, whether British, French, or colonial, referred to Native Americans as "Indians," and this is the term consistently used in contemporaneous written sources. It seemed to me unnecessarily awkward to use terminology in the text that is at odds with the language of source documents, so I have generally used "Indians," while sometimes substituting "indigenous peoples" or "native population." Similarly, I have used the traditional tribal names by which Indian nations were known to Europeans at the time, and which appear in contemporary sources, such as Abenaki, Mohawk, and Chippewa.

Money—income, expenses, and, especially, debts—is central to any discussion of Rogers' career, and it is helpful to have at least a rough idea of what monetary amounts in the eighteenth century translate into in today's money. The benchmark currency in colonial America was the British pound sterling (£), and at least one authority estimates that a British pound sterling at the time of the French and Indian War had a value equivalent to roughly $200 today.[1] In addition to the British pound, each colony had its own currency, also designated in pounds, shillings, and pence. Colonial currencies typically traded at a discount to British currency, usually in the range of 10 to 20 percent, but varying over time and from colony to colony. For convenience and ease of calculation, I have used the ratio £1:$200 throughout this book, but this is only a rough approximation that overstates by some amount values given in colonial currencies.

Eighteenth-century writers, no matter how well educated, were both erratic and idiosyncratic in their spelling, capitalization, and punctuation, and words sometimes had different meanings in the eighteenth century than they have today. In most instances, the writer's message is readily apparent, but, when necessary, I have added a translation or explanation in brackets.

PREFACE

ROBERT ROGERS, commander of Rogers' Rangers during the French and Indian War, is an iconic figure in the history of the American frontier. His fame and reputation at their peak place him alongside legends like Daniel Boone, Davy Crockett, and Kit Carson. Historian John F. Ross wrote that Rogers was, while still in his twenties, "North America's first celebrity."[1] Rogers' biographer Gary Zaboly noted that "[A]fter Benjamin Franklin he was the most famous American-born celebrity of the 1750s and 1760s."[2] In the twentieth century, he was the subject of a historical novel, a feature film starring Spencer Tracy, a television series starring Keith Larsen and Buddy Ebsen, and numerous favorable biographies; more recently, he was played by Angus Macfadyen in the miniseries *Turn*. He is widely regarded as the spiritual father of the U.S. Army Green Berets, the U.S. Navy Seals, and other special operations military units.

Part of Rogers' allure is that his strengths and accomplishments seem so quintessentially American. He was neither wealthy nor well-educated, but a self-made product of the frontier. Although, like many colonials, he was in awe of the British aristocracy, he chafed at the rigid, tradition-bound British military structure and routinely sought to circumvent it. He butted heads repeatedly with Thomas Gage, the supercilious British military commander in the colonies whom Americans have always loved to hate. His quixotic obsession with discovering the Northwest Passage, which inspired Kenneth Roberts' historical novel of the same name, seemed born of the American faith in limitless possibility.

His drive to get ahead, to get rich, to improve his status, would have res-
onated with de Tocqueville.

Yet this quintessentially American celebrity fought as a Loyalist in
the Revolutionary War, during which his principal exploit was the capture, through deception, of the Patriot spy Nathan Hale. Ruined by alcohol and profligate living, he died in obscurity in London, completely
estranged from his American friends and family. What explains his me-
teoric rise and his long, depressing fall?

Rogers undeniably had great personal strengths. He was brave to the
point of near fearlessness. He was physically robust, always the one to
cover the retreat, carry the wounded, or go for help when no one else
could carry on. He was an intrepid explorer who wrote with eloquence
about the splendors of the American frontier. He was bold and uncon-
ventional, good at thinking outside the box. He was an outstanding scout
and intelligence gatherer who provided invaluable service to a British
army inexperienced in woodland warfare.

At the same time, Rogers had enormous weaknesses that undermined
his ability to lead effectively. His boldness was never tempered by judgment, and he was prone to grandiose schemes that came to nothing or,
worse, to disaster. Although he was accomplished at scouting, gathering
intelligence, and conducting small-unit raids, he was at best a mediocre
leader in more significant engagements. His best-known battles were defeats, several of them catastrophic or nearly so, often brought on by his
tactical or strategic blunders. He did not have the discipline, the orga-
nizational or managerial skills, or the strategic vision to be an important
military leader: the Ranger force he created was widely regarded as
worthless except when some portion of that unit was under his personal
command on a specific, well-defined mission.

Rogers' constant self-promotion damaged his reputation with peers
and superiors, who believed that press coverage of minor achievements
had gone to his head. His outside-the-box thinking was generally driven
by the prospect of personal benefit rather than genuine creativity. He
was intentionally and routinely insubordinate, deliberately antagonizing
superiors whose support was necessary for his own advancement.

Rogers was financially irresponsible in the military, in business, and
in his personal life. From 1760 on, he was perpetually in debt and frequently in debtors prison. Compelling evidence shows that these debts
resulted from gambling, extravagant living, and poor business decisions.
His own excuse, that his financial difficulties stemmed from advancing

personal funds to support his professional military obligations and then failing to receive adequate reimbursement from the army, has been accepted uncritically by his biographers but does not withstand analysis.

These professional failings were matched by troubling character traits. Rogers was dishonest and unprincipled, regularly resorting to falsehoods and fraud, especially in financial matters. He was cocky and conceited, with a consistently inflated sense of his own merit. He had a keen sense of playing to an audience, insisting that his financial distress derived solely from his selfless public service or piously assuring his London audience that scalping was a "barbarous custom" of the Indians.[3] In fact, consistent with the brutality of frontier warfare at the time, he routinely scalped his own victims for bounty money. He was a callous, irresponsible, abusive husband and putative father. He was a chronic alcoholic whose drinking sapped his judgment and dominated the second half of his life.

Rogers' personal and professional strengths and weaknesses were largely fixed long before he achieved renown. They are on full display during his participation in a counterfeiting conspiracy in 1754-55, an episode that nearly brought his career to an end before it had begun. These fixed strengths and weaknesses led to a career that peaked early, that was never as successful as he and the press portrayed it, and that degenerated into a long and steep decline.

In all his exploits, Rogers was a fascinating character, embodying the larger-than-life American personality that his admirers find attractive. It is therefore supremely ironic that this deeply American figure never found a comfortable place in America, where his peers viewed him with suspicion and dislike. Instead, it was his aristocratic patrons in London, who knew him mostly from his own self-description, who gave him his most valuable opportunities. He relished being able twice to kiss George III's hand; he aspired to a knighthood; he never stopped penning sycophantic pleas for appointments to powerful British officials; there never was any serious doubt that he would align himself with the Loyalist cause in the colonies. England, not America, provided Rogers his hope for further advancement, and when the British cause failed in America, he became an anathema on both sides of the Atlantic.

PART ONE

RISE TO CELEBRITY

CHAPTER ONE

THE EARLY YEARS

ROBERT ROGERS was born in November 1731 in Methuen, Massachusetts, a frontier town on the Merrimack River about thirty miles north of Boston and about thirty miles southwest of Portsmouth, New Hampshire. He was the fifth of ten children—six boys and four girls—born to James and Mary Rogers.[1] His older brother James, four years his senior, and his younger brother Richard, two years his junior, would both serve under Robert as Ranger officers during the French and Indian War. James, in Robert's shadow for much of his life, emerged during the Revolutionary War. A Loyalist like Robert, who by then had clearly fallen under the influence of alcohol, James proved a more effective proponent of the British cause and ultimately became the leader of a colony of Loyalists who relocated to the northern shore of Lake Ontario after the conclusion of the Revolutionary War.

James and Mary Rogers were Scotch-Irish emigres who came to Massachusetts from the area of Londonderry in the north of Ireland. Able to purchase passage to America, rather than having their passage paid as part of a contract to become indentured servants upon arrival, they were relatively well-off compared to other immigrants.[2] The couple purchased land for a small farm in Methuen.

In 1738, James Rogers and a close friend, Joseph Pudney, purchased shares of land totaling about 365 acres each in a tract known as "Great Meadows" about thirty miles northwest of Methuen. In the spring of 1739, Rogers and Pudney relocated their families to Great Meadows.[3] If Methuen was a frontier town, Great Meadows was almost completely isolated. No one else lived in the immediate vicinity. The nearest town, Rumford, now Concord, New Hampshire, was ten miles away and reachable only by a long hike through wilderness.[4]

In connection with his move to Great Meadows, James Rogers sold the family farm in Methuen, receiving cash and land in exchange. A portion of the purchase price was a sixty-acre parcel of undeveloped land in Merrimack, Massachusetts, which James put in trust for Robert, who would become the legal owner upon reaching age twenty-one in 1752.[5] Presumably James made similar arrangements for other of his children.

When the Rogers and Pudney families moved to Great Meadows in 1739, the parcel was still part of Massachusetts Bay Colony. It became part of New Hampshire in 1741, when New Hampshire became a colony of its own. The Rogers and Pudney families prospered in their new homes, planting orchards, growing crops, and raising livestock.

Frontier life inevitably involved an uneasy relationship between indigenous populations and European settlers. Mutually beneficial trade encouraged peaceful co-existence. But competition for scarce resources—hunting and trapping rights being particularly important to the Indians—could easily lead to disputes that triggered violence even in the most peaceful of times. The worst frontier violence tended to accompany chronic outbreaks of warfare between the British and the French empires in their rivalry for control of North America. In these wars, the Indians were natural allies of the French. Indians correctly perceived that the French had limited interest in seizing Indian lands for settlement, preferring to engage in trade, especially of furs, that did not threaten Indian land stewardship or traditional hunting and trapping. British colonists, by contrast, were notorious for their voracious appetite for land. When France and England were at war, the French found it relatively easy to recruit Indian allies to raid British settlements, often with devastating effect. Everyone on the frontier knew the most significant events in this history of episodic conflict, both important victories and important defeats.

Most recently the British and French in North America had fought Queen Anne's War, which ended in 1713. There followed an extended period of relative amity on the Massachusetts and New Hampshire frontiers. In 1744, however, King George's War broke out, and the frontier population nervously braced for Indian raids. Initially, none were forthcoming, but by 1746 raiding began in earnest, and at times of maximum danger Rogers, Pudney, and other settlers would abandon their farms and move their families and livestock temporarily to the relative safety of Rumford. Rumford contained multiple buildings fortified for defensive purposes and served as a muster point for mounted volunteers to patrol the vicinity.[6]

During stays in Rumford, the teenaged Robert and his brothers performed garrison duty and, on occasion, accompanied patrols by mounted militia. Robert does not appear to have engaged in fighting, but he would have heard detailed descriptions of Indian raids and their effects.[7]

In early 1748, when the war was winding down and the worst danger seemed to have passed, the Rogers and Pudney families briefly returned once again to their farms. A late Indian raiding party targeted the area south of Rumford. Warned by a patrol that had discovered signs of the raiders, the families fled back to Rumford. Raiders ravaged the undefended properties, burning buildings, chopping down orchards, and stealing valuables.[8] Although Rogers and Pudney eventually rebuilt, the loss was painful and the event traumatic.

After King George's War, the area around the Rogers and Pudney farms saw a dramatic influx of settlers, among them the family of Archibald Stark.[9] Robert soon became close friends with one of Archibald's sons, John.

Caleb Stark, John Stark's grandson, leaves the following portrait of Robert Rogers during this period, presumably drawn from family oral history: "He was six feet in stature, well-proportioned, and one of the most athletic men of his time—well known in all the trials of strength or activity among the young men of his vicinity, and for several miles around."[10] Although no contemporaneous portrait of Rogers exists, characterizations of him stress his size and strength. A London newspaper described him as "a handsome Giant,"[11] while *The Scots Magazine* described him in 1775 as "a strong, robust, and bold man."[12] Physical strength would feature in many of his exploits, and his bearing would influence many of his interactions with contemporaries. To strength and athleticism, and perhaps because of them, one can add the traits of self-confidence and fearlessness, although in him these traits too easily veered into conceit and recklessness.

Apart from his limited service as a teenager in King George's War, little is known about Rogers' doings prior to the early 1750s. His own description of his teens and early twenties is generic: "Between the years 1743 and 1755, my manner of life was such as to lead me to a general acquaintance both with the British and French settlements in North America, and especially with the uncultivated desart, the mountains, valleys, rivers, lakes, and several passages that lay between and contiguous to the said settlements. Nor did I content myself with the accounts received from Indians, or the information of hunters, but traveled over large tracts of the country myself, which tended not more to gratify my curiosity, than to inure me to hardships, and, without vanity, I may say, to qualify me for the very service I have since been employed in."[13] Presumably, these extensive travels were not idle wanderings but purposeful undertakings such as hunting, trapping, and perhaps trading.

Rogers' friend John Stark engaged in similar roaming. In April 1752, on a hunting and trapping trip some fifty miles north of Great Meadows with his brother and two friends, Stark was surprised and captured by Indians. Although Stark attempted to deceive them, the Indians soon discovered the remainder of the party, killing one and capturing another, with only Stark's brother escaping.[14]

Although different Indian bands of varying size lived along the frontier and periodically fought with English settlers, one of the best-organized, most warlike, and most feared were the Abenaki. Abenaki raiders destroyed the Rogers and Pudney farms in 1748. The tribe's chief town was St. Francis on the St. Francis River, south of the St. Lawrence River in Quebec and north of the New Hampshire border. St. Francis was a permanent settlement every bit as substantial and well-organized as its European counterparts. The town contained more than fifty large houses, most of squared timber, but some of plank and some of stone, arranged along a main avenue and a central square, on which stood a council house and a wood-framed Roman Catholic church steepled and painted white. The town was served by missionary priests of the Society of Jesus, known as Jesuits, the Abenaki having converted to Catholicism in about 1700. The town had a population of about nine hundred, including roughly 120 fighting men.[15]

Reflecting the fluid intermingling of populations on the frontier, one of the principal war chiefs of the Abenaki, Joseph-Louis Gill, was European, the son of two European captives who had been adopted by the Abenaki. Gill married the daughter of an Abenaki chieftain and they had several children.[16] Tribes commonly adopted captives, as manpower shortages chronically bedeviled frontier Indian groups.

The Abenaki who captured Stark and his companion were from St. Francis. They marched the pair north to the town. A white captive, particularly one found bearing arms on Indian land, could expect in wartime to be tortured and killed, but with England and France temporarily at peace Stark and his companion were slated for ransom, not death. Stark's stoic bravery particularly impressed his captors, who treated both prisoners well. Stark remembered his three-month sojourn with the Abenaki fondly all his life.[17]

Stark and his companion, along with other captives, were ransomed in July 1752. In the ransom negotiations, the Abenaki complained bitterly about incursions on their lands, forbidding British settlers to "kill a single Beaver, or take a single stick of timber on the lands we inhabit." They made clear, however, that they would be happy to sell or trade such items. The Abenaki were particularly upset by colonial surveying parties, which they took as evidence of the settlers' predatory intent toward Indian lands.[18]

Despite the Abenaki objection, Stark and Rogers participated early the next year in a covert surveying expedition to an area of rich meadowland along the Connecticut River known as the Lower Coos. The expedition's goal was to survey a passage to the Lower Coos from more settled areas further south, then to survey a location for a possible settlement at the Lower Coos, "the finest land on the Continent" for farming. Stark was the expedition's "pilot," or guide. Rogers was a "guard." Despite attempts at secrecy, the Abenaki learned about the expedition after the fact and threatened war if the settlement proposition went forward. The plan was abandoned.[19]

In the winter of 1752–53, Robert's father James went to visit an old friend, Ebenezer Ayer, at Ayer's hunting camp near the Rogers farm. James was wearing a bearskin coat and hat. In the half-light of dusk, Ayer mistook his friend for a bear and shot him. James Rogers died a short while later.[20]

When an inventory of James Rogers' estate was completed in the summer of 1753, it was valued at £1,944, "a considerable amount in those days."[21] The beneficiaries were wife Mary and his sons.[22] They had had six, but one, John, appears to have died in childhood.[23] Robert presumably expected to inherit a proportionate share of this "considerable amount."

CHAPTER TWO

THE

COUNTERFEITER

I N LATE 1754, Robert Rogers found himself in a difficult situation. Like many colonial Americans, he aspired to wealth and believed land ownership was the quickest and surest way to achieve it. In November 1752, Robert, having reached his majority, became the legal owner of a small parcel of land in the town of Merrimack, Massachusetts, that his father had previously placed in trust for him. A year later, after James Rogers' death, an acquaintance, William Alld, offered to sell Robert a larger, more attractive, adjacent parcel of two hundred acres for £320. Rogers jumped at the opportunity. Perhaps he planned to use his expected inheritance to cover much of the purchase price. He gave Alld a note for £320, with the first half to be paid by May 31, 1754.[1]

By the due date, Rogers had paid only £67. With Rogers in default, Alld sued to collect the entire £320 in September 1754. Rogers, who had no ability to pay, risked having a large judgment entered against him just as he was entering adulthood.[2]

At about this time, one of the great rogues of American colonial history, John Sullivan, was in New Hampshire seeking collaborators to help distribute counterfeit currency to be printed on plates he had created.

In New Hampshire, as in other colonies, counterfeiting was a capital crime. Sullivan appears to have been in New Hampshire for months, boarding with different residents for a week or so before relocating. At each stop, as an enticement to his hosts and their neighbors, he displayed plates for printing bogus New Hampshire currency and large quantities of already-printed counterfeit money. A significant number of people agreed to join the scheme. Sullivan's last stop was the farm of Edward Martin in Goff's Town, near the Rogers homestead.[3]

Rogers, his younger brother Richard, and other locals came to the Martin farm to meet Sullivan and hear his pitch. Sullivan, going by the alias "John McDaniel," was a colorful but frightening confidence man. As a punishment for past counterfeiting, authorities had cropped his ears and branded his cheeks.[4] He clearly intimidated many meeting-goers. One, John McCurdy, declared he would have no part of the scheme and left. Others appeared hesitant, causing Sullivan to explode in frustration: "Damn you for a pack of fools."[5]

Rogers was receptive. Sullivan gave him a bogus twenty-shilling note for pasturing Sullivan's horse for a few days, a sum suspiciously large—about $200 in today's money—had the note been real. He also asked Rogers to find him three yoke of oxen, promising to pay well.[6] Leaving the meeting, Rogers ran into McCurdy. He asked McCurdy if he knew who Sullivan was. When McCurdy said that he did, Rogers responded "then Damn you say nothing."[7]

Rogers did procure six oxen for Sullivan from his friend John Stark, paying in genuine currency. When he arrived a few days later with the oxen and Sullivan's horse at the location where he had agreed to meet Sullivan, Sullivan had left, likely quitting New Hampshire because his counterfeiting was under investigation. Rogers resold the oxen.[8] Stark later asked Rogers what had become of the oxen. Rogers said he sold them to another party. He complained of having been "Cheated" by Sullivan, who had promised to pay him "a Large Quantity of Counterfeit money" but in his haste to depart had not done so. According to Stark, Rogers said "he would not be Concerned anymore in any such things."[9]

New Hampshire authorities, alarmed by evidence of counterfeiting, were investigating. In early February 1755, they issued warrants for nineteen suspects, including Rogers, and nine witnesses, including Stark. Rogers was arrested and examined under oath on February 7. The four examining justices included Joseph Blanchard, Jr., who apparently had declined an earlier invitation from Rogers to join the counterfeiting conspiracy, and his father, a prominent militia colonel.[10]

Rogers' testimony was self-serving and improbable. Pleading not guilty to the charge of "Making & Passing Counterfeit Bills," he acknowledged meeting Sullivan, who was then, according to all the witnesses, calling himself John McDaniel. Rogers denied knowing that Sullivan "could make money on plates he had or designed." He said he had been hunting near Edward Martin's farm in Goff's Town and had met Sullivan there. He provided basic details of his interaction with Sullivan, including the agreement to pasture Sullivan's horse, an agreement for Sullivan to buy oxen from him at market price, and the departed Sullivan's failure to complete these transactions. According to Rogers, Sullivan assured him the money he would use to pay "would go through all the Laws in Any of the provinces and maintain his money Good." Why would Sullivan make such an odd comment? asked the examining justices. Rogers, who admitted that Sullivan showed him a "book" that was "full" of money, said he asked Sullivan if the money was good.[11]

"Did you ever propose to any Body to become Partners in Counterfeiting Bills?" asked the justices. Rogers had evidently approached Blanchard, so he answered affirmatively. He admitted to having pitched Blanchard on the scheme but insisted he had done so "Only to Discover if [he was] concerned [involved in the counterfeiting]." This was a ridiculous explanation. Rogers' defense was that he did not know that Sullivan was a counterfeiter or that his money was not genuine. Why would he want to discover if the younger Blanchard was "concerned" in an activity of which he was unaware? And Blanchard, one of the examining justices, obviously knew this statement was false. Rogers went on to emphasize that Blanchard had told him "he was not Concerned nor Never Should be in such a Devilish Act and hoped that men would be Honest & Strongly Cautioned me against being concerned in Any Such Thing."[12]

Rogers' denial of any knowledge of counterfeiting was hardly believable given the circumstances of his encounter with Sullivan. The testimony of McCurdy and Stark made clear that Rogers knowingly accepted a counterfeit twenty-shilling note from Sullivan for pasturing his horse and expected to receive an even larger sum of counterfeit currency for the oxen.

The justices found the evidence sufficient to hold Rogers and other defendants, though not Rogers' brother Richard, for trial, to start five days later, on February 12. In the interim, Rogers was released on a £500 bond.[13]

New Hampshire authorities were not yet aware of the most damning witness against Rogers: Carty Gilman, an Exeter, New Hampshire, leather worker. At some point, Rogers had recruited Gilman to join the counterfeiting conspiracy. Gilman would later testify that Rogers gave him counterfeit currency in payment for boots and other goods, as well as an additional sum of counterfeit currency to pass for his own bene- fit.[14] One of Rogers' first acts after his release on bond was to write Gilman, imploring him "for gods sake do the work that you promised me you would"—i.e., destroy any counterfeit currency or other evidence of counterfeiting—"for whie should an onest [honest] Man be Killed."[15] Several months later, when Rogers was already off campaigning in up- state New York, New Hampshire authorities served a summons on Gilman for his testimony and caught him attempting to swallow the in- criminating message from Rogers. The sheriff serving the summons seized not only the note but also a quantity of counterfeit currency in Gilman's possession.[16] Evidently, when Stark testified that Rogers told him he would no longer be "Concerned" in matters involving counter- feit currency, either he was trying to protect Rogers or Rogers had de- liberately misled Stark to protect himself.

In May 1756, New York authorities hanged Sullivan for his counter- feiting activities.[17]

EARLY 1755 saw the colonies beginning preparations for an expected war with France. Massachusetts Governor William Shirley, who was also the senior British military commander in the colonies, began a drive in January 1755 to recruit two thousand colonial volunteers for a campaign in French-held Nova Scotia. Rogers, having penned his appeal to Gilman, hustled south and persuaded a Massachusetts recruiting officer that he could raise twenty-five New Hampshire volunteers to serve in the Massachusetts force. This would entitle him to an appointment as a lieutenant in the Nova Scotia expedition and perhaps put him out of reach of legal proceedings in New Hampshire. For reasons not recorded, his trial for counterfeiting was adjourned and never rescheduled.[18]

New Hampshire authorities were outraged that Rogers was attempt- ing to direct New Hampshire men to a Massachusetts campaign when New Hampshire was attempting to raise its own regiment to help attack

Crown Point, a French-held fort on Lake Champlain. Eager to placate New Hampshire, Rogers turned his men around and enrolled them in the New Hampshire regiment. Governor Shirley ordered his arrest for diverting men who had signed up to fight for Massachusetts. Shirley relented, however, and Rogers, for good measure, recruited twenty-five more men, for a total of fifty, for New Hampshire. This entitled him to the rank of captain of a company in the New Hampshire regiment, commanded by Colonel Joseph Blanchard, one of the justices who had ordered him tried for counterfeiting.[19]

In the spring of 1755, wartime priorities found Rogers, who only weeks earlier had faced trial, almost certain conviction, and career-crippling punishment for counterfeiting, on his way to Albany to join the campaign on the Lake George-Lake Champlain front. His friend John Stark was a lieutenant in the company, while John McCurdy, who had spurned the counterfeiting scheme, was one of the company's privates. Carty Gilman would sign up for service with Rogers a year later.[20] A complete unknown at the beginning of 1755, Rogers, within a year, would be "famous" throughout New England for his scouts and raids in the Lake George-Lake Champlain region.

Rogers' flirtation with counterfeiting features character traits that would recur throughout his career: a penchant for debt, boldness veering into recklessness, a willingness to flout the law and to lie to protect his interests, a view of himself as a victim rather than a wrongdoer, and a Houdini-like ability to escape disasters of his own creation.

CHAPTER THREE

EARLY RANGERING

COLONEL BLANCHARD'S New Hampshire regiment, with Captain Rogers at the head of his own company, arrived in Albany in August 1755. By the end of the month, the unit had moved forward to Fort Lyman, under construction on the banks of the Hudson River north of Albany and eventually renamed Fort Edward. The arrival of Blanchard's regiment allowed the commander of the colonial forces, William Johnson, to move further north to the southern shore of Lake George, where he began the construction of what was to become Fort William Henry, the jumping off point for a planned assault on the French Fort St. Frédéric at Crown Point on Lake Champlain.[1]

William Johnson had emigrated to the colonies in the 1730s, gradually assembling a large estate in the Mohawk River Valley northwest of Albany. He developed friendly relations with the neighboring Mohawk Indians and was adopted into their tribe. He had a Mohawk wife, Molly Brant, who was the older sister of prominent Mohawk chief Joseph Brant, and numerous European and Mohawk mistresses and children. He soon became New York's primary representative to the Mohawk nation. Although he lacked formal military training, Johnson was active during King George's War as a leader of mixed forces of local militia and Iroquois Indians allied with the British. His force at Lake George included almost two hundred Mohawk fighters.[2]

The Mohawks were the easternmost nation of the six-nation Iroquois Confederacy, the most important Indian polity in the northern colonies, and Johnson's close relationship with the Mohawks was instrumental in bringing them and other Iroquois tribes into an alliance with the British. The other five Iroquois nations—the Oneida, the Tuscarora, the Onondaga, the Cayuga, and the Seneca—generally did not actively support the British, but their disinclination to fight their Mohawk relatives kept them mostly neutral rather than allying with the French. Johnson's influence was instrumental in limiting the impact of France's natural Indian alliances, even though most Indians did side with France.

The first major battle of the French and Indian War, Braddock's catastrophic defeat by the French and allied Indians at the Battle of the Monongahela, took place on July 9, 1755. British documents recovered on the battlefield alerted the French to a British plan to have Johnson move against Fort St. Frédéric, and the French shifted significant forces under Baron Dieskau to that front. Although Dieskau's force of 1,500 was smaller than Johnson's more than three thousand, which was divided between Fort Lyman and the southern shore of Lake George, the baron's troops included both many well-trained army regulars and Canadian militia and Indian allies highly experienced in woodland warfare. Dieskau, confident he could outfight Johnson's poorly trained militia, moved in a preemptive strike against the British at Fort Lyman and Lake George.[3]

The Battle of Lake George took place on September 8, 1755. Dieskau's original plan was to bypass Johnson at Lake George, capture Fort Lyman (renamed Fort Edward after the battle), and cut Johnson off from Albany. His Indian allies refused to cooperate with this plan, however, both because they did not want to make a frontal assault on a heavily fortified position and because Fort Lyman, unlike Johnson's camp, was not on Indian land and so was less of an affront to Indian sovereignty. Dieskau acquiesced, turned around, and headed back north, approaching Johnson's camp from the south. Johnson learned of Dieskau's original designs on Fort Lyman but not of his abandonment of that plan. He rushed reinforcements south to aid Fort Lyman, a large body of Mohawks in the vanguard. The French ambushed this force, inflicting heavy casualties and driving it back to Lake George.[4]

A day-long battle ensued, with the French and the Indians attacking Johnson's camp at Lake George. The colonial militia performed better than expected. Johnson successfully fought off the attack and in the process wounded and captured the French commander Dieskau. Although the British colonial forces sustained heavier casualties than the French, it was the French who retreated to Crown Point. They did not resume the offensive for the remainder of 1755.[5]

Victory at the Battle of Lake George restored British spirits badly shaken only two months earlier by Braddock's defeat. Johnson was knighted for his achievement, given a cash award of £5,000, roughly $1 million in today's money, and promoted to the British, rather than colonial, position of Superintendent of Indian Affairs for the northern colonies. In this position, he reported directly to the king, not a colonial governor, and commanded a salary of £600 per year.[6]

Johnson's Mohawks suffered disproportionately in the battle, losing forty dead, including their principal chief, and many others wounded. They left the army to return to their villages to mourn their losses. This left Johnson temporarily without the scouting force on which he relied for intelligence regarding the enemy. That vacuum presented Robert Rogers with the opportunity of a lifetime.[7]

Johnson's military mandate for 1755 was to attack and capture the French fort at Crown Point. To accomplish this, Massachusetts Governor Shirley, overall British commander in the colonies, ordered him to construct a road suitable to convey heavy artillery from Albany to Crown Point and support an attack on the French there. Johnson's dilemma was twofold. He did not have a good sense of the logistics required by his assigned march, nor did he know how large a force opposed him. Dieskau had brought only a portion of his army into action for the Battle of Lake George. Johnson did not know how many fighting troops the baron had in all and whether those men were at Crown Point, Ticonderoga, or the "carrying place," the portage between the north end of Lake George and Ticonderoga on Lake Champlain. Nor did Johnson know if his opponents' plans were offensive or defensive. This void was aggravated by serious problems with Johnson's own forces. Though expected to take the offensive, his army was almost entirely militia rather than British army regulars. The militia regiments, from different colonies, had been late mustering at Albany, and their enlistments would soon begin to expire, leaving only a small window of time for further campaigning. Discipline was poor, morale was low, and Johnson was having difficulty keeping his forward positions supplied.[8] The combination of colonial officers' "Obstinacy and Ignorance" and their troops' "lassitude" and refusal to do construction work prevented Johnson from building an adequate fortification at Lake George.[9] Although Johnson had defeated a smaller French attacking force, it was clear to him that his army was inferior to the French, man for man, in discipline, motivation, and experience. By the end of November, Johnson was asking to be relieved of military responsibilities so he could concentrate on Indian affairs, his area of greatest interest and expertise.[10]

To address at least the informational aspects of Johnson's multiple headaches, Colonel Blanchard proposed Rogers for scouting duty. Despite having ordered Rogers arrested and bound over for trial on counterfeiting charges earlier in the year, Blanchard had plainly concluded, over the course of his regiment's march to the front, that Rogers was a person of talent and bravery. Within a week of the British victory at Lake George, Rogers was off on his first scouting expedition.

His objective was Fort St. Frédéric at Crown Point. His dual mission was to determine whether it was feasible to bring artillery overland from the British position at the southern end of Lake George to Crown Point for an assault on the French fort—it was not—and to assess the strength of French forces at Crown Point. With four hand-picked men, two from his own unit and two from a Connecticut company, Rogers, traveling by night, proceeded by boat down Lake George to its northern end.[11] He left the two Connecticut men with the boat, then trekked overland to Crown Point through territory controlled by France's Indian allies. In darkness, Rogers and his companions passed through two lines of sentries to the walls of the fort, which they explored. They hiked up a nearby hill where, at dawn, Rogers sketched a map of the fort and environs. He determined the French force there to be five to six hundred. The three men withdrew undetected to the north shore of Lake George, en route passing close enough to conclude that the garrison at Ticonderoga included a significant French force whose size they were unable to determine. At the rendezvous point on the north shore of Lake George, Rogers was dismayed to find that the two Connecticut men had fled in the boat, leaving him and his two New Hampshire volunteers to walk back twenty-five miles to Johnson's original camp, where Fort William Henry was under construction.[12]

It requires some context to understand the sheer audacity of Rogers' first scout. The woodlands of the Lake George/Lake Champlain region were controlled almost completely by France's Indian allies, known for their ferocity and horrifying tortures. Colonial troops were terrified of them, especially on small-unit missions. Few people volunteered to scout, many refused to go even if ordered to do so, and those who went under orders typically turned back at the first hint of danger without obtaining any useful information. Individuals and small groups in isolated positions commonly abandoned those positions out of fear, as evidently happened with the two Connecticut men Rogers left with the concealed boat. When the British high command in Albany expressed skepticism about Rogers' reports and requested corroboration by other scouts, one of Johnson's aides responded bluntly that he "did not believe there was another Man in the Army woud go."[13] For Rogers to get to the walls at Crown Point and back without injury was a bold and stunning feat.

A short while later, Rogers was again in the field, this time attempting to determine the strength of French and Indian forces in the Ticonderoga area. With five men, he proceeded to within sight of what was to become Fort Carillon, which the French were just beginning to construct. The British would rename this bastion Fort Ticonderoga after capturing it in 1759. Rogers found French troops involved in constructing the fort. He also reported another body of French and Indians on the north shore of Lake George, controlling the portage linking Lake George and Lake Champlain. These forces appeared to number several thousand.[14] This information was of critical importance to Johnson. Combined with Rogers' intelligence from Crown Point, his new report meant that the French had a force in the field equal in size to Johnson's and, in Johnson's mind, much superior in quality.

As Rogers and his party were returning from the Ticonderoga scout, hiding with their canoe on the north shore of Lake George and waiting for a safe opportunity to paddle back to the British position at the south end of the lake, a canoe with nine Indians and a Frenchman came within range of their hiding place. Rogers' men opened fire, killing or wounding half a dozen of the enemy, then jumped into their canoe to pursue the retreating Indians. Soon additional Indian canoes appeared, and Rogers' men found themselves outnumbered, but they were able to avoid entrapment, out-paddle their pursuers, and return to Fort William Henry with no casualties. The exploit made Rogers a "camp hero," "the army's new champion."[15]

Rogers' information confirmed Johnson's doubts about taking the offensive against the French with his undisciplined, poorly supplied militia

force. Councils of war at Fort William Henry repeatedly voted against
an attack on either Ticonderoga or Crown Point, citing poor roads, insufficient wagons for transport, illness, cold, and hunger among the
troops, poor morale, and other factors.[16] Rogers' intelligence irritated
Johnson's superiors, who regarded the scout's report as an excuse for inactivity. Shirley repeatedly pressed Johnson to attack Ticonderoga,[17] insisting, without citing a basis, that the French had fewer than seven
hundred troops at Crown Point and Ticonderoga combined.[18] When a
French deserter reported that the French had only a few hundred troops
at Ticonderoga, and no artillery, New York political leaders seized on
this information to discredit Rogers. Johnson aide Peter Wraxall, reporting on a meeting with senior officials in Albany, told Johnson the view in
Albany was that "Capt. Rogers Intelligence from Ticonderoga [is] not
to be depended on."[19] New York Deputy Secretary Goldsbrow Banyar
complained to Johnson that he did not "believe a single Syllable of
Rogers' information," arguing that the deserter's information was inher-
ently more reliable.[20] Johnson continued to credit Rogers, "a Brave and
honest Man," and pointed out that other scouts did not get close enough
to the enemy to obtain relevant information.[21] He did send out another
large scouting party that included Connecticut Captains Israel Putnam,
later of Revolutionary War fame, and Samuel Hunt. Putnam and Hunt
were unable to get within sight of Ticonderoga, but they reported a large
French and Indian force at the "carrying place," confirming Rogers' information.[22] As the fall wore on, evidence of French and Indian activity,
including reports from Mohawk scouts, consistently supported Rogers'
intelligence. To his reputation for bravery, he gained respect for being
able to get accurate, reliable information about the enemy.

Rogers continued to scout. In October 1755, with a party of four, including Israel Putnam, Rogers went by boat and foot to Crown Point,
hoping to take a prisoner who could be interrogated. The party crept
to within three hundred yards of the fort, where they hid overnight.
After daybreak, a single French soldier wandered away from the fort.
Rogers jumped from hiding and called on the soldier to surrender. The
man refused and pulled a knife. Rogers killed him with a musket shot
and scalped him within sight of the fort. This alerted the garrison, but
Rogers and his party outdistanced their pursuers, returning to British
lines without casualties. This incident generated Rogers' first press coverage, in the November 3, 1755, issue of the *Boston Gazette*.[23]

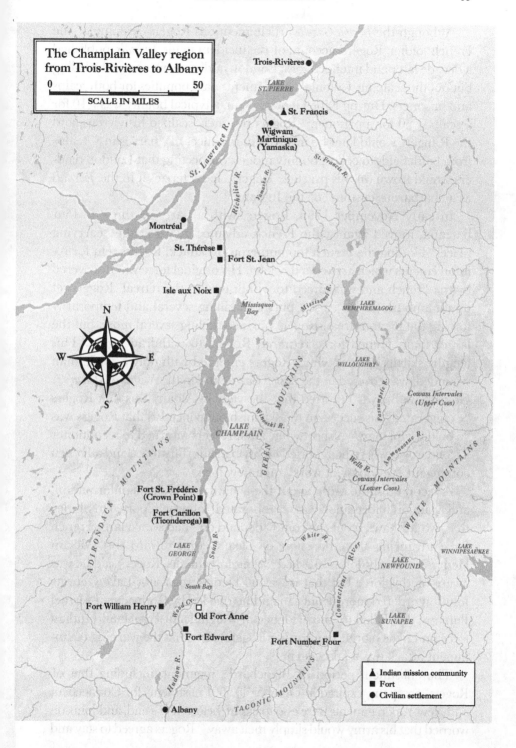

The Champlain Valley region from Trois-Rivières to Albany

0 — 50
SCALE IN MILES

Trois-Rivières
LAKE ST. PIERRE
▲ St. Francis
Wigwam Martinique (Yamaska)
St. Lawrence R.
Richelieu R.
Yamaska R.
St. Francis R.
Montréal
St. Thérèse ■
■ Fort St. Jean
Isle aux Noix ■
Missisquoi Bay
Missisquoi R.
LAKE MEMPHREMAGOG
N
W E
S
LAKE WILLOUGHBY
GREEN MOUNTAINS
Passumpsic R.
Cowass Intervales (Upper Coos)
LAKE CHAMPLAIN
Winooski R.
Wells R.
Ammonoosuc R.
Cowass Intervales (Lower Coos)
ADIRONDACK MOUNTAINS
WHITE MOUNTAINS
Fort St. Frédéric (Crown Point) ■
Fort Carillon (Ticonderoga) ■
White R.
LAKE WINNIPESAUKEE
LAKE GEORGE
South R.
Connecticut River
LAKE NEWFOUND
South Bay
Fort William Henry ■
Wood Cr.
□ Old Fort Anne
Fort Edward ■
Fort Number Four ■
LAKE SUNAPEE
Hudson R.
● Albany
TACONIC MOUNTAINS

▲ Indian mission community
■ Fort
● Civilian settlement

Although the *Boston Gazette* article mentions Rogers' scalping of the French soldier, Rogers' account of the incident in his *Journals*, published a decade later and intended for a London audience, mentions the killing but not the scalping. Colonial governments paid bounties for both scalps and prisoners. During King George's War, a typical bounty was £10 for a scalp, £20 for a prisoner.[24] Rogers routinely scalped his victims, and the Rangers would later be involved in instances of "harvesting" scalps from battlefields to collect bounty money. Suspecting that London readers would frown on this practice, Rogers characterizes it in the *Journals* as a "barbarous custom" of the Indians.[25]

In early November 1755, Rogers, with a party of thirty in four bateaux, moved against the French advance guard at the "carrying place." Finding the French too numerous to attack, Rogers sent for reinforcements which arrived a day later. His original force was discovered by the French and was forced to withdraw. On the retreat, Rogers set up an ambush for his closest pursuers, killing several and temporarily forcing the foe to retreat. Rogers pursued, killing several more, but the larger main French force required Rogers to withdraw again. This lengthy skirmish, from which Rogers emerged with only a single man wounded, was covered in the *Boston Gazette* and in the *New York Mercury*.[26] Goldsbrow Banyar reported that the view in Albany was that Rogers "exaggerated" his success in the skirmish but conceded that Rogers was "a bold useful man." A short while later, Rogers returned to reconnoiter Ticonderoga, where he reported eighty bateaux, fifty tents, and a French contingent "very busy at work" on a new fort.[27]

A second dispute arose about the accuracy of Rogers' information, and again his information was corroborated. Johnson reported to Shirley that two Mohawk scouts he could "depend on" had seen a large French force advancing along the shore of Lake George toward Fort William Henry. Nervously, Johnson asked for reinforcements. Rogers said he was aware of this force but that it was at Ticonderoga, not Lake George. Johnson ordered more scouts, including one led by Connecticut's Israel Putnam, that failed to find evidence of a significant French and Indian force on Lake George, confirming Rogers' view that the warning of imminent attack was a false alarm.[28]

The enlistment period of Blanchard's regiment, including that of Rogers' company, expired in October 1755. Enlistments for Connecticut and New York regiments were also to expire before year's end, and Johnson worried that his army would simply melt away.[29] Rogers agreed to stay and continue scouting through the winter and recruited militiamen to stay with him. Originally numbering ninety-five, this force by late November had shrunk to thirty-two,[30] whether because men deserted or because their commitment to stay was equivocal or of limited duration, and they took advantage of the fact that their enlistment period had expired to go home.

No clear arrangement was made for payments to troops who stayed through the winter of 1755–56. Rogers, who hardly expected to be responsible personally for paying these men, may have guaranteed that they would be paid.[31] No colony wanted to shoulder the entire (but fairly modest) burden of paying these troops, and, despite Rogers' repeated requests, not until early 1763 did New Hampshire finally appropriate the necessary funds.[32] Rogers does not appear to have sustained any significant out-of-pocket expense for the 1755–56 winter troops, but he was dogged about payment for years by demands and lawsuits, to his obvious and legitimate aggravation.

AFTER a month's leave, Rogers returned to the field in December 1755. In January 1756, on a scout with seventeen men, he captured and destroyed two sleighs with provisions on Lake Champlain, taking two prisoners. The *Boston Evening Post*, calling him "Capt. Rogers, the famous scouter," recounted the ambush on February 9, 1756.[33] Rogers staged more raids into enemy territory over the winter, burning buildings and killing livestock, while not engaging in significant combat.[34] In Boston to meet with Governor Shirley in March 1756, Rogers gave the *Connecticut Gazette* an account of these raids. In a story dated March 29, 1756, the *Gazette* reported Rogers' description of these raids, commenting that Rogers "has made himself famous in these Parts of America, by his Courage and Activity with his Scouting Parties near Crown Point."[35]

In addition to press attention, Rogers was also beginning to receive tokens of appreciation from the army and from the provincial government of New York. On March 1, 1756, the *Boston Gazette* reported that fellow officers in Albany had presented him with a "handsome Suit of Cloathes" and a spread of refreshments "for Him and His Men."[36] On February 27, 1756, the New York General Assembly voted him a cash gift of 125 Spanish pieces of eight for his "Extraordinary Courage, Conduct, and Diligence." The award was approved by Massachusetts Governor Shirley, the senior British military officer in the colonies.[37] The sum, the equivalent of about £40, or about $8,000 in today's money, was no mean reward for a twenty-four-year-old militia captain. Rogers penned a modest thank-you, promising to "exert my utmost in faithfully serving my God, my King, and Country, as an honest soldier" and expressing hope to have "the Pleasure of seeing our French and Indian Enemies subdued this Spring." The *Connecticut Gazette*, likely furnished with a copy of the letter by Rogers during his March 29 interview in Boston, printed a copy of it on April 3, 1756.[38] By now, in the words of one biographer, Rogers was already "North America's first celebrity."[39]

What explains this phenomenon? Rogers' accomplishments at this point, while attention-getting for their audacity, were of scant military significance. He had killed or captured perhaps a dozen of the enemy in small ambushes and skirmishes. His intelligence-gathering had strengthened Johnson's resolve in refusing to launch an ill-advised offensive, but the strategic balance on the Lake George/Lake Champlain front remained as before.

Part of the answer is context. As one biographer put it, "Robert Rogers' deeds . . . , small-scale though most of them were, gave the American colonists a morale boost through an otherwise inactive and discouraging winter."[40] Braddock's defeat had been an unmitigated disaster. Johnson's victory at Lake George had been welcome but not decisive, and he had not been able to follow up on it. On all other fronts, British and colonial forces were enduring a complete lack of success. Johnson's correspondence with his military and political superiors paints a depressing picture of an army almost paralyzed by incompetence, fear, and low morale. He complained that his troops were homesick and disinclined to work, that they refused to undertake dangerous scouting assignments because their enlistments were about to expire, and that if ordered to advance against the French they would refuse.[41] By contrast, Johnson found Rogers "the most active man in this Army."[42] His energy and his exploits were a lone bright spot for the British cause. His reputation in the colonies undoubtedly benefited from the fact that he was a homegrown product of the frontier.

An additional reason for Rogers' outsize fame is likely that then, as now, the people who get the most publicity are those who most avidly seek it. It is fair to wonder how the details of Rogers' exploits reached the Boston and New York press and to suspect that Rogers played a role. On at least one occasion, the March 29, 1756, *Connecticut Gazette* story, Rogers was the declared source of a favorable press report about him. His thank you note to the New York General Assembly reads as if intended for a wider audience, and Rogers likely gave a copy of it to the *Connecticut Gazette*, which published it within days of interviewing him.

The most interesting assessment of Rogers comes from William Johnson, who in later years became one of his greatest antagonists. In 1755, Johnson clearly held Rogers in high regard, and not solely because his intelligence reports supported Johnson's own views. Johnson repeatedly praised Rogers in his correspondence with his superiors. In an October 13, 1755, letter to New York Governor Charles Hardy, Johnson says that Rogers' "Bravery & Veracity stands very clear in my Opinion & of all who know him, though his Regt. is gone he remains here a Volunteer." Johnson continues: "I have mentioned Capt. Rogers more particularly as I have Understood some insinuations have been made to his Disadvantage. I believe him to be as brave & honest a Man as any I have equal knowledge of, & both myself & all the Army are convinced he has distinguished himself since he has been among us, superior to most, inferior to none of his Rank in these troops."[43] "Insinuations . . . to his Disadvantage" can only refer to Rogers' counterfeiting activities, known first hand to several members of the New Hampshire regiment, including its commanding officer, and presumably the subject of barracks commentary within the army. Like Colonel Blanchard, Johnson grasped the gravity of the charges against Rogers but believed that his rare bravery and energy justified overlooking his past indiscretions, at least in a time of crisis.

Johnson never repudiated his appreciation of Rogers' bravery and energy. He did come to question the man's honesty and his capacity for command responsibilities. In Johnson's view, Rogers' abilities and accomplishments, while genuine, did not make him a full-blown success as a leader. Reflecting on Rogers later in life, he said: "He was a Soldier in my Army in 1755, and as we were in great Want of Active men at that time, his readiness recommended him so far to me that I made him an officer, and got him continued in the Ranging Service, where he soon became puffed up with pride and folly from the extravagant encomiums & notices of some of the Provinces, this spoiled a good Ranger for he was fitt for nothing else, neither has Nature calculated him for a large Command in that Service, he has neither understanding, education, or principles."[44]

Johnson's roots were no more patrician than Rogers', and his criticisms cannot be lumped in with British aristocrats' reflexive disdain for colonials. Like Rogers, Johnson spent most of his adult life on the frontier. Like Rogers, he had a deep knowledge of and respect for Indians. Like Rogers he was the target of disdain in the British military hierarchy, whose denizens muttered that he lacked the gentleman's education and the social standing requisite for command. Johnson and Rogers should have felt a natural mutual affinity, and the fact that there was none suggests Johnson's negative view rested on more than prejudice.

IN MARCH 1756, Massachusetts Governor Shirley summoned Rogers to a meeting in Boston. In early 1755, Shirley had ordered Rogers arrested for diverting troops Rogers had raised for the Massachusetts militia to Colonel Blanchard's New Hampshire regiment. In the fall of 1755, Shirley had been among the skeptics challenging Rogers' reports of large French and Indian forces at Crown Point and Ticonderoga. Now Shirley, apparently on Johnson's recommendation, formally appointed Rogers a Captain of Rangers in the provincial forces and authorized him to raise a company of sixty-five officers and men at a rate of pay double that paid privates in the colonial forces, who earned more than privates in the British regular army. This new company of Rangers would replace the volunteers who had stayed with Rogers over the winter of 1755–56. Until now, Rogers had been a militia officer. Now he was an officer in what was intended to be an elite force of Rangers. In addition to premium pay, each man was given a one-time special allowance for weapons, clothes, and equipment. Rogers made his younger brother Richard his first lieutenant and his friend John Stark his second lieutenant. The three officers set about recruiting the new company, which included, as a private, Carty Gilman, who a year earlier had attempted unsuccessfully to swallow Rogers' note asking him to destroy evidence in the counterfeiting investigation.[45]

While in New Hampshire and Massachusetts recruiting, Rogers was asked to join the Portsmouth, New Hampshire, Masonic Lodge and happily agreed to do so. The chaplain to the lodge, Arthur Browne, was a prominent Portsmouth minister who five years later would become Rogers' father-in-law.[46]

Rogers returned to the Lake George front in late April or early May to find France's Indian allies creating havoc. In April, a war party ambushed and wiped out a sixteen-man patrol south of Fort Edward; another killed or captured six of Rogers' troops camped on an island in Lake George. In May, raiders killed twelve troops and took four prisoners in an ambush north of Fort Edward. A prisoner he had taken near Ticonderoga alerted Rogers to that raid, but he was unable to move fast enough to intercept the raiders and prevent their attack or to overtake them and free their prisoners. In late June, Indians attacked a mounted patrol just north of Albany, killing eight and taking five prisoners. In September, Indians ambushed and decimated a fifty-person scouting patrol north of Fort William Henry.[47]

Preventing Indian depredations was not specifically part of Rogers' mandate in 1755 and 1756, but these incidents illustrate how, for all Rogers' daring exploits, Indians and Canadian partisans dominated irregular warfare on the New York frontier, continuing to do so throughout the war.

In July 1756, Rogers embarked on his most ambitious project yet. Until now, Rogers had routinely deployed canoes and bateaux the length of Lake George, but he was only able to make approaches to Ticonderoga and Crown Point by land. Now Rogers took a fifty-man force on a raid in five newly arrived whaleboats. In these craft, lighter and more maneuverable than bateaux, the Rangers traveled up the east side of Lake George, landed, and portaged the boats across six miles of wilderness to Wood Creek, which flows north into the southern end of Lake Champlain, south of Ticonderoga. The portage took four full days, but it put the Rangers with their small whaleboat fleet on Lake Champlain. By night, the Rangers slipped past Fort Carillon at Ticonderoga and past Fort St. Frédéric at Crown Point, then proceeded twenty or twenty-five miles north to a spot astride the French supply lines to the southern forts.[48]

Rogers hoped to capture a thirty- or forty-ton schooner, but two armed lighters, or cargo boats, got between the Rangers and the schooner and prepared to land right where the Rangers were hiding ashore. The Rangers attacked the lighters, killing three crew members and capturing nine, two of them wounded. The lighters contained a large cargo of foodstuffs, casks of brandy and wine, military correspondence, and payroll money for French troops. One wounded prisoner was too severely injured to travel easily; rather than leave him behind, possibly to inform on them, the Rangers killed him. They scuttled the lighters, keeping only the brandy and, presumably, the money and correspondence, and retreated. They hid the whaleboats on the west shore of Wood Creek for future use and returned overland to Fort William Henry on July 15, after an expedition lasting two and a half weeks.[49]

The military loss was modest, but the French were stunned by the appearance of British boats on Lake Champlain, which they had believed to be firmly under their control, and they struggled to understand how the boats got there. Refusing to believe that the boats had been portaged from Lake George, the French concluded that the British must have a hidden base somewhere south of Ticonderoga and sent at least two expeditions to search for that imagined outpost.[50]

Rogers' exploit achieved quick and widespread press coverage, with detailed accounts appearing in the *New York Mercury*, the *Boston Gazette*, the *Boston Evening Post*, and the *Boston Newsletter*. As before, the British war effort in 1756 was characterized by inertia, ineptitude, and flagging morale. Rogers' "very bold and daring Enterprise" was again a rare bright spot.[51]

In his 1756 after-action report, Rogers admitted dispatching the badly wounded French soldier. In 1765, when publishing his *Journals*, he apparently felt that the killing of a helpless prisoner would not sit well with readers. In the *Journals* he reports that of the two wounded Frenchmen, "one of them [was hurt] so badly that he soon died." Similarly, though the Rangers took the scalps of their French victims to collect bounties, the *Journals* make no mention of this.[52]

For the remainder of the summer and fall of 1756, Rogers undertook scouts in the vicinity of the carrying place, as well as Ticonderoga and Crown Point. On one expedition, Rangers killed forty cattle and on several they took a prisoner or two, but none produced significant fighting before the armies retired to winter quarters. In September, Rogers also attempted to repeat his water-borne assault on Lake Champlain. Accompanied by John Stark and a body of Rangers, Rogers recovered the whaleboats he had cached near Wood Creek after his earlier raid and launched them again on the lake. The Rangers rowed up and down Lake Champlain looking for targets. The most promising prey, a schooner, had a strong wind behind it and moved too quickly for Rogers to catch up. The Rangers spent several days looking for supply boats to capture but gave up, contenting themselves with taking a French farm family prisoner. Once again they concealed the whaleboats and returned to Fort William Henry.[53] The French discovered the whaleboats soon after and Rogers was not able to use them again.

IN EARLY 1756, England made command changes in its North America military operations. John Campbell, the Earl of Loudoun, replaced Massachusetts Governor Shirley as overall military commander, with Major General James Abercromby his second in command and Colonel Daniel Webb third in command. Abercromby and Webb arrived in Albany in late June 1756 with two regiments of regulars, and Abercromby served as temporary commander in chief until Loudoun's arrival. Rogers, fresh from his first Lake Champlain raid, called on Abercromby in Albany, and Abercromby immediately authorized the creation of a second Ranger company, to be captained by Rogers' younger brother Richard. Abercromby also ratified an earlier decision by Shirley to create a Ranger company of Stockbridge Indians, and this thirty-person company was added to Rogers' command.[54]

In the fall of 1756, two additional companies, under Captains Speakman and Hobbs, were also added to Rogers' command. Rogers' older brother James became an officer in one of these companies. The quality of these additions was inferior. Unlike the New Hampshire woodsmen Robert, Richard, and John Stark recruited for the first two Ranger companies, the Speakman and Hobbs recruits came mostly from Boston and had little experience with the frontier. Both companies were seriously under strength.[55] From this point forward, as new Rangers were recruited to create Ranger companies or to replace losses in the original units, recruit quality was a concern. By the end of 1756, Rogers commanded a total of five companies, three of them under strength.

In September, Rogers, now leading two Ranger companies and the Stockbridge Indians, was ordered to establish a permanent base camp on an island in the Hudson opposite Fort Edward. The island eventually became known as Rogers Island. A bridge of planks laid over bateaux connected Rogers Island to Fort Edward on the east shore. The Rangers constructed bark huts as shelters while a large barracks building was being constructed for them. They preferred smaller buildings to the barracks, however, and, rather than occupy the barracks, they replaced the bark huts with more substantial but still small log huts arranged in rows. The Rangers shared Rogers Island with Israel Putnam's Connecticut troops. The two groups had scouted together from the outset of their service and continued to do so throughout the war. Speakman's and Hobbs' companies, when they arrived, were assigned further north to

Fort William Henry.[56] Rogers Island served as Ranger headquarters until 1759, when British victories finally pushed the front further north.

In October 1756, Rogers presented a proposal to Loudoun for a dead-of-winter surprise attack on the Indian town of St. Francis, two hundred miles north of Fort Edward. The plan called for a force of two hundred Rangers to assemble at Fort No. 4, about fifty miles east of Fort Edward. Fort No. 4 would serve as the jumping off point for the raid. Initially, Loudoun simply put Rogers off, but Rogers pressed the proposal. Loudoun consulted with Abercromby, his second in command, who advised against the action, principally because Rogers was "the chief man we can depend on for intelligence" and could not be spared for a long and distant campaign. If either man had misgivings about the plan itself, he did not say so.[57]

By the end of 1756, Rogers had accumulated an enviable record. He had been in the field for more than a year, inflicting several dozen casualties on the enemy without losing a single man in battle. His audacious raids had startled and embarrassed the French while delighting the colonial press. He seemed to be the one bright spot, and a colonial bright spot at that, in an otherwise floundering British war effort. He enjoyed the confidence of his military superiors Johnson, Shirley, Loudoun, and Abercromby.

This seemingly sterling record came with caveats. Rogers' combat experience was limited to skillfully executed but small ambushes. It included nothing that could fairly be called a battle. His commands were small; he had not yet led as many as one hundred men in the field, and rarely as many as fifty.

Still, for the moment, the Rogers record was impressive.

CHAPTER FOUR

THE 1757 CAMPAIGN

IN MID-JANUARY 1757, Rogers and eighty-four other Rangers set out on a raid during an otherwise quiet period. Most of the men were from Rogers' two companies stationed for the winter at their island base opposite Fort Edward. They stopped at Fort William Henry to pick up Captain Speakman and twenty-eight additional men from Speakman's and Hobbs' untested companies.[1] This was likely the largest force Rogers had commanded.[2]

In bitter cold amid extremely deep snow, the Rangers advanced down Lake George on skates and on the first night camped on the lake's eastern shore. Rogers deemed eleven men unfit to continue owing to fatigue, injury, frostbite, or poor attitude. He sent them back to Fort William Henry, reducing his force to seventy-four. The next day, the party proceeded to the north end of Lake George and camped again, on the third day moving inland on snowshoes. They made their final camp roughly midway between Ticonderoga and Crown Point.[3]

On the fourth day, the weather warmed significantly. Rain made tramping through the deep snow even more difficult. The Rangers proceeded due east until they hit the western shore of Lake Champlain. In the late morning, they encountered an attractive target on the frozen lake: three supply-laden sleighs evidently traveling from Fort Carillon at Ticonderoga to Fort St. Frédéric at Crown Point. Rogers sent Lieutenant Stark and twenty men north with instructions to attack the sleighs when they came within range, while Rogers and the remaining men prepared to cut off the French line of retreat. The Rangers did not initially notice that the three sleighs were followed at a considerable distance by seven or eight more. By the time Rogers saw them, he was unable to get word to Stark to postpone his attack. Stark easily captured the three sleighs, taking prisoner three soldiers and four civilians, but the second group of sleighs, alerted to the Rangers' presence, fled back to Ticonderoga.[4]

The Rangers interrogated their captives, who reported that Fort Carillon's garrison of 350 had just been reinforced by two hundred Canadian militia and forty-five Indians, with fifty more warriors expected imminently. With the French now on the alert, the Rangers faced a force of six hundred or more blocking their retreat to Fort William Henry. Rogers held a council of war. His officers unanimously recommended that the Ranger force cross Lake Champlain out of sight of the French, then break into small groups and filter back to Fort William Henry along the little-used eastern shores of Lake Champlain and Lake George. It was a basic principle of frontier raiding never to withdraw using the route used to advance because an alert enemy would certainly watch this route and intercept you. Indeed, Rogers' own Rules of Rangering specifically recommended on a scout or raid to "return home in a different Road from the one [you] came in."[5] Indians invariably followed this practice,[6] as did Rangers in most circumstances.[7]

Rogers, however, overruled his officers and ordered the Rangers to return to their previous night's campsite, rekindle campfires, dry rain-soaked guns, and retreat along the path they had broken in their advance. Not only were the French likely watching their line of advance, but smoke from the fires might betray their location. Rogers argued that having functioning weapons was worth the risk, and his supporters have added that he might have believed that it would be easier and quicker to move over a broken track than to struggle through unbroken deep snow.[8] When his officers objected that Rogers' plan was very risky, Rogers quipped that the French would not dare to attack the famous Captain Rogers.[9]

Whether or not Rogers believed the French feared him, he undoubtedly believed he would best them in any fight. In this instance he was, in

the words of Stark's biographer, "careless to the point of rashness."[10] The
Rangers returned to their camp and dried their guns, then started re-
tracing the path of their advance. While they had been drying their guns,
the French, searching further south, found the raiders' path and at an
advantageous spot set up an ambush, as Rogers' officers had feared. Half
a mile into their retreat, the Rangers walked right into the trap.[11]

In the first volley, Lieutenant Kennedy, who had the point position,
was killed. A shot at Rogers, close behind, grazed him in the head. Several more Rangers were hit. The French and the Indians charged, and
the Ranger advance guard fled to the rear. Captain Speakman and the
middle group of Rangers were overrun, with Speakman badly
wounded. Stark, with a substantial rear guard, was not under immediate
attack. He organized a line of defense along a ridge from which he was
able to provide covering fire for the retreating Rangers, who regrouped
along Stark's line of defense. The Rangers killed their three military
prisoners, but not their four civilian prisoners. The battle settled into a
sustained attempt by the French to break or flank the outnumbered
Rangers.[12]

Rogers estimated the size of the French force at 250, more than three
times his own number, but the actual number of French was only a little
over a hundred. Although the French prisoners had reported a large
body of Canadian and Indian fighters recently arrived at Ticonderoga,
the force sent to ambush Rogers was mostly French regulars, supplemented by a comparatively few Canadians and Indians. The regulars
lacked snowshoes, limiting their mobility, and, like British regulars,
fought in formed platoons, a deployment not particularly effective in
woods. Nonetheless, the French had put a score of Rangers out of action
in the opening minutes of the ambush, and their superior numbers
made the Rangers' position perilous.[13]

Rogers was wounded again, this time more seriously: a shot through
his hand and wrist prevented him from firing a weapon. At this point,
competing narratives about the battle emerge. In the Rogers version,
reflected in his 1765 *Journals*, Rogers remained in full command, assuring his troops he was fine and continuing to rally them to hold out until
nightfall. After dark, he led the remaining Rangers, including several
seriously wounded men, in a dangerous, silent withdrawal that required
them to sneak around and behind French lines, then directed their nighttime retreat to the northern shore of Lake George. Given the men's
great fatigue, especially among the wounded, Rogers ordered Stark to

go to Fort William Henry for help while the rest of the Rangers hid. Only when a relief force arrived the next day did Rogers allow himself to be placed in a sleigh with the seriously wounded.[14]

In Stark's telling, rendered by one of his biographers and by his grandson Caleb, Rogers' second wound put him completely out of commission, and Stark, the senior officer still standing, assumed command. Rogers had been prepared to order a retreat in daylight, which likely would have degenerated into an every-man-for-himself rout. Stark insisted on keeping the Rangers fighting as a cohesive unit, threatening to shoot anyone who left the firing line. He ordered the daring nighttime withdrawal and the march to Lake George. Stark slogged twenty-five more miles to summon a relief force that rescued the battered Rangers. In the view of Stark partisans, he was the true hero of the battle, even though Rogers barely mentions him in the *Journals* except as someone to whom Rogers gave orders.[15] Even if Stark did not take over command, his selection of a sustainable defensive position and his post-battle trek of more than twenty-five miles should have earned him special mention.

Whoever did lead the Ranger withdrawal believed he was taking all the wounded with him. He was not. Captain Speakman, whom Rogers believed to have been killed early in the fray,[16] was alive but badly wounded. He lay isolated away from the center of the fighting. Thomas Brown, sixteen, shot twice and unable to walk, and seriously wounded Robert Baker, the lone British regular on the raid, had also become separated from the main Ranger force and were unaware of its withdrawal. Somehow, the three found each other. They lit a fire, perhaps recognizing they had no hope of escape and planning to surrender. Thinking from the silence that the French and Indians might have withdrawn, Speakman called out for Rogers. Brown then noticed an Indian stealthily approaching the fire and rolled into the shadows. As he watched in horror, the Indian stripped Speakman naked and scalped him, then dragged Baker off as a prisoner. Speakman begged Brown to give him his tomahawk so he could kill himself, but Brown could not bring himself to do so. He attempted to escape but, nearly immobilized by his injuries, was captured the next day. Brought back to the battlefield by his captors, he saw Speakman's scalped head impaled on a pole next to his corpse. Brown remained a prisoner for two years, witnessing the death by torture of another Ranger captured in the ambush. He subsequently published a riveting account of the battle and of his years in captivity.[17]

The French ambush resulted in the death or capture of twenty Rangers, including two experienced officers,[18] more than a quarter of Rogers' command. Ten or more Rangers were wounded, several seriously. The Ranger force came perilously close to being wiped out completely, and survivors abandoned the battlefield grateful to escape with their lives. The French, in addition to beating the Rangers soundly, rescued the four civilians taken prisoner when the Rangers captured the sleighs. By all calculations, the Rangers had suffered a stinging defeat by a force only slightly larger than theirs and hobbled by its own handicaps, all because of a tactical blunder in which Rogers, through carelessness or overconfidence, overruled his officers' unanimous recommendation.

Rogers transformed his blunder into a great victory. Without mentioning his officers' advice, he portrayed the French ambush as an unavoidable accident of war. He gauged the French force opposing him at 250, more than double the reality and making it appear he was outnumbered more than three to one. Despite this supposedly enormous numerical disadvantage, he initially estimated that the Ranger force had killed forty of the French. The press inflated this to sixty or more, and by the time Rogers told the story of the ambush in the *Journals*, the number of French and Indian dead had ballooned to 116, with many more wounded. This was absurd, imagining as it did the badly outnumbered Rangers nearly wiping out the enemy force, even assuming that Rogers' exaggerated estimate of its size was accurate. One wonders why the Rangers retreated.[19]

In reality, the French suffered eleven killed, plus three who later died of their wounds, and twenty-odd wounded.[20] Most casualties were French regulars who insisted on fighting in platoon formation in the open rather than taking cover behind trees, as Canadians, Indians, and Rangers did.[21] While these French casualties were greater than necessary, they hardly made Rogers the victor. And there is no need to guess what would have happened if Rogers had followed his officers' advice. While the French were setting up their ambush miles to the west of Ticonderoga, the Rangers would have been several hours' march away to the east, on the far side of Lake Champlain and moving south toward safety. Even if French or Indian scouts had spotted them, the Rangers would have had too great a lead for the main French force to overtake them.

For the colonial press, however, Rogers was the victor. The battle was widely covered, with the papers heaping praise on Rogers and his men.

The *New York Gazette* cited Rogers' "Courage and Conduct," the *New York Mercury* reported that "Rogers behaved extreamely well," while the *Boston Gazette* contrasted "the brave Rogers [who] is acquiring Glory to himself in the Field" with the British Lord Loudoun, who was then in Boston attending "Balls and Assemblies."[22] Even Captain James Abercrombie, nephew of and aide de camp to General Abercromby, and later a severe critic of the Rangers, wrote to Rogers to assure him that "all ranks of people here [in Albany] are pleased with your conduct, and your mens behavior" and to console him for his losses: "it is impossible to play at bowls without meeting with rubs." (Bowls is a British bowling game played on a lawn. Rubs are uneven spots in the lawn that throw the bowled ball off course.) In a report on the battle prepared immediately afterward, Rogers asked that he and the Rangers be granted bounties for the seven French they had taken prisoner when they captured the sleighs, even though they had killed three during the battle and the other four had been rescued. Abercrombie passed on that the request had been granted.[23] Rogers' public reputation was enhanced, not diminished, by his falling into a deadly ambush in his first major command.

IN MARCH 1757, Loudoun authorized the expansion of the existing Ranger companies to one hundred men each but warned Rogers: "You are to enlist no vagrants, but such as you and your officers are acquainted with, and who are in every way qualified for the duty of Rangers."[24] This instruction was apparently a comment on the inferior Speakman and Hobbs recruits.

The wrist wound Rogers sustained in the January 1757 ambush was sufficiently serious to force him to Albany for medical treatment in February. Upon his return to Fort Edward, he contracted smallpox, which left him bedridden for six weeks. After he recovered, he and three of the Ranger companies were ordered to Albany for ultimate assignment to the Louisbourg campaign, leaving just one company of Rangers stationed at Fort William Henry under his brother Richard. Louisbourg, an immense French fortress on Cape Breton Island, Nova Scotia, controlled sea approaches to the St. Lawrence River. The British Louisbourg expedition sailed from New York in nearly one hundred ships in June 1757, and Rogers did not return to Albany until September. Rogers says almost nothing about the summer campaign against Louisbourg in

his *Journals*, and the campaign itself was a fiasco, with the Rangers given
missions that were "far from challenging." Although Loudoun had a
force of almost fifteen thousand troops and more than thirty warships,
the warships arrived late, Loudoun was hampered by disease and bad
weather, and Louisbourg's defenses proved stronger than anticipated.
Loudoun called off the campaign without a major battle. It was another
wasted campaign season for the British.[25]

Not so for the French. Sensing that British forces in the Albany-Lake
George region had been depleted by the demands of the Louisbourg
campaign, Montcalm, the French commander in Quebec, planned an
attack in force. In addition to a large body of French regulars and
Canadian militia, the French recruited a huge number of Indian auxiliaries, luring them from as far away as the Great Lakes with promises
of plunder.

Even before Montcalm's invasion in August 1757, Indians and Canadian partisans dominated the warfare in the Lake George region. They
struck repeatedly behind British lines, making travel between Albany
and Fort Edward and between Fort Edward and Fort William Henry
unsafe except for large, well-armed convoys. Richard Rogers, commanding the lone Ranger company not assigned to the Louisbourg campaign,
contracted smallpox and died in June 1757. His Rangers, and other
colonial ranger forces, were generally unable to obtain meaningful intelligence about French resources and intentions or to disrupt Indian
and Canadian partisan raids.[26]

As it became clear that Montcalm was planning a major attack,
British military fortunes deteriorated further. Colonel Monro, the commander at Fort William Henry, learned that Montcalm intended to
move a large artillery train from the northern shore of Lake Champlain
to Ticonderoga by boat, portage the guns by land to the north shore of
Lake George, then move them again by boat to Lake George's southern
shore to besiege the fort. Monro sent Colonel Parker and a force of 350
provincials, mostly New Jersey Blues regiment, to attack French facilities
at the portage and bar transport of artillery from Lake Champlain to
Lake George. The Parker expedition never made it to the portage.
Falling into an ambush at Sabbath Day Point in the middle of the west
shore of Lake George in July, they were virtually wiped out, with seventy
killed and 150 taken prisoner. The same day, Indians and Canadian partisans attacked a large body of woodcutters within half a mile of Fort
Edward, killing twelve and wounding fourteen.[27]

Montcalm moved against Fort William Henry in early August. His force of more than eight thousand vastly outnumbered Monro's garrison of about twenty-three hundred. Colonel Webb at Fort Edward had, after reinforcement by Johnson, perhaps four thousand troops, with more en route from Albany—they did not arrive until after the surrender of Fort William Henry—but the French troops and the Indian forces stood astride the road between the two forts, and Webb did not believe he had the strength to break through the enemy lines and relieve Fort William Henry. Even Sir William Johnson, arriving with more than 1,500 militia and 150 Mohawk reinforcements, could not induce Webb to attempt a breakthrough to Fort William Henry. Webb has been widely criticized for his inactivity—Monro, not surprisingly, was especially bitter—but at best he could muster a force inferior to Montcalm's in number, split between two locations, and likely of poorer quality. Worse, Webb was under the mistaken impression that Montcalm had a much larger force than he had. Captured French troops told him, perhaps a deliberate deception, that the French army numbered between eleven and twelve thousand. Had Webb sent a strong relief force and been defeated, Montcalm could have captured Fort Edward immediately after Fort William Henry, gaining an unobstructed path to Albany.[28]

Recognizing that Fort Edward was "the lynchpin of the New York frontier," and not wishing to risk it, Webb stayed put. Montcalm's artillery battered Fort William Henry until resistance was untenable. Montcalm had his Indian auxiliaries assemble in view of the fort to signal what lay in store for the garrison if it did not surrender, presented Monro with a captured message from Webb telling Monro he could not expect reinforcement, and offered generous terms of surrender, with the British troops allowed to march out with arms and baggage to Fort Edward. Monro accepted.[29]

Montcalm could not control the Indian auxiliaries. They had been promised plunder and they were determined to have it. The British left behind seriously wounded soldiers to be cared for by the French. As the main body of British and colonial troops was vacating the fort, Indians entered the fort to plunder it, and, finding troops alive in the hospital, killed them. They dug up buried British dead, including Richard Rogers, and scalped the corpses, then, dissatisfied with the limited booty they had been able to seize, began attacking the retreating column of troops who had surrendered. The evacuees panicked, and French guards were unable to halt the Indian attacks. Scores were killed, and hundreds of others taken prisoner. Montcalm made the Indians give up many of their prisoners on the spot, and others were later ransomed in Montreal and returned to the British. In the end, all but about 270 of the occupants of Fort William Henry were accounted for, and not all of those unaccounted for were killed in the post-surrender attack. Whatever the actual numbers, the massacre at Fort William Henry passed into frontier legend.[30]

In one respect, the British obtained an unintended measure of revenge. Richard Rogers and others of the British dead whose corpses the Indians had dug up and scalped had died of smallpox. When the infected scalps were carried back to Indian villages as trophies, they triggered a smallpox epidemic of major proportions.[31]

Rogers returned to Albany and the Lake George front in September 1757. Two years into the war, the British had finally come to appreciate how important it was in woodland warfare to have troops available for scouting, raiding, and other irregular tactics. But they were leery of trusting this role to provincial rangers, whose quality and discipline they regarded as poor. Lord Loudoun had a plan to have two companies in every British regiment trained in ranger techniques by colonials. This would graft rangering responsibilities onto British regulars. Loudoun asked Rogers to assist in this training and he agreed. At Loudoun's request, Rogers put into writing Rules of Rangering, a compendium of scouting and raiding advice that may have been printed or hand-copied and given to trainees. The trainees moved from Albany to Rogers Island, where they camped next to the Rangers and participated with them in scouts. Trainees "graduated" in early November, and, although the program was not continued, and in time Loudoun's plan to have two companies in every regiment trained as rangers was abandoned, the program created a small pool of regulars interested in irregular warfare.[32]

Although the Ranger training program of 1757 was short-lived, variations of Rogers' Rules of Rangering have, in modern times, been distributed widely to a variety of American special operations military units, including the Army Rangers and the Green Berets. The best known version, a "Ranger Creed" containing "Standing Orders" attributed to Rogers and beginning "Don't forget nothing," is a folksy twentieth-century compendium of advice Rogers might have given, tied only loosely to anything he is known to have written or said. It nonetheless emphasizes to recruits that contemporary special operations tactics and procedures have deep roots in American military history.[33]

Appreciation of the need to adapt to the unique features of frontier warfare grew with the arrival of Lord George Augustus Howe in October 1757. Down to earth and well-liked by both British and colonial troops, Howe urged British troops to learn from colonials, emphasized the need to develop forest survival skills, and went on at least one scout with Rogers.[34]

None of this activity in the fall of 1757 overcame inherent British distrust of colonials, a wariness soon underscored by an incident involving Captain James Abercrombie. A nephew of and an aide to General Abercromby, Captain Abercrombie, having gotten on the rangering bandwagon, asked to be sent on a scout with Rogers in November 1757. Rogers was sick again—scurvy—and nominated John Stark as his substitute. Abercrombie did not get on with Stark or the Rangers. The party's objective was to obtain current information about French dispositions at Fort Carillon. Fog prevented a clear view of the fort. Ranger officers rejected as too risky Abercrombie's proposal to sneak up to the fort's walls to take a prisoner or untie and disperse boats moored by the French. The next day, an attempt to ambush woodcutters working outside the fort failed when the Rangers' presence was detected. The French ran back to the fort, with the Rangers in pursuit, yelling loudly. The scout yielded no information of value.

The exercise badly damaged the Rangers' reputation. Abercrombie was appalled by what he regarded as the Rangers' lack of discipline and faulted Stark for not exercising greater authority. He criticized Stark for not posting guards for the Rangers' night camps and for failing to set a rear guard to make sure they were not being pursued when they withdrew from the Ticonderoga area at the conclusion of the scout. He criticized the Rangers for shouting threats at the French garrison at Fort Carillon after the woodcutters retreated to safety there and for generally acting disorderly. Abercrombie contrived to have a dozen Rangers dismissed from the service for poor discipline, and he undoubtedly promoted the view among British officers that, however important rangering skills might be, Rangers were not to be trusted.[35]

While Loudoun, Howe, and others tried to get all British troops, or select units within each regiment, to learn and apply ranger techniques, Colonel Thomas Gage, someday to become the senior British commander in North America, had a different idea. He proposed creating a five hundred-man regiment of light infantry, even offering to advance personal funds, to be reimbursed later, to get this regiment up and running. He hoped British light infantry could replace Rogers' Rangers. Loudoun accepted the proposal, and Gage's 80th Light Infantry Regiment served until the end of the French and Indian War. That regiment never replaced Rogers' Rangers, but it was one more reflection of the British view that rangers, to be effective, either needed to serve under British officers or be replaced altogether by British rangers.[36]

This negative view of the Rangers was cemented by an ugly incident in early December 1757. In early 1757, the command structure of British regular forces and colonial forces had been integrated, subjecting colonial troops to British standards of discipline. Colonel William Haviland at Fort Edward, perhaps reacting to Captain Abercrombie's loud complaints about undisciplined Rangers, ordered two Rangers who had been arrested for stealing rum from British stores to be flogged severely in front of fellow Rangers and placed in the guardhouse. On December 6, angry Rangers destroyed the whipping post upon which the men had been flogged. Rogers was still ill with scurvy, and other Ranger officers did not intervene to quell the protest. Angry Rangers, some armed, marched on the guardhouse, intending to free the prisoners. Ranger officers finally intervened, prevented the release of the prisoners, and persuaded the protesting Rangers to return to their quarters. Haviland got wind of the "mutiny" and had six Rangers he believed to be ringleaders arrested.[37]

Haviland insisted on conducting an inquiry and appointed Rogers to head the investigation. Rogers engineered a whitewash. Witnesses, including the Ranger officers who had persuaded the protesters to stand down, pretended to be unable to identify Rangers who had committed mutinous acts. Rogers concluded there was no basis for any disciplinary action and urged Haviland to drop the matter. This led to a confrontation between Rogers and Haviland, with Haviland accusing Rogers of protecting mutineers, Rogers countering that mass desertions would follow if further discipline were meted out, and Haviland threatening to hang one or more Rangers. Refusing to back down, Haviland formally requested that his superiors convene a court martial. Rogers persuaded Loudoun that this would sap morale and urged the matter be dropped. Loudoun reluctantly agreed, infuriating Haviland all the further.[38]

Rogers may have prevailed short term, but Captain Abercrombie's complaints and the December 6 mutiny caused "almost irreversible damage to [Rogers'] reputation," eroding the good opinion Rogers had built up in 1755 and 1756. Rogers not only made no effort to repair his rift with Haviland—he sought to inflame it. Haviland had imposed a rule that firearms were not to be discharged within hearing of Fort Edward except in an enemy attack. Actual attacks were unnervingly common, so any gunfire was likely to send men running for weapons or shelter and to be highly distracting and disruptive. The Rangers on Rogers Island enjoyed target shooting. Rogers refused to curtail this practice, despite Haviland's rule and despite discussions with him about it.[39]

British commanders were highly dissatisfied with the Rangers but saw no alternative to maintaining them in service and expanding their ranks. General Abercromby, second in command, believed Rogers was essential; "without him these four Companies would be good for nothing." Loudoun considered the Rangers, with their premium pay, "an extravagant drain on the war chest," but authorized Rogers to recruit four more colonial companies and one Indian company, giving the Rangers ten companies in all. As usual, the new Rangers got premium pay.[40] Rogers would later complain that he advanced significant personal funds to promote the recruiting campaign and was never reimbursed, but there is no evidence he raised this complaint at the time. The four new companies went to Canada to join the campaign headed by Jeffery Amherst and James Wolfe, where Wolfe characterized them as "the worst soldiers in the universe."[41]

British officers' uniform disdain for the Rangers undoubtedly arose in part from cultural differences, with the Americans more democratic and suspicious, or at least not in awe, of authority, while the British were more wedded to tradition and hierarchy. None of the Rangers' early critics—Abercromby and his nephew Abercrombie, Loudoun, Haviland—was a person of any great talent, military or otherwise, and their opinions are properly treated with some skepticism. But the consistency of the negative view of the Rangers is striking, and it came to be shared by people who were obviously talented, like Wolfe and Amherst, who had "a very despicable [opinion] of the Rangers."[42] With the likely exception of Haviland, British critics of the Rangers were, at least at this point in his career, appreciative of Rogers' individual strengths. The key factor in assessing whether the Rangers were a rabble in uniform or simply the embodiment of American culture, alien to and under-appreciated by the British, is whether poor discipline diminished their military effectiveness. As subsequent events would show, poor discipline did undermine Ranger effectiveness.

IN LATE DECEMBER 1757, Rogers, with a force of about 125, advanced to Fort Carillon at Ticonderoga for a raid. The Rangers were unable to engage the garrison in any significant fighting, but they took two prisoners, killed seventeen cows, and set fire to several woodpiles. Before withdrawing, Rogers left a note stuck on a slaughtered cow's horn. The note said in part: "I thank you for the fresh meat you have sent me" and "I request you to present my compliments to the Marquis de Montcalm." Rogers signed the note, undoubtedly pleased with his display of cheekiness. The French considered the gesture "a very low piece of braggadocio."[43]

CHAPTER FIVE

THE BATTLE
ON SNOWSHOES

IN JANUARY 1758, Rogers presented a plan to capture Fort St. Frédéric at Crown Point. He proposed to take a force of four hundred men north down Lake George, march inland, bypass Fort St. Frédéric by moving to the west of it, then circle around to the north to put himself astride supply lines serving Fort St. Frédéric from Canada. Here, Rogers hoped to capture one or more French supply sleighs and staff them with French-speaking Rangers as drivers and guards. The sleigh team of raiders would approach the fort from the north, the direction that would seem normal, expected, and non-threatening. Once admitted to the fort, the French-speaking Rangers would hold the gates open, permitting Rogers' men to rush the gates and overwhelm the garrison.[1]

Loudoun had in mind a winter attack of his own—on Fort Carillon at Ticonderoga—for which he anticipated needing substantial support from Rogers and the Rangers. Rogers was not intimately involved in Loudoun's planning and was unaware of the conflict between Loudoun's plan for Ticonderoga and his own plan for Crown Point. The Crown Point plan, if authorized, would have to be led by someone else unless it was delayed to allow Rogers first to participate in the Ticonderoga campaign. Loudoun left it to Abercromby, closer to the scene in Albany, to coordinate the ventures. Rogers believed he had gotten the go-ahead for his Crown Point plan.[2]

As part of Loudoun's attack plan, which Rogers had no hand in preparing, Rangers were to fashion six hundred pairs of snowshoes. In Loudoun's mind, raiders wearing them could, in the event of heavy snow, tramp a path for the raid's other troops and artillery train. But the Rangers constructed only two- to three-hundred pairs of snowshoes, and February 1758 saw snowfalls so heavy as to make the movement of a large force and artillery train extremely difficult. Loudoun's attack on Ticonderoga never came off. Rogers, who may not have known the purpose or urgency of the order to produce snowshoes, caught a share of the blame for the cancellation.[3]

As part of a coordinated offensive, which would bring a large British and colonial force to the front, Rogers' plan to capture Crown Point may have been worth a gamble, regardless of who led it. As a stand-alone project, it was extremely risky. The French had substantial forces at Ticonderoga and at Crown Point. It would be difficult for a four-hundred-man Ranger force to march undetected to Crown Point and capture the French fort by surprise. Even if Rogers could capture Fort St. Frédéric, it is unclear how he could hold it, and reinforcement would be difficult: with the Ticonderoga campaign abandoned, most British and colonial forces would be in winter quarters farther south. The Rangers would be outnumbered and behind enemy lines. With these considerations in mind, Haviland, assigned by Abercromby to control local operations for the rest of the winter from Fort Edward, cancelled the Crown Point raid.

Rogers did not understand this. He believed that the plan to send him with a force of four hundred against Crown Point remained active, and that Haviland at the last minute arbitrarily cut the roster to 180, re-characterizing the mission as a scout in force.[4] A factor in Haviland's thinking was intelligence from Israel Putnam. At Haviland's order Putnam had led 115 men on a scout in force to the north end of Lake George, coming within eight miles of Ticonderoga. Upon his return Putnam reported finding some six hundred Indian warriors there.[5] Haviland sent Rogers on a follow-up scout to the same vicinity with a force of 180 to get further information on enemy dispositions.[6]

Rogers and his men marched out of Fort Edward on March 10, 1758. His detachment constituted "the cream of Rogers' four old companies."[7] They camped halfway between Fort Edward and the ruins of Fort William Henry, then for two nights on the shores of Lake George as they moved north. On the fourth day, they moved inland on snow-shoes from the north shore of Lake George, putting a mountain between themselves and the location to the east where Putnam had seen the Indian warriors. The Rangers rested for several hours that afternoon, planning ambushes to spring on enemy scouting parties the following morning.[8]

Resuming their march, the Rangers proceeded north with a frozen brook to their left and a steep mountain to their right. About 3:00 p.m., a runner from the Ranger advance guard reported an enemy force, mostly Indians, advancing along the frozen brook. The runner put their number at an improbably precise ninety-six. The Rangers set an ambush on higher ground along one side of the brook. When the Indians were well into the ambush, the Rangers, on a signal from Rogers, rose and fired a volley into the Indian column, killing several and sending the rest in headlong flight.[9]

About half the Rangers sprinted after the Indians in a disorganized pursuit, with officers seeming to exert no control. Rogers apparently stayed behind to scalp victims felled in the first Ranger volley, leaving his men without a commander.[10] The Indian column the Rangers ambushed turned out to be the advance guard of a larger French and Indian force, led by the well-known Canadian partisan Jean-Baptiste Levrault de Langis "Langy" Montegron. The Ranger advance guard had not detected the larger force. The onrushing Rangers collided with Langy's advancing force and, before they could organize themselves, were largely wiped out. Within minutes, fifty Rangers were killed, captured, or isolated to be finished off later.[11]

Rangers at the rear formed a defensive line as best they could. Survivors of the fighting farther forward retreated to that line, but with fifty or more Rangers out of action French and Indian numerical superiority grew steadily more decisive. The Rangers' defensive arc was ever more hemmed in, and by 4:30 p.m., after a battle of an hour and a half, Rogers concluded he could hold out no further. At that point, the enemy surrounded twenty men under Lieutenant William Phillips protecting one of the flanks. Offered clemency, Phillips surrendered. Rogers then ordered what disintegrated into an every-man-for-himself flight from the battlefield. Survivors were to make their way to the spot on Lake George where they had cached their sleighs and supplies.

Not many made it. In mid-March, it was still light in late afternoon, depriving the Rangers of the cover of darkness. The French and the Indians hunted them down, making the withdrawal "almost as harrowing as the battle itself," "the lowest moment of the [Rangers'] existence." Rogers said later that "several" Rangers were captured during the retreat, likely a gross understatement.[12] In all, at least 130 Rangers were killed or captured in the battle, more than 70 percent of Rogers' command.

Many Rangers, including Rogers, shed their outer jackets as too cumbersome or attention-getting. Officers may have shed theirs out of fear of being identified by rank and mistreated if captured. As the Rangers were fleeing, Indians discovered in a Ranger officer's jacket, possibly Rogers', scalps presumably taken from Indians killed in the initial ambush. Enraged, the Indians attacked and killed many of their prisoners, including most of Lieutenant Phillips' detachment, who had been promised quarter. The recovery of Rogers' jacket led to claims that he had died in the fighting.[13]

It is not known what route Rogers took to the meeting place. He seems to have traveled alone. He needed more than three hours to reach the rendezvous, where he found several wounded Rangers, who must have moved more slowly than Rogers, already there.[14] Rogers never explained how he escaped, and several variations of a legend developed. The route south from the killing ground to the meeting place passed a mountain abutting Lake George. That peak terminated in a sheer, six-hundred-foot granite cliff dropping off to the lakefront. The cliff is now known as Rogers' Rock. According to one story, Rogers, pursued by Indians, came to the cliff's edge, jumped, and survived without injury. A less melodramatic version posits that he descended a steep path by clutching onto trees and bushes. A third has Rogers summiting the rock, then reversing his snowshoes and tramping back down, leaving two snowshoe trails leading to the cliff's edge but none descending and confusing pursuers. No evidence supports these stories, and there is no reason to think there was anything heroic about Rogers' escape. In fact, his absence of leadership during the frantic retreat raises questions of its own.[15]

A total of about fifty Rangers, four of whom later died of their wounds, eventually reached the meeting place. Rogers sent two uninjured Rangers to Fort Edward for help, then remained hidden with the survivors on the lake shore that night. The next day the group struggled south along the lake until they met a relief party headed by John Stark. The group returned to Fort Edward the next day.[16]

Rogers and the Rangers suffered "a crushing defeat" at the Battle on Snowshoes.[17] Since the Ranger force at the battle included a high percentage of the Rangers then in service on the Lake George front, the debacle temporarily disabled the Rangers as a fighting force, and the loss of a large number of experienced officers made rebuilding a challenge.

Rogers later insisted that Haviland announced publicly after Putnam's scout that Rogers "should be sent to the French forts with a strong party of 400 Rangers."[18] But given that Loudoun's Ticonderoga raid was off, an attack on Crown Point made little sense, and a raid on Ticonderoga, never a Rogers assignment, made even less sense. If Rogers merely was going on a scout in force, as Putnam had, four hundred was too large a contingent. Clearly, Haviland understood he was sending Rogers on a scout.

In his *Journals*, Rogers estimates the force opposing him at about seven hundred, mostly Indigenous warriors, but Rogers' biographers put the number at about three hundred, while French sources put the number at 230 or 250. Rogers estimates that he killed about 150 enemy, including forty in the initial ambush, while wounding a like number. French and Indian dead may have been as few as eight, and certainly not much more. Rogers could perhaps be forgiven for estimating the French and Indian force at almost three times its actual size, but his enemy casualty estimates, likely ten times the reality, seem invented. One suspects that he estimated 150 French and Indian dead because that figure was larger than Rogers' own acknowledged casualty count. Despite insisting that he gave as good as he got against a greatly superior enemy force, however, Rogers recognized that the venture had been "an unfortunate scout."[19]

In addition to exaggerating enemy numbers and losses at the Battle on Snowshoes, Rogers gives a misleading account of his own role in the battle and its aftermath. In the *Journals*, he portrays himself as having been in complete control of the Ranger force start to finish. In fact, the initial rout of the Rangers appears to have been decisive and complete, with Rogers at the rear exercising no control over his troops, before he realized what was happening. When it became apparent by late afternoon that the diminished Rangers could not hold a defensive line, Rogers says he "thought it most prudent to retreat, and bring off with me as many of my party as I possibly could." But Rogers brought off no one. The retreat was a "harrowing" helter-skelter flight in which everyone was left to his own devices. Rogers concludes that "[w]e came to Lake George in the evening," suggesting a body of troops under his command, when in reality survivors, including Rogers, straggled in one by one, Rogers later than most.[20]

What really happened? Rogers presents the Battle on Snowshoes as another of war's unfortunate hazards, a body of troops unexpectedly confronted by a greatly superior enemy and suffering the consequences. Given the actual size of the French and Indian force, however, it is apparent that a cohesive Ranger force of 180 should have been able to hold its own against the enemy and, if not defeat them, at least withdraw without excessive loss. The decisive fact about the Battle on Snowshoes is not that the French and Indians had greatly superior numbers—they did not—but that Ranger discipline broke down, with Rangers rushing blindly to take scalps while their commander remained at the rear exercising no control. This failure of command control cost fifty men their lives in minutes, giving the enemy a decisive advantage and making the battle an unavoidable defeat.

Press coverage, as usual, missed this. The *Boston Gazette* reported: "All the Accounts from the Westward agree that the Party of 180 Men under the command of Major Rogers, behaved in the most gallant and heroic Manner in the late engagement," proving that "our Provincial troops are fully a Match, when not greatly out-numbered, for any Canadians or Savages that might be brought against them."[21]

Rogers, knowing the facts did him no credit, sought to shift responsibility onto Haviland. Haviland may have borne as much responsibility as Rogers for the men's feud, but it is difficult to assign him any blame for the Battle on Snowshoes defeat. Rogers complained that public declarations by Haviland that Rogers was to set off on a four-hundred-man mission gave away the game to the foe. But no evidence shows the French had advance knowledge of Rogers' expedition and there is ample evidence that French and Indian scouts first alerted the French to Rogers' advance as it was happening. The force attacking Rogers was not the six hundred Indians Putnam had reported from his earlier scout, but a recently-arrived force that no one could have predicted. Rogers maintained that the French were expecting a force of four hundred. As a result, he claimed, his original force should have been augmented, not slashed by more than half, calling Haviland's decision to reduce his force "incomprehensible." He seemed to be suggesting Haviland was sending him on a suicide mission, for which, Rogers said, he "doubtless had his reasons, and is able to vindicate his own conduct."[22] The French complement at the Battle on Snowshoes—about 250 men—shows that the French were not expecting a much larger attack.[23]

Rogers' suicide-mission allegation ignored the fact that British regular officers and men from Fort Edward accompanied the expedition and were casualties of the battle. Once the British commanders at the front had cancelled the plan for an assault on Fort St. Frédéric and reduced Rogers' mission to a scout—the term even Rogers uses to describe the mission—a force of 180 was both typical and appropriate. Lamenting his losses while emphasizing those he supposedly inflicted on the foe, Rogers wrote, "I will not pretend to determine what we should have done had we been 400 or more strong."[24] Obviously, the Rangers would have done better had they been a larger force. But, knowing four hundred men were attacking them, the French would have responded with more soldiers or stayed within the safety of their fort. The Battle on Snowshoes defeat flowed from poor discipline and leadership.

AS Rogers was about to set out on the expedition that led to the Battle on Snowshoes, the British government announced the replacement of Lord Loudoun as commander in chief in North America, reflecting government unhappiness with Loudoun's lethargy against Louisbourg and his loss of Fort William Henry. Abercromby took over. He planned a massive summer campaign against Ticonderoga. Following the Snowshoes debacle, Rogers set about trying to reconstitute the Rangers as a scouting and fighting force. He was elevated to major, apparently after threatening to resign to become a colonel in the New Hampshire provincial forces if denied promotion in the Rangers.[25] Although he never rose above the rank of captain in the British army, from this point on he was routinely addressed as "Major."

With most of the best Ranger officers and experienced men dead or captured and Rogers scrambling to replace them, Ranger quality, always problematic, appears to have deteriorated further. Perhaps as a result, the Rangers, scouting in advance of the Ticonderoga campaign, sustained modest but painful defeats. In May 1758, twenty-six Rangers, mostly Stockbridge and other Indians on a scout to Ticonderoga, were ambushed in their camp, losing four killed and nine captured. In mid-

June, a scouting party under Rogers was attacked while Rogers was off with two men making observations and sketches. Rogers was cut off, wounded, and nearly killed or captured, and the Ranger force lost five killed and three captured. Later that month, an entire seventeen-member Ranger scouting party, including two officers, was surrounded and captured on Lake George. As one of Rogers' biographers put it, "the balance of power in the partisan war still lay on the side of the French."[26]

On July 5, 1758, the Ticonderoga campaign began. A British force of almost sixteen thousand men, assembled at the site of the former Fort William Henry, proceeded down Lake George in more than one thousand bateaux and other watercraft. Rogers and the Rangers formed the left flank of the advance guard, while British light infantry—presumably Gage's regiment—formed the right flank of the advance guard. On the second day, the British flotilla reached the northern end of Lake George. Rogers participated in a scouting party that spied a few French troops and Indians at the proposed landing place. Their numbers not being enough to impede a landing, the British, with the Rangers in the lead, began to disembark.[27]

Upon landing, Rogers and the Rangers were ordered to seize high ground about a mile north of the landing spot, then proceed east across the La Chute River, where Rogers was to construct a crude bridge. Moving further east, he was to occupy high ground within sight of a sawmill at the La Chute falls, where the French under Montcalm were expected to make a stand. Several provincial regiments followed closely behind, trailed in turn by British regulars under Lord Howe. From the west, a large French and Canadian scouting force of about 350, either lost or caught off balance and out of position by the speed of the British advance, ran into the British army moving north from the landing site. A sharp battle broke out engaging the provincial units behind Rogers and the British regular units under Howe. Colonel Lyman, commanding one of the provincial regiments, asked Rogers to shift position and attack the left flank of the French force. Leaving 150 men to hold the high ground near the sawmill, Rogers obliged, joined the battle, and killed several enemy. Howe, rushing to the sound of the fighting, crested a small rise and was shot dead.[28]

The French force was badly mauled, with most of its men killed or captured, while the British and colonials suffered only minor casualties. But the loss of the energetic, well-liked Howe was devastating and the chaos and violence of unexpected battle in deep woods unnerved British regulars. Many retreated to the landing spot to regroup. By mistake, British and colonial forces attacked one another, causing casualties and further confusion. The following morning, Abercromby ordered more units back to the landing spot. These missteps hobbled the British force, bought Montcalm time to strengthen his defenses at Ticonderoga, and undoubtedly sapped British morale.[29]

The Rangers had been comparatively minor participants in the fight against the French scouting force. The night after that clash, however, they returned to the battlefield, according to multiple sources, to "harvest" scalps from French dead in order to collect bounties.[30]

Montcalm had fewer than four thousand French and Canadian troops with him at Ticonderoga and virtually no Indian auxiliaries. The Indians, overawed by the British attacking force's size, were still angry at having been deprived of booty they thought they had been promised a year earlier, when they joined the attack on Fort William Henry. Many of Montcalm's officers recommended abandoning Fort Carillon and retreating to Crown Point. The stuttering British attack gave Montcalm another option. Fort Carillon stood on a peninsula bounded on the north and northeast by Lake Champlain and on the south and southeast by the La Chute River, which flows from the northern end of Lake George to the southern end of Lake Champlain. The fort was vulnerable to artillery fire from the far shore of the La Chute, but Abercromby had not yet positioned his gunners. The only land approach to the fort was across a narrow neck to the west. While Abercromby took an extra day to regroup, Montcalm set his entire force to block the land approach by felling trees and building an abatis, a tangle of trunks with sharpened limbs poking outward. He constructed a fortified line immediately behind the abatis, all about half a mile from the fort itself.[31]

To British officers assessing the French defenses at Ticonderoga from a mountain overlooking the peninsula, the abatis did not appear formidable. Abercromby was persuaded that the British, with greatly superior numbers, could penetrate the abatis and the fortified line behind it, then take Fort Carillon by storm. Continuing to leave his artillery undeployed, Abercromby ordered a frontal assault on the abatis on July 8. Rogers and other provincial and British forces were assigned secondary roles as skirmishers, away from the charge.

The attack was a catastrophe. Begun before all the British and provincial units were in place, the advance proceeded piecemeal in an uncoordinated fashion. Wave after wave of British and colonial troops

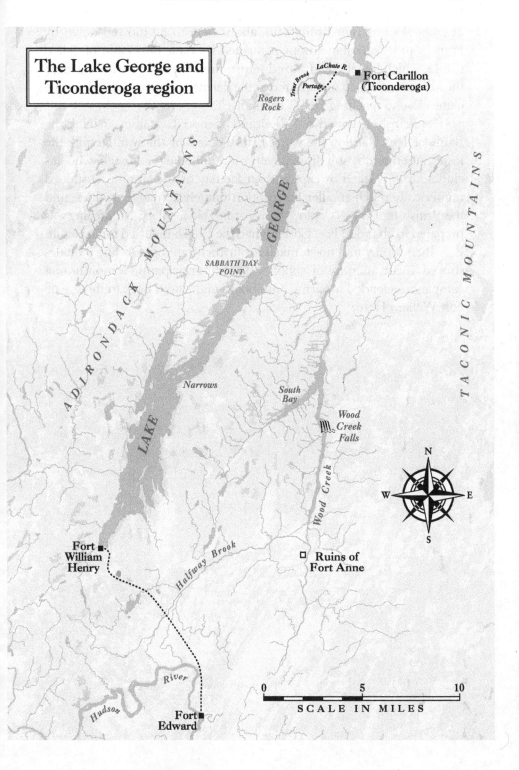

The Lake George and
Ticonderoga region

attempted to march through the abatis only to be mowed down by
French and Canadian troops protected by their barricade of felled
trunks, which largely neutralized return fire. Any troops who did clear
the abatis were killed or captured at the defensive barricade, and no one
came close to reaching Fort Carillon itself.[32]

The British sustained two thousand or more casualties, making the
Battle of Fort Carillon the worst British defeat of the war. Despite the
losses, Abercromby still dramatically outnumbered the French, who, including troops killed or captured on the day of the landing, sustained
numerically much smaller but proportionately similar casualties, and
the British had yet to deploy their formidable artillery. Montcalm was
prepared to abandon Fort Carillon had the British renewed their assault.
But Abercromby had no stomach for further fighting. On July 9 he destroyed a vast quantity of supplies brought anticipating a month-long
campaign, reloaded his army onto boats, and rowed back to the site of
Fort William Henry.[33]

CHAPTER SIX

FORT ANNE, TICONDEROGA, AND CROWN POINT

AFTER their surprise victory at Ticonderoga, the French launched major attacks behind British lines targeting the supply route between Fort Edward and the main British force camped at the site of Fort William Henry. The French objective was to drive the British from Lake George to Fort Edward and Albany. On July 17, 1758, at Halfway Brook, midway between Fort Edward and Fort William Henry, Indians and Canadian partisans attacked a colonial regiment under Colonel Joseph Nichols. The unit lost more than twenty men killed and captured, including two officers. Sent in pursuit, Rogers and a force of Rangers and other colonials could not catch the raiders.[1] Ten days later, near the same spot, an even larger body of Indians and Canadian partisans attacked a supply train of almost forty wagons rolling from Fort Edward to Fort William Henry. The train had a relatively light guard of fifty provincials and twenty Rangers, but it included more than one hundred civilians, including drivers, supply personnel, and some thirty women and children, the former part of a nursing force being sent north to minister to British casualties from the Ticonderoga. The enemy partisan force overwhelmed the supply caravan, capturing all the wagons, killing more than one hundred troops and civilians, including sixteen Rangers, and taking most of the rest prisoner. The attackers captured mounds of booty, including British army payroll money and parts of General Abercromby's personal baggage. They butchered the 150 oxen that had been hauling the wagons.[2]

Rogers and the Rangers, accompanied by other colonial and regular units, including Connecticut troops under Israel Putnam, were ordered out in pursuit. Chasing the raiders up the east shore of Lake George and east to Wood Creek, Rogers' force arrived at Wood Creek to find that the partisans and Indians had reached their boats and were rowing and paddling back to the safety of Fort Carillon. Rather than return to Fort Edward, Rogers and his force of about seven hundred got orders to remain in the field, patrol south of Wood Creek, and return to Fort Edward from the east. They encountered small bands of Indians they were unable to capture and who undoubtedly reported their presence, but found no large enemy force. In fact, Captain Joseph Marin, a well-known Canadian partisan leader, had set out in early August with about three hundred Canadians, Indians, and French regulars for a third major raid. Rogers and Putnam, unaware of this party's presence in the vicinity, worked their way south along Wood Creek and camped for the night of August 7 at the site of an abandoned bastion, Fort Anne.[3]

On the morning of August 8, the Rogers/Putnam force moved out of their camp, Putnam and his Connecticut men in front, Captain James Dalyell and a body of Gage's light infantry, together with other British regular units, in the middle, and Rogers and the Rangers in the rear. Not long into its march, the column stepped into an ambush set by Marin. In the initial fighting, Putnam and others were taken prisoner, some of his men were killed, and the Connecticut troops were put to flight. The British regulars and light infantry held firm, allowing Rogers and the Rangers to come up. A sharp fight ensued. By all accounts, Rogers exhibited great coolness under fire. He may have personally shot and killed a six-foot, four-inch sachem, "the Largest Indian Ever Rogers saw," who had been anchoring the Indian defense, although most likely credit for this belongs to one of Dalyell's men. At some point, a sizable group of about fifty Canadian militia fled the battlefield. Eventually, the larger numbers of British and colonial troops tipped the balance, forcing Marin to withdraw with significant casualties.[4]

Estimates of the number of combatants in the Battle of Fort Anne vary. Rogers said the British and colonial forces numbered 530, but other contemporaneous British and colonial estimates put the number higher, above six hundred and perhaps seven hundred or more. Although the British and colonials, including Rogers, estimated the French force at five hundred or more, the French put Marin's force at three hundred. Estimates of casualties also differ. At the time, British and colonial sources reported more than one hundred killed or missing, although some labeled missing later appeared, so that actual British and colonial battle losses likely did not exceed seventy-five, in addition to wounded. French estimates of Marin's losses—as few as ten killed—are absurdly low. Rogers' estimate of two hundred French killed is too high. The true number of dead on the French side was at least fifty—the number of scalps Rangers were reported to have taken on the battlefield—but likely fewer than one hundred. In other words, casualties were similar on both sides, although Marin's losses represented a larger percentage of his smaller force.[5]

Technically, the Battle of Fort Anne was a British victory. The British drove the French from the field and inflicted at least as many casualties as they received. Rogers was uncharacteristically subdued in describing the battle, emphasizing more the stoutness of the defense his troops put up in avoiding being overrun than any affirmative defeat of the French. In part this may have reflected the fact that the British and colonial side sustained painful losses, especially the capture of Israel Putnam. Putnam experienced several brushes with death at Indian hands during his captivity, but within months he returned to Fort Edward in a prisoner exchange.[6]

The other explanation for Rogers' reserved description of the Fort Anne "victory," never mentioned in his *Journals*, is that the battle and its losses came about because of Rogers' carelessness, and everyone under his command knew it. Apparently convinced there was no significant enemy force within hearing, Rogers, on the morning of August 8, either proposed or agreed to compete in a shooting match with a British officer. According to some sources, the contest prompted target shooting by other Rangers, and the ruckus alerted Marin to the enemy's nearby presence, inspiring his ambush. The fact that a senior officer's carelessness caused the battle was sufficiently unusual to merit comment in at least half a dozen contemporaneous accounts. Reverend John Cleaveland, a chaplain serving Massachusetts units participating in the battle, was particularly scathing. He regarded the French ambush as "a judg't of God upon us" for Rogers' carelessness and lamented, "O when will men be wise?"[7]

As at Ticonderoga, the Rangers methodically worked their way through the Fort Anne battlefield taking scalps for bounties. More troublesome, certainly for twenty-first century sensibilities but also likely for eighteenth-century observers, was the claim of Rogers' mutilation of a Canadian corpse. A captured Canadian partisan identified one of the fallen Canadians as Captain Marin. Rogers skinned the corpse's head from the neck up, stretched it to dry, then carved "Marin" into the dried skin, a grisly trophy. As it turned out, Marin had escaped; the corpse was someone else's.[8]

THE Battle of Fort Anne was the last significant engagement of the 1758 campaign season on the Lake George front, with the rest of the year seeing only small-scale scouting and skirmishing. The British evacuated their large forward camp at the site of Fort William Henry, falling back to Fort Edward and Albany for the winter. Results on the Lake George front had been dismal, but elsewhere the British fared better. Amherst captured Louisbourg in July 1758, opening the way to Quebec; British and colonial forces on Lake Ontario captured Fort Frontenac.[9] The end of 1758 also brought command changes. Abercromby was recalled and, in December 1758, Amherst became British commander in chief for North America. In February 1759, Thomas Gage was named commander of British forces for the northern district.[10]

In January 1759, Rogers settled his accounts with the paymaster in Albany. He expressed no dissatisfaction with the outcome and made no mention of supposedly unreimbursed recruiting expenses from early 1758, about which he later complained in the *Journals*. Rogers next returned his attention to recruiting. Although his nominal Ranger strength on the Lake George front was six hundred, deaths from battle and disease, injuries, illness, and desertions had reduced the Rangers to only about two hundred effectives. Rogers had recruiters hard at work around New England, and they had reportedly enlisted four hundred men to fill out the companies. Rogers wrote to Colonel Roger Townshend, an aide to Amherst, in February 1759 requesting permission to leave Fort Edward, return to New England, and supervise the mustering of recruits and their dispatch to Fort Edward. He suggested first going to New York to meet with Amherst to propose further augmentation of the Rangers. Townshend, on behalf of Amherst, tartly denied Rogers' request to leave Fort Edward. He said that Ranger recruits had been notified by newspaper advertisement to muster at Fort Edward, noting with annoyance that he and Amherst had had to do so because Rogers had not identified his recruiting officers or provided their contact information. He told Rogers to put his proposals for additional Ranger units in writing and said that Amherst would see Rogers "at another time."[11]

The 1759 recruiting program appears to have reprised all the shortcomings of earlier such efforts. In February, Amherst asked Rogers for his recommendation regarding the suitability of Captain Jacob Cheeksaunkun, known as Captain Jacob, and a company of Stockbridge Indians for a campaign against Ticonderoga. Rogers was in favor. Amherst also consulted Gage. "These Indians were last Campaign so great a nuisance to the Army & did no Manner of service," Gage wrote. "[N]either orders nor Entreaty's could prevail on them to do service always lying drunk in their Hutts, or firing round the Camp." Amherst authorized Rogers to retain the Stockbridge company despite Gage's advice but wound up being highly dissatisfied with that unit's performance.[12]

Results were just as bad with newly enlisted colonial Ranger recruits. Although Rogers assured Amherst he had exceeded his recruiting goals, Gage doubted the new Rangers would show up on time and in force: "When you are better acquainted with them, you will find them not very alert at obeying orders, especially when at a Distance & at home." Again Gage's misgivings proved accurate. In April, Gage reported to Amherst that "[t]here is such confusion in the Ranging Companies that it's difficult to ascertain their numbers; they have no person amongst them enough acquainted with regular Service to put them in a proper order." When the new Rangers had mustered fully for the campaign, Rogers remained severely short-handed, and had to recruit more than 130 volunteers from other units. The quality of new recruits was abysmal. A British physician posted in Albany reported in June 1759: "Rogers's Rangers are far from compleat and have so many Boys among them that they are not worth a Farthing." Amherst was equally caustic in a letter to New York Lieutenant Governor James Delancey. Complaining that one Ranger scouting party had reported enemy forces south of Lake George without attempting to determine their number, while another had been completely wiped out by a "small" party of the enemy, Amherst fumed, "I do not give the least credit to any Ranger report, from all I have seen of them they are the most Careless, Negligent, Ignorant Corps I ever Saw, and if they are not beat on all Occasions I really cannot find out the reason they are not. M. Rogers a good Man, but I must Rub his Corps up or they are worse than Nothing."[13]

At the end of the 1759 campaign, Amherst asked the men of the four active colonial Ranger companies on the Lake Champlain front to continue in service. Fewer than half agreed. Amherst discharged the remainder, complaining directly to Rogers: "I hope [your officers] will be able to Raise better men than those who now Demand their Discharges, of which the greatest part is the worst Trash that I believe was ever Collected in any Corps." Rogers promised to do better, and reported in the spring of 1760 that he was discharging Rangers unfit for service and filling his ranks with "good men."[14]

Despite his strong reservations about the Rangers, Amherst recognized Rogers' talent and energy. For years, he wove Rogers into the British drive to conquer Canada, although Rogers exasperated him with demands for money from the army to cover ostensible expenses. Playing on Amherst's good will, Rogers peppered Amherst for more than a decade with proposals for appointments, awards, or recommendations to which Amherst eventually stopped responding.

Gage seems to have disdained Rogers from the outset, a view that persisted through his career. His opinions seem to have derived mainly from the view, almost universal among British officers, that all colonial ranger forces were too disorganized and undisciplined to be militarily effective, but he also personally disliked Rogers.

To Amherst, the new British commander-in-chief, Gage scorned the Rangers' fighting ability. When Amherst, early in his tenure, expressed hope that the Rangers could overtake and punish Indian raiders, Gage, recalling events of late 1758, commented, "I despair of this being done by Rangers only Judging from the many Pursuits of those People after Indians during my Service in this Country, in which they have never once come up with them."[15]

As to Rogers personally, Gage was harsh. Advising Amherst in the spring of 1759 that he had sent Rogers to Fort Edward to put his camp in order, he added that he had also ordered the British officers at Fort Edward to take responsibility for putting the Ranger camp in order, "as I know [Rogers] to be a true Ranger & not much addicted to Regularity." At another point he said, "Rogers is a good man in his way, but his schemes are very wild and he has a new one every Day."[16]

Gage, like Loudoun, Abercromby, and Haviland, was not a person of great talent or distinction. At Braddock's defeat on the Monongahela in 1755, Gage commanded the British advance guard, and his failure to seize and hold unoccupied high ground, together with his troops' disorderly flight at the battle's start, contributed significantly, perhaps decisively, to the defeat. Following the British capture of Ticonderoga and Crown Point in the 1759 campaign, Gage's next assignment was to lead a British force down the St. Lawrence to capture La Galette, but he failed to do so, much to Amherst's annoyance.[17]

On the other hand, Gage was well-liked and highly regarded by British peers, and he became good friends with Sir William Johnson, a colorful, unpolished product of the frontier, not unlike Rogers, which suggests that simple class snobbery was not behind Gage's dislike of Rogers. Gage's assessments reflected consensus in 1759, and, by the 1760s, even appear mild, as more people came to question Rogers' honesty and integrity.

Scouting in anticipation of the summer assault on Ticonderoga, the Rangers delivered mixed results. In February 1759, with Rogers sidelined again, this time with frostbite, Rangers at Fort Edward refused to go on scouts because they felt the new commander, Colonel Haldimand, proposed giving them too few men, perhaps setting them up to face superior numbers of Indians and Canadian partisans. Understandably, this refusal to execute orders infuriated Haldimand and Gage. In March, Rogers and a party of ninety ambushed French woodcutters on the east shore of Lake Champlain, opposite Fort Carillon, killing eight and capturing seven, then successfully fought off a large party of pursuers. But in May, Captain Jonathan Burbank, on a scout with thirty Rangers, was ambushed and the entire party killed or captured. Indians, mistaking Burbank for Rogers, mutilated his corpse "in a shocking Manner." That July, a Ranger party of mostly Stockbridge Indians, carelessly canoeing on Lake George in the open by day, was attacked and overwhelmed, losing five dead and at least five more captured.[18]

AMHERST began his advance on Ticonderoga on July 21, 1759. He had about twelve thousand men, compared to Abercromby's sixteen thousand a year earlier. The French force opposing him at Ticonderoga was only 2,300, compared to four thousand in 1758. More importantly, the French were without Montcalm, who was in Quebec trying to defend that city against Wolfe, while Amherst was a much more able commander than Abercromby. The French were under orders to abandon both Fort Carillon and Fort St. Frédéric at Crown Point and retreat to the north shore of Lake Champlain as soon as the British arrived in force at those strongholds.[19]

General Gage's 80th Light Infantry regiment was at the front of the British flotilla moving down Lake George, with Rogers and his men in the second rank. When it came time to land at the north end of Lake George, Rogers was again in the lead, at the head of a mixed force of Rangers, light infantry, and regulars under the overall command of Colonel Haviland. As Rogers had done the year before, he proceeded toward the sawmills, capturing an unguarded bridge over the La Chute River, then repelling a French counterattack attempting to retake the bridge. He took up a position at the west end of the Ticonderoga peninsula, opposite the fortifications that had defeated the British in 1758, while Amherst brought up his artillery.[20]

On the night of July 23, under cover of an artillery barrage from Fort Carillon, the French largely abandoned the fort. Most of the garrison boarded boats that moved off to the north, leaving a skeleton force of four hundred inside the fort with instructions to evacuate the bastion and blow it up once the British had their artillery in place. Hoping to cut off this remaining force, Amherst, on the night of July 26, ordered Rogers, with sixty men in a gunboat, to eliminate a boom blocking the water approach to Ticonderoga from the south. This would allow British watercraft to move further down Lake Champlain, encircle the fort on the water side, and prevent the remaining French troops from escaping. Before Rogers could reach the boom, huge explosions destroyed Fort Carillon and its remaining troops pushed off in boats. Rogers cut the boom and harried the retreating French, forcing several boats ashore and taking sixteen prisoners. The main French force escaped.[21]

During the artillery duel that preceded the demolition of Fort Carillon, a cannonball killed Amherst's aide Colonel Roger Townshend, one of relatively few British casualties. Roger's brother Charles, a prominent member of Parliament, held various cabinet positions in the 1750s and 1760s.

Only days after abandoning Fort Carillon, the French evacuated and blew up Fort St. Frédéric as well, retreating to the north end of Lake Champlain without any further resistance.[22] The British successes of 1758 (Louisbourg, Frontenac) and especially 1759 (Ticonderoga, Crown Point, Niagara, Quebec) were in large measure the result of a shift in global British strategy in early 1758. In late 1757, England had suffered a stinging defeat at the hands of the French in Hanover in the European theater of the Seven Years' War. This caused England to reassess its military objectives and to shift its focus from Europe to the conquest of Canada.[23] Canada's civilian population had always been only a small fraction of that of British North America, allowing England to raise far more provincial troops than France. Beginning in early 1758, England began to supplement this manpower advantage by pouring in additional regular regiments. By the end of 1759, England's numerical advantage was becoming decisive, the French were in retreat on all fronts, and it was apparent, in hindsight, that the end of French Canada was near.

As Amherst was moving his army forward to occupy Crown Point, news arrived that Sir William Johnson had captured Fort Niagara on Lake Ontario. Originally second in command in the siege of Fort Niagara, Johnson took over after the original commanding officer's death in combat. Before a British officer of higher social standing could arrive and take over command, Johnson soundly defeated a French, Canadian, and Indian column marching to the relief of Fort Niagara, killing more than three hundred enemy and capturing another one hundred, including the partisan leader Marin, who had fought Rogers at the Battle of Fort Anne. With the prospect of relief eliminated, Fort Niagara's garrison of six hundred had to surrender. Johnson had recruited a very large body of Mohawk and other Iroquois to supplement the British and colonial force attacking Fort Niagara. These Indians, in turn, persuaded hundreds of Iroquois aligned with the French to desert, not only Indians serving with the fort's garrison but also Indians accompanying the French relief force that Johnson defeated. His stature with the Iroquois, together with his stand-alone military skills, were decisive in the Fort Niagara victory. That win, in turn, was the greatest British victory of the French and Indian War until the capture of Quebec a short while later. The taking of Fort Niagara boxed Montreal in from the west, cut it off from western forts, and gave the British complete control of the Ohio valley.[24]

Rogers plainly considered himself to be Johnson's equal in merit and stature. A simple listing of Johnson's actual accomplishments, however—the 1755 victory at the Battle of Lake George, the capture of Fort Niagara, his invaluable service as Indian Superintendent, including the mobilization of hundreds of Mohawk and other Indian warriors to fight on the British side—makes clear that Johnson and Rogers were in completely different leagues.

CHAPTER SEVEN

THE
ST. FRANCIS RAID

HAVING captured Ticonderoga and Crown Point and having ordered Gage to advance down the St. Lawrence River from the southwest to capture La Galette, Amherst now grew anxious for news from Wolfe and the status of his campaign against Quebec. The direct route to Quebec from either Crown Point or the British forces on Lake Ontario passed through several hundred miles of enemy territory. Amherst asked for Ranger volunteers to serve as messengers to Quebec and back, but no one came forward; the assignment was too risky. In theory, a messenger could proceed to New York or Boston, sail from either port to British-controlled eastern Canada, and approach Wolfe from the rear, but the roundabout trip was too time-consuming to be useful. Amherst hit upon an alternative. He would send two officers, accompanied by several Indian guides and under a flag of truce, to carry peace proposals to the Indians in southern Quebec. The expedition's true purpose, however, was not to make peace with the Indians but to inveigle the peace commissioners, Captain Kennedy and Lieutenant Hamilton, safely through hostile French and Indian territory to Quebec.[1]

The plan backfired when Abenaki Indians refused to honor the flag of truce, took the Kennedy-Hamilton party prisoner, and handed the captives over to the French. Amherst was furious: how could the Indians have known the white flag was a ruse? He was determined to teach the Abenaki a lesson. Sensing an opening, Rogers dusted off and pitched Amherst on his 1756 proposal for a Ranger attack on St. Francis, the principal town of the Abenaki. St. Francis, a prosperous town of well-built houses, a Catholic church, and a large council house, lay south of the St. Lawrence River, northeast of Lake Champlain. Amherst authorized the plan, which Rogers subsequently acknowledged as his idea, indicating that he was responsible for the consequences.[2]

The Ranger expedition, as Amherst conceived it, had a legitimate military purpose beyond mere retaliation. The French had significant forces at Montreal and Isle aux Noix, a fort and military complex at the north end of Lake Champlain, where the lake drains into the Richelieu River. These forces could be sent to Quebec to support Montcalm or up the St. Lawrence to counter Gage. A raid in force to the territory south of the St. Lawrence, targeting both French and Indian settlements, might draw large numbers of French from Montreal and Isle aux Noix, perhaps reducing French capacity to reinforce other fronts. Amherst recorded in his diary that his mandate to Rogers was to "destroy the St. Francis Indian Settlements and the French settlements on the South side of the River St. Lawrence." His written instructions to Rogers were to "march and attack the enemy's settlements on the south-side of the river St. Lawrence."[3] Rogers saw his mission as simply a score-settling exercise punishing the Abenaki for decades of raiding in New England. He never had the slightest doubt that he would make St. Francis his primary target. Amherst was plainly concerned about the Rangers' desire to visit retribution on the Abenaki. "Take your revenge," he instructed Rogers in his written order, but "it is my orders that no women or children are killed or hurt."[4]

In their haste to get the raid off the ground, neither Rogers nor Amherst appears to have thought through the logistical problems the undertaking presented. So far in the war, Rogers had been operating in a narrow corridor stretching about fifty miles from Fort Edward to Crown Point. He knew this territory intimately. More importantly, the corridor was small enough that reinforcements or a retreat to safety were always within a one- or two-day march. St. Francis, in contrast, was 150 miles from Crown Point as the crow flew. The first half of the expedition, down Lake Champlain, was controlled by the French navy; in 1759, the British had only small transport vessels inadequate for confronting armed sloops and gunboats. The second half of the march was over land almost completely unfamiliar to Rogers and the Rangers. Indians and Canadian partisans controlled this segment of the route. Rogers knew that he could expect no reinforcement if his party were discovered. The proposed raiding force of two hundred was large enough that it would have difficulty operating undetected in enemy territory for an extended period. The force was small enough that, if detected, it could not expect to hold its own against greatly superior enemy forces.

Rogers set about assembling an attack force. Ranger ranks remained depleted and insufficient, so the party incorporated Captain Amos Ogden and a detachment of the New Jersey Blues regiment, Lieutenant William Dunbar and a detachment from Gage's 80th Light Infantry regiment, and men from other British and colonial units. Captain Stark, Rogers' best Ranger officer, declined to participate, pleading rheumatism; his grandson Caleb maintained that Stark declined at least in part because he knew the target to be St. Francis. He did not wish to participate in a punitive attack against people who had shown him so much kindness during his 1752 captivity.[5]

The raiders set out in whaleboats on the night of September 13, 1759. Their objective was Missisquoi Bay at the extreme northeast corner of Lake Champlain, some seventy-five miles north. To evade French naval forces, they had to travel at night and rest by day, and even moving by night they risked detection, especially in the lake's very narrow southerly portions. Limited to traveling in the dark and beset by foul weather, they averaged only seven or eight miles a night, needing a full ten days to reach Missisquoi Bay.[6]

En route Rogers had to send back to Crown Point a significant number of men unfit to continue. An unspecified disease disabled thirty men, including many Stockbridge Indians. A firearms accident disabled others. Several men were too weak to walk; healthy men had to carry them in litters and guide the invalids back to Crown Point. By the time Rogers' force reached Missisquoi Bay, he was down to fewer than 160 men.[7]

Rogers reached Missisquoi Bay on September 23. The troops pulled the whaleboats ashore and hid them, along with provisions for the return trip to Crown Point. Rogers expected to be gone from Missisquoi Bay for at least several weeks. Knowing that if in his absence the enemy found his cache, his preferred line of retreat would be cut off, he left two Stockbridge Indians to watch the boats and provisions; if the Rangers' cache was discovered they were to immediately run after and alert the main party.[8]

Rogers' precaution was all too necessary. The landing spot was not heavily populated, but neither was it entirely deserted. As the Rangers were landing, Abenaki hunters heard oars pulling boats and, concluding that an enemy force might be about, hurried to Isle aux Noix to report their suspicions. The next day, a Canadian patrol discovered an oar of English manufacture floating near the landing site. The patrol's report prompted superiors to dispatch Ensign Langy, the Canadian partisan who had defeated Rogers at the Battle on Snowshoes, from Isle aux Noix to investigate. Langy quickly found and burned the boats and appropriated or destroyed the provisions, then returned to Isle aux Noix. The commander there sent multiple messengers to alert French and Indian forces in the region. He ordered Langy, with a force of 350, to pursue the raiders; another four hundred men were to set an ambush at the landing site. Enemy forces numbering five times the size of his own command now blocked Rogers' intended line of retreat.[9]

Eighteen months earlier, Rogers had complained bitterly that Colonel Haviland had sent him on a suicide mission when he ordered Rogers with a force of 180 to scout the environs of Ticonderoga. Now he found himself with fewer men in a far more serious predicament much farther from reinforcement, entirely by his own choice.

Having learned from his Indian watchmen that they had been found out, Rogers and his officers considered their options. Reversing their route was out of the question. Making a stand to fight the force pursuing them was also not attractive. Even if they could defeat any immediate pursuers, they would still be far behind enemy lines and close enough to major enemy troop concentrations to be easily cut off and destroyed. Rogers must have calculated that food for the retreat would be a major issue, but he also likely figured the Rangers could replenish at St. Francis—if they could capture the town. That made the most attractive option forging ahead, taking St. Francis and resupplying, then retreating southeast toward Fort No. 4, away from the largest concentrations of enemy fighters.[10] The only other alternatives would have been to abandon the raid and head straight for Fort No. 4 or to retreat overland toward the British-controlled portion of Lake Champlain. The first option would have involved a 150-mile trek over unfamiliar territory, but likely would have avoided significant enemy forces. The second option was shorter, but it still would have involved a week's march and a greater risk of enemy attack.

The raiders decided to forge ahead. Rogers sent a group of sick and injured back to Crown Point with a messenger, Lieutenant Andrew Mc-Mullen, who was to explain their situation, their plan to continue to St. Francis, and their probable retreat by way of Fort No. 4. McMullen was to ask that a detachment bringing provisions by canoe paddle from Fort No. 4 up the Connecticut River to wait for them sixty miles north at the Lower Coos, the meadowland Rogers had helped to survey in 1753. Rogers' command was now down to 142.[11]

The long slog to St. Francis was hellish. Rogers' party had to traverse an enormous spruce bog in water nearly a foot deep relieved only by scant hummocks of dry land. At night, the troops cut boughs and fash-ioned hammocks to try to keep dry while they slept. All day they marched in shin-deep water. The terrain's one advantage was that it caused Langy to lose their trail; the Rangers did not know it, but they were no longer in danger of imminent attack.[12]

The bog crossing took ten days, during which their provisions ran out. When they reached solid ground, another challenge confronted them. The town of St. Francis was on the east bank of the St. Francis River; the Rangers were on the west bank. The river, swelled by recent rains, was deep and fast-flowing. The Rangers may have contemplated, or even started, building rafts, but they likely lacked adequate tools, and they now were so close to St. Francis that the clatter of wood chopping risked alerting the foe. Instead, they explored upriver until they found a spot that was barely fordable—five feet deep. Forming a human chain, they managed to inch their way across.[13]

The Rangers marched to within sight of St. Francis late in the after-noon of October 3.[14] After dark, as the main body rested, Rogers and Lieutenant George Turner and Ensign Elias Avery, disguised as Indians, entered the town to reconnoiter. They found the Indians engaged in a social event in the council house that included dancing. Sources differ as to whether the fête was a wedding, a harvest festival, or the celebration of a hunting party's return. Rogers and the other spies returned to the main camp at 2:00 a.m. At 3:00 a.m., Rogers had his men take up po-sitions about five hundred yards from the town.[15]

In addition to Rogers, Turner, and Avery, another outsider entered St. Francis that night: a non-Abenaki Indian, thought to have been a

Stockbridge Indian from Rogers' own force. The Indian warned villagers, possibly through a young girl who had left the council house to rest, that they were about to be attacked. Some families heeded the warning and hid in a nearby ravine, apparently a traditional emergency refuge. Although the story of the mysterious stranger warning St. Francis is supported only by Abenaki oral tradition, Rogers' biographers credit both the story itself and the likelihood that the advance notice allowed significant numbers of villagers to escape death or capture as events unfolded.[16]

The Ranger force attacked the next morning in predawn half-light. The attack came as a complete surprise to those left in the town, and they were overwhelmed. Resistance from the council house was quickly suppressed. Some villagers tried to escape downriver by boat, but were pursued and shot and their boats sunk. The battle was over by 7:00 a.m. Rogers reported killing "at least two hundred" Indians and capturing twenty women and children, but sustaining only trifling losses: a single Stockbridge Indian killed.[17] Captain Ogden had serious but not mortal head and upper body wounds, and half a dozen men reported minor wounds or injuries.[18]

WITH the battle over, the Rangers faced the most difficult part of the mission: getting out alive. Interrogation of prisoners and former captives revealed the presence nearby of a large French force, well-positioned to block a direct retreat to Lake Champlain, where, in any event, the Rangers knew their whaleboats and supplies had been discovered and destroyed. As Rogers had anticipated, their only real option was to retreat southeast toward the Connecticut River and Fort No. 4, two hundred miles away. The Lower Coos, where Rogers had asked that provisions be sent—assuming his messenger had gotten through—was 140 miles away.[19]

The most pressing issue was food to fuel the long, arduous retreat. The Rangers had exhausted the provisions they were carrying on the way to St. Francis. Fortunately, the Abenaki had been laying in food for winter: three storehouses of corn and possibly other foodstuffs. Rogers ordered his men to fill their knapsacks.[20]

Some men, especially the British troops, did. Many Rangers and other provincials, however, stuffed their bags with loot. The Catholic church had many valuable items, including silver chalices and candlesticks and a ten-pound silver Madonna, all of which were taken. Looting was not limited to the church. St. Francis was a wealthy town, and descriptions of the amount and types of plunder taken, including money, wampum, and other valuables, make clear that the town's fifty solidly built houses were thoroughly ransacked. The looting appalled British troops, not because of moral scruples but because a successful escape demanded that the Rangers gather all the food they could carry. There is no record of Ranger officers attempting to stop the looting or to ensure that every man in the party was packing a full measure of provisions.

Plundering done, the Rangers burned the town, church and all. Of the twenty female and child prisoners, Rogers released fifteen, taking along on the retreat five or six, including the Abenaki chief Gill's wife and two sons. Presumably, Rogers believed them valuable as hostages. The Rangers had freed five captives held by the Abenaki, and these, too, joined the retreat.[21]

For eight days, Rogers held his party, numbering about 150, together. During this time, the enemy pursued but apparently did not attack, whether because they had not yet caught up or because their force was too small to risk attacking the entire Ranger party. In mid-October, with food again exhausted, Rogers reorganized the group into nine small detachments, each headed by an officer, on the theory that smaller groups would have better luck hunting and foraging. Four of these, including Rogers', headed due south at intervals, their objective the rendezvous at the Lower Coos on the Connecticut River. Three groups followed Indian trails southeast, planning to reach the Connecticut River further upstream and follow that waterway down to the Lower Coos. Two groups headed southwest toward Lake Champlain, hoping to follow its eastern shore south until they reached British-held territory.[22]

The fortunes of Rogers' command now deteriorated sharply. Food quickly became an acute issue. Virtually no game was to be found, reducing the men to scrounging for edible vegetation. French, Canadian, and Indian pursuers harried them, led by a Canadian partisan named Dumas, who had patched together a force of sixty. The French, not knowing Rogers had gotten word of the destruction of his whaleboats and supplies, kept most of their forces near his landing spot on Lake Champlain, expecting him to retreat in that direction. When the Rangers split up, Dumas struck hard. He attacked a detachment of twenty headed by British light infantry Lieutenant Dunbar and ranger

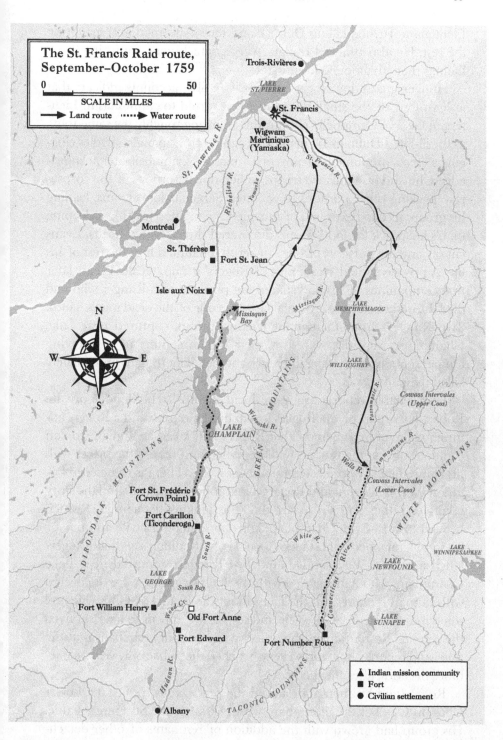

The St. Francis Raid route,
September–October 1759

0   50

SCALE IN MILES
→ Land route   ·····▶ Water route

Trois-Rivières

LAKE ST. PIERRE

St. Francis

Wigwam
Martinique
(Yamaska)

St. Lawrence R.

St. Francis R.

Richelieu R.

Yamaska R.

Montréal

St. Thérèse
Fort St. Jean

Isle aux Noix

Missisquoi R.

Missisquoi
Bay

LAKE
MEMPHREMAGOG

N
W   E
S

GREEN MOUNTAINS

LAKE
WILLOUGHBY

Passumpsic R.

Cowass Intervales
(Upper Coos)

Winooski R.

LAKE
CHAMPLAIN

ADIRONDACK MOUNTAINS

Fort St. Frédéric
(Crown Point)

Fort Carillon
(Ticonderoga)

South R.

Wells R.

Ammonoosuc R.

Cowass Intervales
(Lower Coos)

WHITE MOUNTAINS

White R.

LAKE
WINNIPESAUKEE

LAKE
NEWFOUND

LAKE
GEORGE

South Bay

Fort William Henry

Wood Cr.

Old Fort Anne

Fort Edward

Fort Number Four

Connecticut River

LAKE
SUNAPEE

Hudson R.

TACONIC MOUNTAINS

Albany

▲ Indian mission community
■ Fort
● Civilian settlement

Lieutenant Turner, killing Dunbar and ten of his men and scattering the rest. He also attacked Ensign Avery's detachment, capturing five.[23] Dumas then abandoned his pursuit.

Hunger gnawed at Rogers' troops. Credible accounts indicate that at least four of the small detachments resorted to cannibalism. Lieutenant George Campbell's contingent, following roughly the same route as the ill-fated Dunbar-Turner group, came across mangled bodies clogging a creek, presumably victims of Dumas. As Campbell later acknowledged, he and his famished troops wolfed down portions of the corpses raw, packing other portions to eat later. Sergeant John Evans, leading his group, recalled extremes of hunger. One night, searching a sleeping man's knapsack for food, Evans discovered three severed heads. Evans cut off and ate portions of one, an act that haunted him the rest of his life. A private named Ward, part of Rogers' group, recalled years later that companions of his had shared out portions of a Ranger who had died the night before. Ward breakfasted on one of the dead man's hands. Two Rangers from Lieutenant Jenkins' group, captured near Lake Champlain, were discovered by their Indian captors to be carrying human remains, according to French sources. The Indians immediately killed the pair.[24]

Less reliable reports are more lurid. Scottish Highlander private Robert Kirk, part of the Rogers group on the retreat and a Rogers admirer, claimed in a memoir that Rogers had killed an Indian woman captured during the retreat, butchered her, and shared the pieces with his companions, who roasted them over a fire. There is some corroboration for this account and Rogers' biographers appear to find the story credible. Other sources assert that the Jenkins detachment, which headed toward Lake Champlain, killed and ate Gill's wife and one of his sons, kidnapped as hostages. Abenaki oral tradition says that Rangers killed and ate a boy captive, and two Rangers captured near Lake Champlain, who had traveled with the Jenkins group, were discovered with human remains, but the facts about the deaths of Gill's wife and son remain unclear.[25] Gill's wife and son do not appear to have survived the retreat. No participant breathed a word about cannibalism at the time, and reports about these events reached the public only years, sometimes decades, after the fact.

Rogers and his men approached the rendezvous spot at the Lower Coos on October 20, more than two weeks after the St. Francis battle. His group had grown with the addition of remnants of other detachments. Advancing, the Rangers found a still-warm campfire, but no relief party and no supplies. They heard shots. Thinking them to be signals from the rescue party—they may actually have been hunters—the Rangers fired but got no response. The rescue party had left only hours earlier, taking the provisions back to Fort No. 4.[26]

Rogers' messenger, Lieutenant McMullen, had made it to Crown Point with Rogers' request that supplies be sent from Fort No. 4 to the junction of the Wells River and the Connecticut River at the Lower Coos. Amherst dispatched a Lieutenant Stevens to go to Fort No. 4, organize a relief party to carry provisions to the rendezvous, and remain there "so long as You shall think there is any probability of Major Rogers's returning that way." Rather than go all the way to the rendezvous, Stevens, accompanied by a handful of men, stopped several miles short, allegedly concerned about rapids on the Connecticut River. He hiked to the actual rendezvous daily for several days to see if anyone was there and to fire signal shots. Stevens, not knowing Rogers was near but having heard McMullen's account of Rogers' plan, decided that if Rogers did retreat to that location he should already have arrived, so he left. When he reported to Amherst at Crown Point that he had failed to connect with Rogers, Amherst, still unaware of Rogers' fate, commented in his diary: "he should have waited longer." Stevens' premature departure, which made the famished Rangers wait two more weeks for food, caused multiple deaths from starvation.[27]

Rogers and party waited at the Lower Coos for several days hoping relief would arrive. When it became apparent that no help was on the way, Rogers had only one option: someone would have to make the sixty-mile trip downriver to bring help from Fort No. 4. Most of Rogers' troops were too exhausted to move. The robust Rogers was likely in the best condition of anyone. Captain Ogden also agreed to go. Ogden had been so weak from his wounds that Rogers had earlier carried him on his back fording streams and rivers, but he had recovered. Rogers selected another Ranger and a captive Indian boy, likely Gill's second son, and the party constructed a small raft and headed down the Connecticut River.[28]

The raft trip was an ordeal of its own. The second day out, the party was barely able to jump off the raft and flounder to shore to avoid being swept over a falls. The raft broke to pieces on rocks. The men, too weak to use hatchets to build a raft, were reduced to felling small trees by burning them off at the base, then burning the trunks into appropriate lengths they bound with vines. They nearly lost the second raft to another falls but wrestled their craft and themselves ashore in time. Ogden used an improvised rope to lower the raft over the cascade to Rogers, who was able to recover it. They reached Fort No. 4 at the end of October, nearly a month after the battle.[29]

Supply canoes were dispatched upriver to the survivors at the Lower Coos. Rogers followed two days later with supplies to collect survivors from his band and search for other survivors. In between, Rogers wrote his report of the raid to Amherst and sent it to Crown Point with Ogden.

Amherst had been waiting anxiously for news of Rogers. On November 2, 1759, he reported to New York Lieutenant Governor Delancey that he had heard that Rogers had attacked an Indian settlement, which Amherst presumed to have been St. Francis, but that Indian and Canadian pursuers "fell upon Major Rogers in his retreat to New England and killed several of his party. . . . What this will turn out," Amherst concluded, "will not be known till Some of his party Come in." On November 13, Amherst reported that Ogden and others from the Ranger party had made it to Crown Point with the first reports of the mission. Amherst was stunned by the loot that Ranger survivors brought in.[30] He commented that they were carrying "more Indian Riches than I thought any of their Towns would have contained." Ogden assured him that "their Houses were very good."

Then Ogden reported the military results: the Indians, "of Course all Drunk," had been surprised sleeping and slaughtered without being able to reach their weapons and had lost "about 200" dead. Relieved, Amherst assumed that the handful of Rangers killed on the retreat had been killed "by a Hunting Party," saying, "I don't doubt but the [rest of the] party will all come in safe." He offered the same optimistic prediction to Rogers: "I am in hopes all the rest will get in very safe. I think there is no danger but they will . . . ."[31]

They didn't. When the final losses were tallied, Rogers calculated he had had forty-nine men killed or captured. His biographers put the number somewhat higher, at fifty-five or sixty. Any of these numbers is more than a third of the force that attacked St. Francis. Part of the disagreement about total losses may result from the fact that several men captured near Lake Champlain, including Rogers' later accuser Sergeant Lewis, apparently were released almost immediately in a prisoner exchange, and it is unclear whether they should be counted in the casualty total. Many, if not most, other prisoners were tortured to death by vengeful Abenaki. Apparently only two survived to return eventually to the British side. Of the total deaths, about half were due to starvation or exposure, the remainder to Indian attack.[32]

Rogers, writing his official report from Fort No. 4 a month after the battle, declared he had killed "at least two hundred" Abenaki in the St. Francis attack. Ogden, sticking to the party line, reported the same casualty estimate to Amherst. This number of warriors slain would have completely annihilated the Abenaki as a fighting force, making the raid a stunning, lop-sided, decisive military victory. But was it?

Sources agree that when the Rangers attacked St. Francis, there were few if any fighting men there. At the time of the British attack, one group of Abenaki fighters was at Wigwam Martinique, an Indian village ten miles west, closer to Rogers' landing spot and believed erroneously by the French to be his likeliest target for attack. Others were with the French forces at Isle aux Noix. A French source states that St. Francis, at the time of the attack, had been "denuded" of warriors.[33]

How many Abenaki actually died in the attack? Abenaki oral tradition says thirty.[34] A Jesuit missionary priest, Pierre-Joseph-Antoine Roubaud, served the village. He was away at the time of the attack but returned to the ruins the next day. He reported ten men and twenty-two women and children killed.[35] Another French source says that the raiders "killed around thirty women & old people," suggesting that even the male victims were not warriors.[36] One of Rogers' biographers concedes that the French casualty estimates were "accurate enough."[37]

How could Rogers have come in good faith to report "at least two hundred" Indians killed? His mostly sympathetic biographers offer a variety of explanations. Knowing beforehand how many warriors were thought to reside in St. Francis, he may have assumed he had killed most of them.[38] He may have based his casualty estimate on the number of people he had seen during his reconnaissance the night before, unaware that many residents had fled thanks to the mysterious warning.[39] When the town was torched, flames may have consumed many bodies, hampering his effort to get a valid count.[40]

These theories do not hold up. The Rangers were familiar enough with St. Francis—many colonials had lived there as captives—to know that its entire fighting force did not approach two hundred. In the middle of a wartime campaign season, many if not most of the warriors would be expected to be away fighting. If Rogers was relying on his observations from the night before, he would have seen that few warriors were present.

The lack of significant Ranger casualties makes clear that the Rangers encountered no major opposition: no matter how profound the element of surprise, a force of 140, in an age of single-shot weapons, could not have annihilated two hundred well-armed opponents without sustaining significant casualties. Recognizing that the absence of Abenaki opposition was unusual, Rogers, again echoed by Ogden, suggested an explanation: they were all drunk or hung over and had been killed before they could reach their weapons. This was improbable.

Following the January 1757 ambush and after the Battle on Snowshoes, Rogers had greatly overestimated the losses he inflicted on the enemy, but in both instances he had retreated from the battlefield in the dark and could not have been expected to accurately tabulate enemy losses. At St. Francis, by contrast, the Rangers occupied the battlefield for several hours after the battle, unopposed and in daylight. The conclusion is inescapable that Rogers' estimate of "at least two hundred" Indian dead was a deliberate lie, intended to soften the blow when the details of his harrowing retreat came out.

The circumstances of Rogers' first report to Amherst confirm this. When Rogers reached Fort No. 4, he knew that French and Indian pursuers had attacked Ensign Avery's detachment and captured five men; survivors of that attack had joined Rogers' detachment.[41] He had no details on the fates of the seven or eight other small groups of survivors, but he knew they were being hunted aggressively. He knew, too, that starvation was a grave risk; men in his detachment had died of starvation and others were starving. Rogers could be optimistic about the survival only of his own detachment of perhaps thirty or forty, and even they were at risk until rescuers from Fort No. 4 could reach them. Rogers likely feared the worst for his fragmented command, and if the reality was not quite as bad as he feared, it was bad enough. A claim to have decimated the Abenaki in the fight would in some measure balance out the horrendous loss of life he knew was bound to come to light, and the press coverage and popular acclaim greeting his victory would shield him from critical scrutiny.

Rogers clearly meant his initial account to Amherst of the St. Francis raid to cover up the truth. First, he reports that before the attack, he "found the Indians in a high frolic or dance. . . . At half an hour before sunrise, I surprised the town when they were all fast asleep." This was done "with so much alacrity by both the officers and men, that the enemy had not time to recover themselves, or to take arms for their defense, till they were chiefly destroyed." Then, "[a] little after sunrise I set fire to all their houses, except three, in which there was corn, that I reserved for the use of the party." Rogers concludes that "[t]he fire consumed many of the Indians who had concealed themselves in the cellars and lofts of their houses. About seven o'clock in the morning the affair was completely over, in which time we had killed at least two hundred Indians, and taken twenty of their women and children prisoners."[42]

The discovery of the Indians "in a high frolic or dance" explains how he could surprise and defeat them so easily; they had likely gotten drunk and at the time of the attack were sleeping off their bender. The claim that the Indians were "chiefly destroyed" before they could reach their weapons reinforces this idea and explains the Rangers' improbably light casualties. The specific hour he gives for torching the town allows no time for the rampant looting that actually took place, while the reference to numerous Indians consumed by fire suggests a preemptive defense if fewer that two hundred bodies turn up. The reference to at least two hundred killed, of course, establishes the raid as a stunning victory, while the reference to women and children taken prisoner suggests both that the dead were all warriors and that Rogers was scrupulously following orders not to harm women and children. Indeed, confronted later with French protests that at St. Francis Rogers had killed non-combatants—and few others—Amherst did not believe the charge.[43]

Amherst was not the only person Rogers wished to influence with his letter. He knew that the St. Francis raid would be a major news story. His letter to Amherst in its entirety quickly reached the press. As early as November 3, only days after Rogers' arrival at Fort No. 4, an unidentified soldier there sent the *New York Gazette* an account of the raid closely tracking Rogers' account to Amherst. This informant either had a copy of Rogers' letter, had spoken in depth with Rogers, or both. It would be helpful to Rogers if Amherst formed a positive view of the raid before negative news trickled in. It would be even better if Rogers were already enjoying public acclaim for his tremendous victory before all the facts were known.[44]

Rogers' account misled his superiors only briefly. When all information on the retreat from St. Francis was in, it was the accepted British army conclusion that the provincial soldiers' greed, packing loot rather than food, contributed significantly to the retreat's descent into nightmare.

Other criticism surfaced. According to a Sergeant Lewis of the 80th Light Infantry detachment, Rogers forcibly redistributed food among the troops, taking provisions from soldiers who had prudently packed as much food as possible and issuing it to soldiers who had foolishly packed plunder. Rogers angrily denied the accusation and sought to have Lewis court-martialed for slander. Amherst persuaded Rogers to let the matter drop. Lewis had retreated with a detachment led by Lieutenant Jenkins, one of the groups reduced to cannibalism. Reliable accounts record that at least two men in this group, when captured, were found to be carrying human remains. Whether or not Lewis engaged in cannibalism, he was plainly traumatized by the retreat, and whether or not his allegation against Rogers was true, it reflected British troops' deep anger at the Rangers for exacerbating the horrors of the retreat with their greed.[45]

Sobered as the magnitude of his losses began to register, Rogers wrote to Amherst in December 1759 in a penitent tone: "The Misfortunes attending my Retreat from Saint Francois cause me great uneasiness, the brave men lost I most heartily lament, and fear your Excellency's Censure as the going against that place was my own proposal, and that I shall be disappointed of that Footing in the Army which I have long endeavor'd to merit."[46] Rogers may have waxed penitent, but his primary concern appears to have been his "Footing in the Army"—i.e., his prospects for promotion, which he feared had been damaged—rather than the many unnecessary dead. Amherst responded, "I am Sorry to See you have so many Men Missing, this will I hope be a Lesson to all other Parties to Secure Provisions and themselves, instead of Loading themselves with Plunder, by which they must be Lost, if an Enemy pursues."[47]

Rogers, however, continued to duck the issue of looting. Asked by Amherst to respond to a French complaint that important records had been destroyed when St. Francis burned, Rogers responded that it never occurred to him that the town might contain important records and that he had ordered it burned to prevent looting. Amherst, of course, knew all about the looting and had already remarked to Delancey on the riches Rangers carried off.[48]

If the British command understood that the retreat from St. Francis had been a major calamity, they also likely recognized Rogers' claim of a stunning victory, with two hundred Abenaki warriors killed, for the fabrication that it was. By now the British knew the French viewed the attack on St. Francis as a small-scale slaughter of non-combatants, and must have concluded that Rogers' rosy presentation of the battle had been invented.

While the British high command was increasingly skeptical, and while Rogers seemed penitent, the press, aware only of the facts as Rogers presented them, was thrilled. Rogers' victory over the Abenaki was greeted with "a chorus of acclaim," fixing him "in the spotlight of celebrity." The *New York Mercury* printed verbatim Rogers' report to Amherst on the raid. The *New York Gazette* printed an account of the raid, largely taken from Rogers' letter, written by a soldier at Fort No. 4. The *New Hampshire Gazette* gave front-page coverage to a lengthy report on the raid, which also appeared in the *Boston Gazette* and the *Boston Evening Post*. Newspapers inflated the number of Indian dead from Rogers' fictitious two hundred to an even more improbable three hundred or more. "What do we owe such a beneficial Man; and a Man of such enterprizing Genius?" wondered the *New Hampshire Gazette*.[49]

Money? Fearful a few months earlier of Amherst's censure and for his standing in the army, Rogers filed a petition with the Massachusetts legislature in March 1760 "praying that a suitable Reward may be granted by this Government to himself and his Men for their service in destroying the Indian Town of St. Francois." The petition was dismissed without comment.[50]

Anxious to neutralize criticism, Rogers sought court martials of two men: Lieutenant Stevens, who failed to wait for him at the Lower Coos with desperately needed food supplies, and Sergeant Lewis of the 80th Light Infantry regiment, who accused him of taking food from the men of that regiment and giving it to Rangers who had loaded up on plunder. Rogers even had Lewis, just back from his harrowing near-death experience on the retreat, arrested and confined to the stockade until a court martial could be arranged. Gage offered to organize the court martial but pointed out that assembling the relevant witnesses in one place would be difficult. Amherst, who had written in his diary that he believed Stevens had left too soon, and who had twice shared his disapproval of Stevens' conduct with Rogers, agreed to the Stevens court martial, but demurred as to Lewis, telling Rogers "it is not in the power of that Serjeant to hurt Your Character."[51] Given that Amherst had already chastised Rogers for the Rangers' ill-disciplined plundering, it is unlikely that he regarded Rogers as blameless, but while a trial of Stevens for dereliction of duty could serve as a useful warning to other officers, a Lewis court martial risked focusing official attention on the disorderly retreat, with who knew what result.

Stevens' court martial was duly held in April 1760. Several witnesses disputed the assertion that there were turbulent waters at the approach to the rendezvous, casting doubt on Stevens' claim that fear of his supply canoes being overturned was his reason for stopping miles short of the rendezvous. There was inconsistent testimony about just how long he waited for Rogers. Unexpressed, but clearly influencing the proceeding, was the suspicion that Stevens, scared of being alone in Indian territory with only a small patrol, was looking for an excuse to return to the safety of Fort No. 4. He was convicted.[52]

R OGERS' attack on St. Francis was hardly the stupendous victory he claimed, and today no one disputes that conclusion. The Abenaki were not eliminated as a fighting force, St. Francis was rebuilt, and "Rogers' revenge [was not] the truly punishing blow he had hoped it would be."[53] Instead, Rogers' generally sympathetic biographers argue that the St. Francis attack was a "psychological" victory.[54]

If "psychological" victory means that enemy morale was materially undermined, this claim is dubious. The Abenaki were certainly angry about the destruction of St. Francis—and took their anger out on Ranger captives—but there is no evidence they were intimidated. Claims that Indian support for the French diminished in the final months of the war more likely reflect the fact that the Indians saw which way the wind was blowing in the war writ large, not the impact of the relatively minor battle at St. Francis.[55]

If "psychological" victory, however, means that the St. Francis attack boosted colonial morale by appealing to public and press interest in getting revenge against traditional Indian adversaries, Rogers' biographers may well be right. The destruction of St. Francis was plainly hugely popular, and the public and press were likely largely indifferent to Abenaki casualties, and whether they were warriors or non-combatants. What gratified the colonial psyche was the image of St. Francis in flames. Even here, though, the public and press might have balked had they known the true cost of this "psychological" victory, and the very limited concrete results it achieved.

Was the satisfaction of having destroyed St. Francis worth the fifty or sixty lives lost, and the horrors visited on the survivors of the retreat? Rogers clearly worried that the game was not worth the candle for his superiors, and objectively he was right. The St. Francis raid achieved

very little, at a cost that was unjustified. Take away the fictitious annihi-
lation of the Abenaki fighting force and the St. Francis raid was simply
another destruction of an undefended Indian village. Such "victories"
were common in the European subjugation of North America but, in
the absence of a significant military victory, they did not win press or
public acclaim for their leaders.[56] Rogers' false claim to have destroyed
the Abenaki fighting force made him a hero.

The plan to attack St. Francis was one of the wild schemes that Gage
had warned of. Its fundamental flaw was that Rogers and the Rangers
had no plausible exit plan. Even if the Rangers could have advanced
undiscovered to St. Francis, the attack on St. Francis would raise an
alarm, they would be 150 miles and a fifteen- or twenty-day march behind enemy lines, and their preferred escape route would be blocked by
enemy forces outnumbering them at least five to one. Rogers did not
initially contemplate a withdrawal in the direction of Fort No. 4, but if
he had he would have recognized that this alternative had its own serious
disadvantages.

Successful retreat would be even more difficult if the Rangers were
encumbered by wounded, as they would have been had St. Francis actually been defended. And, if so, the risk of discovery by scouts, pickets,
or hunters, depriving Rogers of the element of surprise, would have
been enormous. To the extent that the attack on St. Francis made any
limited sense, it could only have succeeded if the town was largely or
entirely undefended, and Rogers must have known this. His reconnaissance on the night before the attack likely was intended to confirm that
there would be no serious resistance. Even though he was correct in this
assessment, the flaws were so serious that the attack, on balance, was
still a military failure.

Rogers, who had proposed the raid and who had been thinking about
it for years, was principally responsible for the plan's flaws. Amherst,
however, usually meticulous and foresightful in his planning, approved
Rogers' proposal without questioning it and bears at least some responsibility for the failed outcome. It is likely because he recognized his own
share of the blame that Amherst failed to deliver the "censure" that
Rogers expected.

None of these considerations can detract from the remarkable
courage and perseverance of the Rangers, and Rogers personally, on
the St. Francis campaign. It is difficult not to be moved by the narrative
of the Rangers' interminable slog across the marsh, their improvised

crossing of the swollen St. Francis River, the image of Rogers carrying
Ogden on his back to ford streams during the long retreat, the unbear-
able hunger of the retreat, and Rogers' final sixty-mile improvised trip
by raft to secure help. The Rangers', and Rogers', efforts were heroic,
even epic. But this does not mean that the attack on St. Francis was a
sound military plan; the hardships and horrors the Rangers overcame
were of their own creation.

William Shirley, 1694-1771, was Governor of Massachusetts and military commander in North America at the start of the French and Indian War. He created the first provincial Ranger unit, under Rogers' command, in 1756. (*New York Public Library*)

Frederick Haldimand, 1718-1791, was commander of Fort Edward, and Rogers' commanding officer, in 1758. He held a variety of later military appointments in North America and became Governor of Canada in 1778. (*New York Public Library*)

William Johnson, 1715-1774, friend and adopted member of the Mohawk tribe, was Superintendent of Indian Affairs for the northern colonies from 1756 until 1774. An early supporter of Rogers, he later became one of his severest critics. (*New York Public Library*)

Thomas Gage, 1721-1787, held various military positions in the colonies during and after the French and Indian War. He disliked Rogers intensely. (*New York Public Library*)

John Campbell, Earl of Loudoun, 1705-1782, succeeded William Shirley as military commander in North America in 1756. (*New York Public Library*)

Marquis de Montcalm, 1712-1759, was French military commander in North America from 1756 until 1759. The victor at the siege of Fort William Henry in 1757 and the defense of Fort Carillon in 1758, he was killed defending Quebec in 1759. (*New York Public Library*)

Jonathan Carver, 1710-1780, was mapmaker for the Tute-Carver expedition in 1766-67. (*New York Public Library*)

Charles Townshend, 1725-1767, a Member of Parliament who held various cabinet positions in the 1750s and 1760s, was Rogers' most important London patron. He supported Rogers' proposal for an overland expedition to discover the Northwest Passage. (*New York Public Library*)

Israel Putnam, 1718-1790, scouted and fought alongside Rogers during the French and Indian War and later became a prominent Continental Army officer during the Revolutionary War. (*New York Public Library*)

Lord George Augustus Howe, 1725-1758, was well-liked by both British and colonial troops and urged British troops to learn woodland warfare tactics from their colonial counterparts. He died during the 1758 Ticonderoga campaign. (*New York Public Library*)

Lord Jeffery Amherst, 1717-1797, was British military commander in North America during the final years of the French and Indian War. Appreciative of Rogers' personal bravery and enterprise, he had a poor opinion of the Rangers and believed Rogers' claims for reimbursement from the army were grossly inflated. (*New York Public Library*)

William Howe, 1759-1814, was the commander of the British land forces in the colonies during the early years of the Revolutionary War. He recruited Rogers to command a Loyalist regiment known as the Queen's American Rangers. (*New York Public Library*)

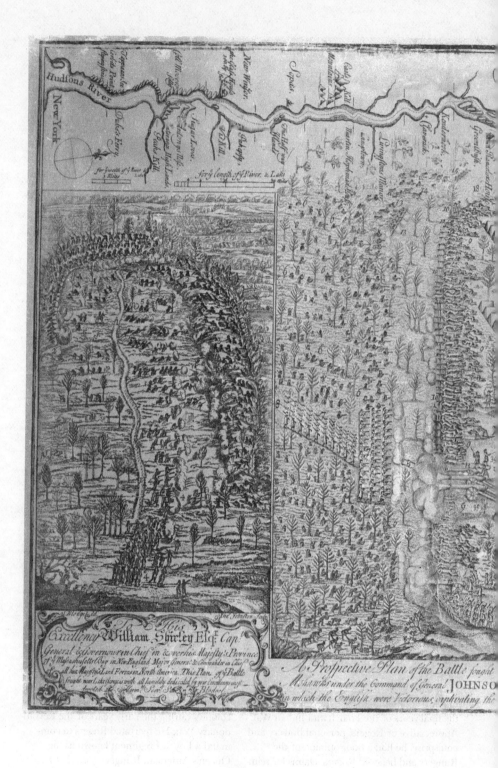

A Prospective Plan of the Battle fought
Mohawks under the Command of General JOHNSO
in which the English were Victorious, captivating the

KE GEORGE on the 8th of September 1755, between 2000 English with 250
2500 French and Indians under the Command of General DIESKAU
General with a number of his Men, killing 700 and putting the rest to flight.

"A Perspective View of the Battle fought near Lake George on the 8th of Sepr. 1755." Drawn and published at the time, it was dedicated to William Shirley. The map at top shows the Hudson River from New York City to Lake George, with plans of Fort William Henry and Fort Edward. In the aftermath, William Johnson realized that the British needed men who knew the frontier well. As a result, within a week of this important British victory, Robert Rogers was given his first scouting expedition to Fort St. Frédéric at Crown Point. (*New York Public Library*)

Battle of Rogers' Rock, Lake George, March 1758. This battle is often also referred to as the Battle on Snowshoes. (*New York Public Library*)

Robert Rogers, 1731-1795, in a fanciful portrait done in London in 1776. There is no known portrait of Rogers drawn from life. (*New York Public Library*)

John Stark, 1728-1822, Rogers' neighbor, friend, and best Ranger officer, declined to participate in the St. Francis raid. He became a prominent Patriot militia commander during the Revolutionary War. (*New York Public Library*)

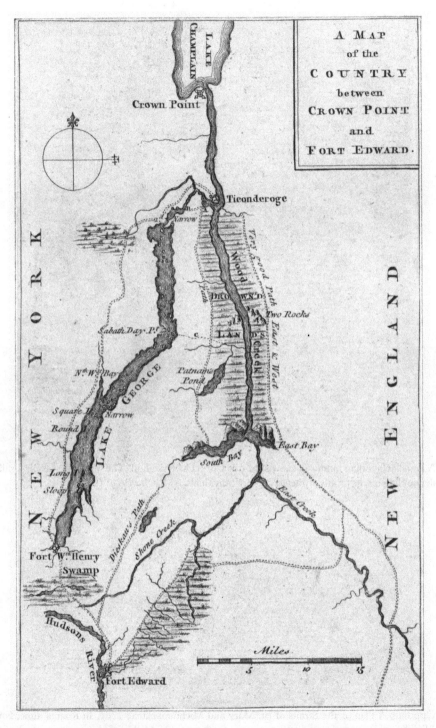

"A Map of the Country between Crown Point and Fort Edward," 1772. (*New York Public Library*)

A French Canadian hunter in snow shoes, by Cornelius Krieghoff. The fur trade was physically demanding but its profits attracted rugged individuals. (*Public Archives of Canada*)

Opposite: A Plan of the Straits of St. Mary and Michilimackinac 1761. In Rogers' time, Fort Michilimackinac was located at the extreme northern tip of Michigan's lower peninsula. It was later moved to Michilimackinac [Mackinac] Island, to the northeast. (*Norman B. Leventhal Map & Education Center, Botston Public Library*)

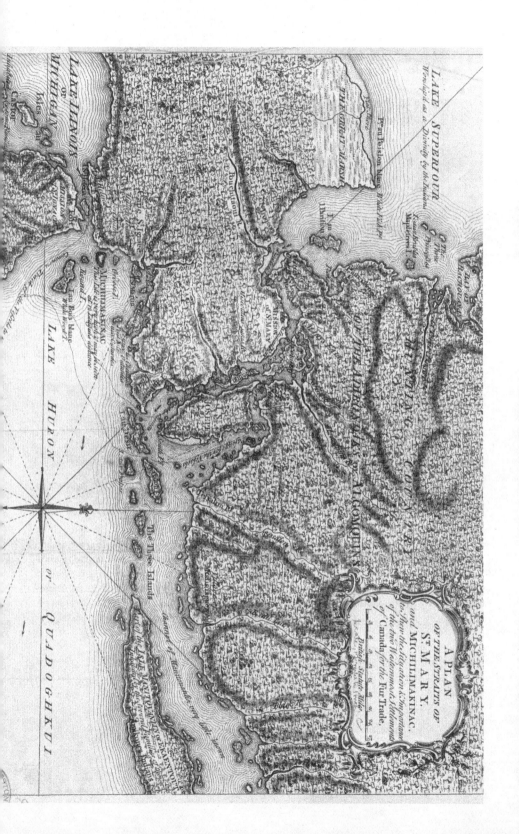

LAKE SUPERIOUR
Wrsaliped as a Divinity by the Savages.

LAKE ILLINOIS
OR
MICHIGAN

LAKE HURON
OR
QUADOGHAVI

A PLAN
OF THE STRAITS OF
St. MARY,
and MICHILIMAKINAC.
to shew the situation & importance
of the two Westernmost Settlements
of Canada for the Fur Trade.

British Statute Miles

A Rifleman of the Queen's Ranger, ca. 1780, from an original by James Murray. William Howe commissioned Rogers a lieutenant colonel in July 1776 and authorized him to recruit a battalion of Loyalists to be known as the Queen's American Rangers. When the unit was found to be composed of recruits and officers who were unqualified for their positions, Rogers was relieved of duty in January 1777. Under new leadership, the Queen's Rangers became one of the finest Loyalist units to serve alongside the British army. (*Public Archives of Canada*)

CHAPTER EIGHT

THE 1760
CAMPAIGN

AFTER returning from St. Francis and recuperating, Rogers addressed his army expense accounts for 1759. The initial reviewer was John Appy, secretary to General Amherst. Biographers of Rogers are not kind to Appy. One says that Appy was "a born accountant" who "had a field day with Rogers' '59 accounts" and who could "salute his commander in chief with the accounts limply impaled on his terrible pen." Another calls him a "stone-hearted bureaucrat." Unquestionably, "[t]ime and again Appy found fault with [Rogers'] accounting."[1]

Two major items were at issue regarding the 1759 expenses. The first was Rogers' request to be reimbursed for money he spent on equipment for the St. Francis expedition, on the mission to rescue survivors of the raid, and on the cost to clothe survivors. Amherst readily allowed payment for these items, and Gage, although chastising Rogers for poor record-keeping, paid.[2]

Expenses Rogers claimed to have incurred for the 1759 Stockbridge Indian Rangers were more problematic. Gage had advised against recruiting these Indians. Rogers asked reimbursement for £1521 in advances he said he had made to recruit the Stockbridge Indians. The sum seems extraordinarily high. In early 1758, Lord Loudoun, then British commander in North America, had authorized Rogers to advance a month's pay to new recruits as an incentive to sign up. At the per diem pay of two shillings six pence, this amounted to not quite £4 per recruit. Assuming a comparable rate of pay for the Stockbridge Rangers, and a comparable advance of one month's pay, Rogers, to recruit 100 men, might have advanced about £400, nowhere close to the £1,521 sought. Moreover, any pay advanced should properly have been withheld by Rogers from soldiers' pay, not recovered from the army. Appy initially insisted on documentation that Rogers had authority to receive this money on behalf of the Indians, which Rogers reasonably claimed was impossible. Amherst sent these issues back to Gage and Appy to resolve. Gage promised to do so.[3]

An Amherst letter to Rogers about the recruitment of Stockbridge Indians for the 1760 campaign hints at least partly at what underlay the 1759 dispute. In a letter dated March 9, 1760, Amherst authorized Rogers to instruct Stockbridge Indian Lieutenant Solomon Uhhau-nauwaunmaut, known as Lieutenant Solomon, to raise a body of Indians for the campaign, but on strict conditions, apparently because the British army had serious issues with the quality and/or equipment of the 1759 Stockbridge Indian recruits, and doubts as to whether the army should be responsible for paying recruits who were in fact useless. Wrote Amherst: "[I]f he chooses to accept [command of the Indian Rangers], it must be on condition of bringing to the field none but good men, that are well inclined, and that are hale and strong. Whatever number he or any of his friends can raise that will answer this description, I will readily employ . . . . All others that are too old or too young, I shall reject, nor shall I make them any allowance of payment, altho' they should join the army; so that, in order to prevent his having any difference with these people, it will behove him to engage none but what shall be esteemed fit for service."[4]

The issue of costs involving the 1759 Stockbridge Indian Rangers was deferred. It is not clear what that resolution was. In May 1760, Rogers wrote a memorial to Amherst complaining about still being owed money—but for pay due to Rangers who stayed with him to scout over the winter of 1755–56, an outlay for which no colony wanted to accept responsibility. This issue was eventually resolved at no monetary cost to Rogers, and he made no other complaint about claims he submitted at the end of 1759. When he reached an all-encompassing settlement with the army in May 1761, he agreed that the sum paid satisfied his claims from the beginning of his service through the date of the settlement.[5]

After settling his accounts, Rogers headed for Crown Point with thirteen new recruits as yet not equipped with weapons. They attached themselves to a fourteen-sleigh supply train headed for Crown Point with no armed escort. Rogers had in his baggage payroll for the Rangers and cash from settling his accounts. The party was behind British lines but in an area known for Indian and partisan raids. On Lake Champlain, halfway between Ticonderoga and Crown Point, raiders came at the sleighs. The attackers were mostly Indians led by the Canadian partisan Ensign Langy. Langy's force killed five men and captured four, along with several sleighs, including the one carrying the money.

Rogers' location and actions during the raid are unclear. He hurried afterwards to Crown Point, now commanded by Colonel Haviland. Rogers asked Haviland for enough troops to pursue and attack the raiders, but Haviland, whose minimal winter garrison was depleted by illness, said he had no men to spare. Privately, Haviland confided to Gage that he thought a pursuit "had little possibility of success" and that he did not believe Rogers had had a large amount of money stolen: "I don't Credit it, as he is so very easy and indifferent about it."[6]

In his *Journals*, Rogers later recorded the amount lost as 1,196 New York pounds, of which 396 belonged to him. Rogers complained falsely in the *Journals* that these personal funds were "entirely lost," but Rogers was reimbursed in full when he settled his accounts in 1761—years before the *Journals* came out.[7]

In April 1760 the French, attempting to retake Quebec, had drawn British occupiers into a set-piece fight outside the city walls like the previous year's Wolfe-Montcalm battle. They defeated the British, who retreated into the city. The French began a siege; if they brought in naval reinforcement, they might recapture Quebec. Amherst wanted to support Quebec's defenders any way he could. On a scout in early May, Rogers observed that the French had pulled most of their forces from Isle aux Nois, leaving the region lightly defended. After his scout, Rogers came to New York. He met with Amherst, who proposed that Rogers take three hundred men to raid behind enemy lines between Isle aux Noix and Montreal in hopes of drawing the French away from the siege at Quebec.[8]

Thus began Rogers' role in the final campaign to take Canada, an obscure chapter in his French and Indian War service but arguably his finest hour. He did nothing flashy, particularly newsworthy, or militarily decisive, but in a workmanlike manner he effectively harassed a foe already on his back foot.

By June 1760 the British had a fleet on Lake Champlain consisting of a 155-ton brig, *The Duke of Cumberland*, and multiple armed sloops. This force outmatched its French counterpart and gave the British control of the lake from Crown Point to Isle aux Noix. Rather than row laboriously in whaleboats at night, Rogers and 270 men boarded the lake fleet's vessels and in two days reached Missisquoi Bay. Rogers dropped off fifty men under Lieutenant Robert Holmes with orders to march on Wigwam Martinique and destroy the village. Rogers and the larger force proceeded to land on the west shore of Lake Champlain about ten miles southwest of Isle aux Noix. The fleet was to remain at the north end of the lake to support the Ranger parties, retrieve them after their raids, and return them to Crown Point.[9]

The Holmes party got lost and never made it to Wigwam Martinique, returning to the Missisquoi Bay rendezvous, where a sloop took them aboard. Rogers tried but failed to slip past Isle aux Noix undetected. The French sent a force of three hundred, mostly Indians, against him. Although outnumbered, Rogers had a good defensive position, protected on one flank by a bog that ran down to the lake. He sent seventy men in a flanking maneuver to attack the enemy rear, catching them by surprise. In a sharp battle, Rogers put the larger French and Indian force to flight, killing, by his estimate, forty or fifty. (The actual number was likely smaller.) Rogers lost seventeen men killed, but he remained in possession of the battlefield, and the French at Isle aux Noix lacked the forces to counterattack. Rogers bypassed Isle aux Noix as planned and approached forts further down the Richelieu River toward Montreal. Deeming St. Jean too heavily defended, Rogers marched to Fort St. Therese and waited for an opportunity to attack. When hay wagons approached and the garrison opened the gates, the Rangers rushed the French, catching them by surprise. The Rangers captured the fort and its twenty-four-man garrison without a shot.[10]

The Rangers captured sixty civilians and destroyed the fort and adjacent farms, as well as such supplies as they could find. Rather than return to their landing site, they released the civilians and marched their military prisoners to Missisquoi Bay. A French force of eight hundred, sent from further north, nearly caught the Rangers, who outdistanced them and were boarding British boats at Missisquoi Bay when the French appeared. The Rangers escaped without incident. Other than the casualties of the earlier battle at the landing site, Rogers had not lost a man, while sowing alarm with his destruction of Fort St. Therese and drawing off many enemy troops.[11]

The contrasts between the well-planned, successful raid behind enemy lines in 1760 and the ill-conceived attack on St. Francis in 1759 are striking. A descendant of Rogers' older brother James describes the campaign as the "most brilliant and successful action by the rangers during the war," and if the label "brilliant" is a bit overdone, the operation was certainly competent and well-executed. In 1760, Rogers knew from reconnaissance that the Isle aux Noix area was lightly defended, at least temporarily, so that he did not face the risk, once behind enemy lines, of being cut off by a superior force. In 1760, the British controlled Lake Champlain. This meant Rogers' force would be spending far less time in the field, greatly simplifying supply issues, and that he was never more than a day's march or two from safety. He was even able to transfer his wounded from his one significant battle to nearby British support ships before proceeding. He attacked Fort St. Therese only when he also had an overwhelming numerical advantage, after declining to attack the better-defended Fort St. Jean.[12]

Throughout the war, Rogers butted heads with Haviland, his antagonist since the Ranger "mutiny" in late 1757. In 1760, Amherst squarely sided with Rogers in this dispute. Rogers' raiding force, which was supposed to number three hundred, started with only 270: Haviland refused to make up the difference with forces he led. Amherst evidently chastised Haviland for being uncooperative. Ignoring his own refusal to supply Rogers more men, Haviland told Amherst the problem was Indian Rangers who failed to make a timely appearance, adding that when a new contingent of Rangers appeared, Haviland sent them after Rogers, too late for the initial battle but in time for the capture of Fort St. Therese. Amherst was not mollified. He sent a follow-up letter on June 10, 1760, emphasizing the importance of supporting Rogers, whose raid, as hoped, had alarmed the French. Two weeks later, Amherst sent another letter stressing that "Major Rogers has done very well." Amherst then ruled for Rogers on a seniority issue. Although Rogers had been elevated to the rank of colonial major earlier, Haviland claimed this rank was temporary and that in terms of seniority Rogers should be considered a captain. Amherst affirmed that Rogers was to be treated as a major and made a point of letting Rogers know he had given this instruction.[13]

The main British assault on Isle aux Noix got underway in mid-August. The campaign was under Haviland, Amherst having taken command of the British force heading down the St. Lawrence and approaching Montreal from the southwest. Haviland's total troop strength was about 3,500 versus 1,500 French defending Isle aux Noix. Rogers and the Rangers were in the vanguard and among the first British troops to land on the northern shore of Lake Champlain. The landing force, led by British Colonel William Darby, marched north from the landing site until they were opposite the fort at Isle aux Noix, where they dug in. The landing and march went unopposed, and Haviland was advised "that there was not the least danger to apprehend from the enemy."[14]

At Isle aux Noix booms blocked narrow channels on either side of the island, preventing British gunships from getting behind the fort. The French naval force, such as it was, was moored north of Isle aux Noix, behind the booms. After days of erecting batteries and beginning to shell the fort, Colonel Darby conceived a bold plan. With British grenadiers and Rangers, Darby led a surprise nighttime attack on the ships from the land side. A cannon shot severed the cable restraining the largest French ship. Wind from the west blew that gunboat to the east shore of the lake, where Darby captured it. Three other French vessels fled north toward the Richelieu River but ran aground. Darby sent Rogers to capture the northernmost boat, which he did by having Rangers armed with tomahawks swim to the vessel under cover of fire from the shore. Darby captured the other two grounded boats. The French apparently put up little or no resistance, with fifty men aboard the boats surrendering and British attackers sustaining no casualties.[15]

A day later, the French abandoned Isle aux Noix and retreated north to Montreal. Rogers was sent in pursuit, with instructions to proceed no further than St. Jean. Rogers found the fort in flames and the French retreating further. Based on prisoner interrogation, Rogers concluded the French retreat was disorganized, slow, and vulnerable to an attack that would "make [their] dance a little merrier." Leaving part of his force at St. Jean, Rogers, defying orders, led a force of about five hundred after the fleeing French, who numbered about 1,500. He attacked and scattered the French rear guard and was hoping to bring the main French force to battle, but the French retreated across a bridge which they destroyed, taking up a fortified position on the far shore. Rogers prudently declined to attack and returned to St. Jean, where Haviland,

undoubtedly mindful of Amherst's admonition to support Rogers, ratified the other man's rationale for exceeding his orders as justified.[16]

The British closed rapidly on Montreal from three directions. On
September 8, 1760, the French signed articles of capitulation. England
and France did not sign a treaty until 1763 but fighting in North America was effectively over.

Robert Rogers was now "the war's most famous North American
hero."[17]

PART TWO

LOSING HIS GRIP

CHAPTER NINE

DETROIT

T HE fall of Montreal ended the war in North America, but French troops holding several forts on the western frontier did not know. Amherst ordered Rogers to take a force of two hundred Rangers west to announce France's surrender and install British regulars from Fort Pitt at the western forts. Rogers left Montreal on September 13, 1760. Rangers not accompanying him on the mission were demobilized and sent home the following month.

The war's end would extinguish Rogers' army commission; once this assignment was over he faced a return to civilian life. In Montreal, preparing for the trip west, Rogers consulted Chevalier de Longueuil, a former commander at Fort Detroit, the largest of the French forts that Rogers was to visit. Longueuil said Fort Detroit held an enormous inventory of furs which, with the collapse of French authority, the commander would be prepared to sell Rogers at favorable prices. Rogers knew the Canadian partisan Marin had gotten rich trading fur while commanding western posts for the French. He prepared to do likewise. His clerk in Montreal, Paul Burbeen, was an agent for Abraham Douw, an Albany merchant who was among Rogers' sources of loans.[1] On Rogers' behalf, Burbeen wrote to Douw, "Major Rogers desired me to inform you that the tour he had undertaken was exceedingly agreeable to him & he expected to make a Fortune by it, he had with him the French Officer that Commanded at Fort Detroit who has promised him about Three Hundred Thousand wt of furs at a very low price—and he desires that if he should have Occasion for any money before he could see you that you would supply him and he will allow as heretofore."[2]

Alas, the Articles of Capitulation by which France ceded Canada to England stated that furs stored at western forts by French-Canadian traders remained the traders' property.[3] French commanders had no authority to sell the furs, and the traders, with long-established transport routes to Montreal, where long-established networks of purchasers waited, had no incentive to cut deals with Rogers.

Rogers' journey to Detroit took more than two months, mostly by boat along the Great Lakes. En route in Fort Niagara, he formed a trading company, Rogers & Co., with traders named Cole and Stevens and a Ranger officer named McCormick. The firm purchased £3,423 in trade goods on credit. In his capacity as commander of the expedition to Detroit, Rogers caused the army to purchase £932 in supplies from Rogers & Co. He hired men and equipment to haul to Detroit the goods sold to the army and those still belonging to Rogers & Co., charging the cost to the army, giving Rogers & Co. free shipping. As one of Rogers' biographers put it, with understatement, these transactions "walked close to the line ethically."[4]

From Fort Niagara, Rogers proceeded to Presque Isle, off present-day Erie, Pennsylvania, where he turned south to Fort Pitt to present Amherst's orders to commander General Robert Monckton. Passing along additional orders, Monckton dispatched British regulars under Captain Donald Campbell to join Rogers at Presque Isle and ultimately to garrison Fort Detroit and any other formerly French forts. Also joining Rogers at Presque Isle was George Croghan, deputy to Superintendent of Indian Affairs William Johnson. Croghan was to make contact on behalf of England with Indian tribes in the Detroit vicinity. He had sent emissaries ahead to invite Indians to meet him at Fort Detroit for a council.[5]

On the way to Detroit, Rogers had multiple friendly meetings with local Indians, who provided gifts of food and expressed pleasure at the British victory. In *A Concise Account of North America*, Rogers claims that one of these Indians was Pontiac, who became the leader of Pontiac's War in 1763. The simultaneously published *Journals* does not make this claim, and there is no evidence showing whether this meeting occurred.[6]

Rogers reached Detroit in late November. The French commander initially told Rogers to keep his distance, wary that the claim of an English victory was a ruse and noting that Rogers had not brought along a French officer to corroborate Rogers' claim. When Rogers presented a confirmatory letter from the French governor in Montreal, the commander surrendered. Rogers reports that a crowd of seven hundred Indians gave a shout of approval for the British, greatly surprising the French.[7]

Once established in Detroit, Rogers engineered two additional large purchases from Rogers & Co. Captain Campbell, the newly installed British commander at Fort Detroit, purchased £500 in supplies from Rogers & Co. And Croghan spent lavishly on gifts for Indians attending his council, purchasing the goods from Rogers & Co. He told Johnson that Campbell, presumably in consultation with Rogers, had ordered him to go all out with gifts, and to buy them from Rogers & Co. The bill was £586, more than $100,000 in today's money. British policy at the time was to reduce sharply the value of gifts given Indians, and Johnson was sufficiently alarmed by the cost of the December 1760 gifts that he asked Amherst whether to pay the charges. Amherst authorized him to pay.[8] Policy issues aside, Rogers had managed to dispose of half or more of Rogers & Co.'s inventory to the army and office of Indian Affairs by interposing Rogers & Co. as an unnecessary profiteering intermediary.

Besides Fort Detroit, Rogers was to announce the British victory to three other French bastions: Fort Miami, at present-day Fort Wayne, Indiana; Fort Ouiatenon, eighty miles beyond Fort Miami; and Fort Michilimackinac at the Mackinac Straits in northern Michigan. In early December, Rogers dispatched small parties to accept the surrender of the first two forts. He set off with a larger party to Fort Michilimackinac. He was turned back by weather without reaching Michilimackinac and returned to Detroit, arriving on December 21, 1760.[9]

On his last day in Detroit, December 23, Rogers concluded the purchase, sight unseen, of two enormous tracts of land from the Chippewa Indians. A 30,000-acre parcel was deeded personally to Rogers. A second parcel of 20,000 acres was deeded to Rogers, John Baptiste Cadotte, and Alexander Henry. Cadotte and Henry were well-established frontier traders whose relationship with Rogers is unclear. Nor is it clear who paid for a substantial array of goods—60 lbs. of vermillion, 300 barrels of rum, 400 lbs. of gunpowder, 500 lbs. of shot, 30,000 beads of wampum, and more—given in consideration. The lands were on the southern shore of Lake Superior, in Michigan's Upper Peninsula, and were rich in copper and iron ore deposits.[10]

What is one to make of Rogers' extensive personal business dealings on this army mission? Croghan, appalled, complained to Sir William Johnson that "ye Expence of this Journey [to Detroit] will be Much More than I Expected" because of the quantity of gifts he was required to purchase from Rogers & Co. and dispense to the Indians. He noted that he had been importuned to speculate in Indian lands. Indians, he reported, offered him "ye Finest Island I Ever see . . . Butt I Did Nott Chuse to Except it as people Might say I went a Land Jobing when I Should have Done My Duty."[11]

In his report to Johnson on the Detroit expedition, Croghan also urged Johnson to manage trade with the Indians closely to avoid "Irregularitys" that would cause "his Majestys Indian Intrest in Gineral [to] Suffer." He recommended banning sale of alcohol to Indians.[12] In his own dealings, Rogers favored trader flexibility and a hands-off government approach, and, as his Chippewa land purchases make clear, alcohol was a trading commodity of choice.

While in Detroit, Rogers heard stories from French-Canadian traders, who had heard them for many years from Indians, about a west-flowing river originating far to the northwest of Detroit and emptying into the "Western Sea," a large bay believed to extend northeast into the interior of North America from the Pacific Ocean. The phrase "Western Sea" appears to refer to the Puget Sound/Salish Sea/Strait of Georgia region, although that actual body of water does not penetrate the continent but bends northwest around Vancouver Island and back to the Pacific.

Multiple French expeditions had failed to find the "River of the West,"[13] which, according to the lore Rogers heard in Detroit, originated in the Lake of the Woods, or at Lake Winnipeg, or possibly among highlands in northern Minnesota, on the far side of a divide from the headwaters of the Mississippi. It is not clear if the Indians or the French believed the "River of the West" to be associated in some way with the fabled Northwest Passage, or simply a storied route to the Pacific from the center of the continent. Rogers immediately made the connection to the Northwest Passage, although basic facts of geography, likely not known to him, made such a connection impossible. The Lake of the Woods drains north into Lake Winnipeg, which drains north via the Nelson River into Hudson Bay. Rivers reaching both lakes on their western sides are all east-flowing, not west-flowing, and even if a transcontinental waterway linked the Pacific Ocean to Lake of the Woods or Lake Winnipeg, the further leg to the North Atlantic would be missing, because the Nelson River, which connects Lake Winnipeg to Hudson Bay, is navigable only by canoe, and then only with multiple portages. A river having its headwaters in northern Minnesota and flowing to the Pacific was theoretically possible, but it, too, would lack a connection to the Atlantic.

Rogers was not deterred but fascinated. He embraced the "River of the West" story, tinkering with it as he absorbed information that he modified to imagine a link to the quest for the Northwest Passage. He learned that the river was called "Ourigan"—presumably the Columbia. He came to understand that it originated west of the forks of the Saskatchewan River in central Saskatchewan, much further west than Lake Winnipeg or Lake of the Woods. Eventually, he concluded that the best way the reach the "River Ourigan" would be to follow the Missouri River to its headwaters, cross the Rocky Mountains, and on the far side search for the elusive waterway. His biggest innovation was to postulate that the legendary river flowed to the "Western Sea," which connected directly to Hudson Bay. Whoever found the "Western Sea" would be on the cusp of discovering a true Northwest Passage. Rogers obsessed about this thesis for fifteen years.

Rogers arrived at Fort Pitt from Detroit in mid-January 1761, traveling overland via Albany to Philadelphia, reaching that city in mid-February. The trip from Montreal to Detroit to Fort Pitt took him 1,600 miles, and although it was along known routes and in peacetime, his journey was nonetheless a significant accomplishment.[14] Rogers received a commission as a captain in the British regular army in February 1761. A British army commission stood sharply apart from one in the colonial military forces. Very few colonial officers received these highly coveted designations. Rogers' appointment signaled that he enjoyed Amherst's special favor. Among other things, the commission paid a handsome salary of £560 per year—and entitled Rogers, upon his retirement, to half pay of £280 per year for life to the extent he was not on active duty at a higher salary. Because they carried substantial financial rewards potentially lasting a lifetime, British army commissions could also be bought and sold, subject to appropriate approvals by superiors.

Ordered to join a campaign against the Cherokee Indians in South Carolina, Rogers was first given time to attend to various personal and professional matters in the Northeast.[15] In March 1761, he formed a new trading partnership, Askin & Rogers, with John Askin to engage in fur trading in the colonial west. Askin had been a sutler to Rogers and the Rangers during the 1760 campaign. Rogers gave Askin a power of attorney to collect money owed him by Cole, one of the partners in Rogers & Co. Rogers formed another partnership with McCormick, the Ranger officer and partner in Rogers & Co., and borrowed £5,000 to fund McCormick's purchase of trade goods and boats for shipping them.[16]

These transactions hint at trouble in the management of Rogers & Co., perhaps because Cole had taken control of the company and diverted to himself business that should have gone to the partnership. Finding Cole and obtaining payment for money owed Rogers from Rogers & Co. proved troublesome and the money, when finally obtained, was a disappointingly small sum. The relationship between Askin & Rogers and Rogers' new partnership with McCormick was murky. The idea seems to have been that McCormick would buy goods from Askin & Rogers, trade those goods for furs, then sell the furs to Askin & Rogers, which would also do business on its own.

In all, Rogers borrowed almost £8,500, more than $1.5 million in today's money, to fund these trading ventures between October 1760 and March 1761. He does not appear to have been actively involved in any of these businesses, but rather was lending his name and his credit and leaving day-to-day affairs to others. The investments did not fare well. When James Gordon, an Askin employee, tracked Cole down and forced an accounting with Rogers in early 1763, Rogers received £975, "a rather inconsiderable return on the original investment." Rogers' return appears to have been less than "inconsiderable," as money he borrowed to fund Rogers & Co. seems to have remained at least partially unpaid in 1763.[17]

According to one commentator, "[t]he firm of Askin & Rogers had a more disastrous end than did Rogers & Co." Pontiac's War in 1763 disrupted the fur trade and caused Askin & Rogers significant losses. The firm shut down in 1764. Although they evaporated more slowly than had Rogers' hope for a quick killing in fur trading in Detroit in 1760, his longer term partnerships all withered over time. As one historian put it, "As each new opportunity presented itself Rogers saw a fortune for himself and his friends just around the bend. Each time, however, the reality was little more than a load of debts and a fresh host of creditors. Rogers' abilities were not those conducive to success in trade."[18]

Besides committing more fully to fur trading through partnerships with Askin and McCormick, Rogers also explored land ownership. He decided to apply to the state of New York for permission to buy a large tract on the Mohawk River, within the Mohawks' traditional holdings. Rogers persuaded Goldsbrow Banyar, a senior New York official whom he knew from the early days of the French and Indian War, to sign his petition and share the costs of the venture, assuring Banyar that Sir William Johnson, Superintendent of Indian Affairs and a long-time friend of the Mohawks, would lend his support. Other partners joined the venture. Although granted the right to survey, the partners saw their application die more than a year later because of objections by the Mohawks, who were suspicious after having been taken advantage of in past land ventures. Johnson, always solicitous of the Mohawks, but also likely influenced by Croghan's unflattering reports about Rogers' wheeling and dealing on the Detroit expedition, supported the Mohawk objections and withheld the expected support.[19]

CHAPTER TEN

SETTLING
ACCOUNTS

IN EARLY MAY 1761, Rogers presented the British army with his largest claim yet for reimbursement, mostly involving demobilization of the Rangers following the British victory in North America. Rogers' previous claims had been much smaller and had generally been resolved to his satisfaction.

In May 1761, Rogers claimed to be due about £6,300, about $1.2 million in today's money. After multiple reviews, the army allowed payment of about £2,200. Rogers' chroniclers describe him as "thunderstruck" and "outraged" at having so much of his claim denied, and attribute Rogers' subsequent chronic debt to the army's obduracy, one of them concluding that this denial marked the beginning of "Rogers' eternal torment" of indebtedness. Much of his biographers' ire falls on John Appy, the "stone-hearted bureaucrat" who initially reviewed Rogers' claims.[1] This view of Rogers' May 1761 settlement with the army is profoundly mistaken and fails to examine the admittedly abstruse details of Rogers' claim and its disposition. It also obscures the true reasons for Rogers' historic indebtedness: gambling, poor business decisions, and extravagant personal spending.

Whatever Rogers thought about the ultimate settlement of his claim, Appy was not to blame. Yes, he constantly pressed Rogers for receipts documenting outlays he claimed to have made. This is not bureaucratic nitpicking, it is standard business practice. Nor can Rogers be excused because "his ranger's life" made it impossible to be "consistently scrupulous" about maintaining records.[2] Rogers did not spend the money for which he sought reimbursement in the heat of battle, but in British forts and colonial towns, or on recruiting expeditions. Documenting expenses was a minimal skill expected of every officer. If Rogers did not appreciate this responsibility in 1755, he certainly was aware of it in 1759 and 1761.

Appy also apparently demanded proof of matters that, in retrospect, can be made to look obvious, but the questions he raised were generally legitimate and he did not press them unreasonably. The majority of Rogers' claim related to Rangers captured by the French and held until the war ended. Rogers sought back pay on those men's behalf, plus reimbursement of money Ranger officers had sent them to buy food and other necessities while in French custody. Had these prisoners been stricken from the British payroll, Appy wanted to know, or had Ranger officers already been issued pay on their behalf? Were they really prisoners, or were they deserters? Did they really need money for food, or did the French feed them? Amherst originally supported Appy in demanding answers to these questions, but both bowed to a three-officer review panel's finding that the relevant facts were adequately shown, and no payment was denied because of them.[3]

Few, if any, of Rogers' claims were denied for poor record-keeping or other failure to show facts to Appy's or Amherst's satisfaction. The army accepted affidavits in lieu of receipts, took statements about prison conditions, and verified through payroll records that pay had not already been issued.[4] Claims were not denied for lack of proof, but because they were deemed not allowable.

Rogers' biographers assume that his claim for £6,300 represented money he actually spent, or charged to his personal credit, so that he would either lose this money or be responsible for the debt if the army did not reimburse him.[5] This was not so. Most of Rogers' claim, and most of the amount disallowed, was not for money Rogers spent, but for money he claimed was owed Rangers and which he wanted so that he could distribute it to them, even though they had been demobilized and were scattered across the colonies. Denial of these claims never cost

Rogers a penny. One suspects that Rogers' push to be awarded large amounts of money for supposed distribution to demobilized Rangers was driven by cash flow problems at his fur trading business. One biographer suggests that his business partner Askin, "pretty much of a schemer" according to his employee James Gordon, may have assisted Rogers in preparing the May 1761 claim "and perhaps in cooking the books here and there."[6]

The process by which Rogers' claim was adjudicated, far from being stacked against him, was scrupulously fair. Amherst, the ultimate decision-maker, was Rogers' strongest supporter in the entire British army. Although Amherst had a poor opinion of the Rangers, and told Rogers so bluntly, he had a high opinion of Rogers. It is not credible that Amherst was out to shortchange Rogers, and the record makes clear that Amherst did not simply rubber-stamp subordinates' recommendations; he himself reviewed Rogers' claims. When Rogers protested Amherst's initial rulings on Rogers' claims, Amherst appointed a three-officer panel to review those rulings. The panel was highly favorable to Rogers. One member was a Ranger officer, another a British officer known to be a friend of Rogers.[7] Although the panel upheld Amherst on most contested points, it recommended in Rogers' favor on others, one of them quite large, and Amherst adopted these recommendations.[8]

THE two largest items by far in Rogers' May 1761 claim, mentioned above, relate to ninety-nine Rangers taken prisoner during the war and held by the French until after they capitulated in August 1760. Rogers was en route to Detroit when these Rangers were repatriated and eventually demobilized and sent home, and he returned to Albany long after their demobilization. Rogers sought £2,268 in back pay for these Rangers. He also sought £1,377 for money sent them by Ranger officers to buy food and other necessities in captivity. Neither Rogers nor anyone else had disbursed any of the back pay sought. With respect to the money sent to imprisoned Rangers, Rogers did not list himself as one of the officers who sent the money. Although he said in correspondence relating to his claim that he had later spent some of his own funds to support captured Rangers after their release, such amounts were undocumented and would have been small, as Rogers was in Detroit when these prisoners were freed, and by the time he returned east the former prisoners had left the army.[9]

Appy saw instantly that these claims amounted to double counting; if the Rangers were awarded full back pay, the cost of their support should be deducted, as was done during normal service. This seems so obvious that it is difficult to believe that Rogers' request for both amounts was an innocent mistake. Rogers, when confronted, quickly conceded that Appy was right, assuring him in a letter that he never intended the Rangers to get both back pay and reimbursement for support costs, but only "their net pay for the time they were Prisoners." The claim for money advanced for their support, Rogers now said, was only to illustrate that they had living expenses and needed their pay to cover them.[10] In other words, if full back pay were granted, money advanced to the Rangers for their support should be deducted from it and used to reimburse parties who advanced it. This concession meant that Rogers' claim was overstated by at least £1,377, and in reality totaled less than £5,000. This fact has not previously been recognized.

There were other problems with both prongs of Rogers' claim relating to the former prisoners. With respect to back pay, the prisoners had no clear entitlement to it. The British army had, on occasion, given repatriated prisoners back pay, but inconsistently and with no right to back pay implied. In this case, Rangers themselves were not demanding money, only Rogers. There was no obvious way to distribute the money, as the demobilized Rangers were scattered and Rogers soon would be heading for South Carolina. The three-officer panel recommended that if awarded back pay at all, the former prisoners should not be reimbursed at full Ranger premium rates, which may have been appropriate for men on active duty at the front, but which seemed excessive for men who had been idle, even if the idleness was not their fault.[11]

With respect to money spent to support captured Rangers, less than half the claimed amount was documented. The largest undocumented claim, 350 guineas (about £370) Colonel Peter Schuyler said he spent on captive Rangers, and which Rogers said he owed Schuyler, had been spent by a scion of one of America's wealthiest families. This does not mean that Schuyler was not entitled to the money, but it does mean that if Rogers did not get the money and pass it on to him, Schuyler could easily absorb the loss. Schuyler never pursued Rogers for his 350 guineas.[12]

The army jerry-rigged a solution that seems fair, especially to Rogers. The army awarded him the full amount of documented claims for money sent captive Rangers—£525. Presumably, Rogers would distribute this money to Ranger officers who made the documented expenditures. Full back pay, £159, went to three captured Ranger officers. Rogers was then given an additional lump sum £709 as back pay for the ninety-six sergeants and privates among the prisoners, reflecting regular army pay rates, not premium Ranger rates. This money awarded to Rogers, enough to cover all claimed undocumented payments, including Schuyler's, was essentially discretionary. Assuming he accepted their claims, Rogers could reimburse officers who had made undocumented payments to support captive Rangers. Alternatively, he could try to find individual Rangers to give them their back pay. Or, as most likely happened, he could keep the money or a portion of it. The sum of these payments, £1,393, exceeded the amount Rogers attributed to prisoner support, and included more than 60 percent of the back pay award he had sought. Rogers, who acknowledged he was not entitled to both reimbursement for money spent on prisoner support and to back pay for prisoners, agreed the award satisfied his prisoner claims.[13]

Rogers lost no money and may have gained some. He had not personally advanced any funds that needed to be reimbursed. He faced no financial risk relating to claims that others might later assert against him. If he declined to reimburse officers who said they had made undocumented expenditures, he was protected by the army's finding that these claims could not be reimbursed without proof. If individual Ranger enlisted men demanded back pay, Rogers could point to the fact that they had no clear right to back pay and had been provided support in captivity. Rogers in fact faced no further claims relating to captive Rangers.

The resolution of the captive Ranger issues settled claims totaling £3,645 for a total of £1,393. Most of this cut reflected what Rogers acknowledged as double-counting. Rogers appeared satisfied and raised no further argument.

There remained claims totaling £2,655. One, by Rogers, covered personal funds he said had been stolen from him by Indian raiders while he was returning from Albany to Crown Point in December 1759. It was not clear that the army had to cover this. Unlike the payroll money stolen at the same time, and which the army owed Rangers, Rogers' funds were personal property and he was no different from a private citizen whose property was destroyed in wartime; the army had no obligation to make such an individual whole. The army did not insist on this legal position. Reviewers did balk at the absence of proof for Rogers' ostensible loss. Haviland had questioned at the time whether Rogers had really lost money in the raid. The three-officer panel thought this was nitpicking and that the loss was adequately shown. It recommended awarding Rogers the full amount. Amherst allowed Rogers £404.[14]

Appy and Amherst had also agreed to pay £52, as documented, for snowshoes assembled by Rangers, likely in 1758, and delivered to the army. The panel thought Rogers had adequately shown additional sums owed, bringing the total due for the footwear to £99, which Amherst awarded.[15] This was likely a windfall for Rogers. He had not worked on the snowshoes, and the Rangers who had, had done so on army time. The army also awarded Rogers about £300 for a host of miscellaneous expenses and claims, bringing his total award to £2,183.

Two claims disallowed did not reflect outlays by Rogers, but additional money he claimed was due Rangers and should be given him for disbursement. The largest, for £615, was due to Rangers who scouted with Rogers over the winter of 1755–56. The New Hampshire volunteers who joined Rogers' company in the spring of 1755 had enlisted for six months and their enlistments expired that fall. When the army asked him to stay through the winter, Rogers agreed, and recruited about thirty New Hampshire troops to join him. The obligation to pay these troops had always been murky; the men were from New Hampshire, they were stationed in New York, and the overall British commander was Governor Shirley of Massachusetts, who had directed Rogers in the spring of 1756 to raise a replacement body of Rangers. Rogers clearly was not responsible for paying these troops, but the colonies dithered and blamed each other. Troopers hounded Rogers, some suing him personally. Rogers did not pay the men, repeatedly telling them that he could not pay them until he himself had been given money to do so. The aggravation lasted years.[16]

But Rogers had not advanced his own money to the 1755–56 Rangers, and his claim that they were owed a total of £615 appears to have been highly inflated. A year earlier, Rogers had told Amherst the amount owed was £406.[17]

The army's response to this claim did not hinge on the amount due. The army said that Massachusetts, New Hampshire, or New York, or perhaps proportionately all three, should be paying, not the British army. Amherst in a personal letter expressed sympathy for Rogers' predicament, which he acknowledged was a "hardship." He granted Rogers a month's leave to resolve the matter but said he could not release British army funds to pay the claim. Rogers used the leave to petition the New

Hampshire Assembly to pay the 1755–56 Rangers. When New Hampshire finally appropriated funds in 1763, the colony calculated the amount due as £235, and this sum put the issue to rest once and for all. Rogers lost little if any money of his own.[18]

Rogers also sought £325 to distribute to Rangers demobilized in October 1760. He argued it was traditional to give discharged troops an allowance for the cost of getting home, and proposed the Rangers get an additional four weeks' pay, from October 25, the date they were discharged, through November 20. Rogers represented that he and other Ranger officers had given demobilized Rangers an unspecified amount of travel money. Rogers had left for Detroit more than a month before the Rangers were discharged, and returned months after the men had mustered out, so it is unlikely that he personally paid out any travel money. He never attempted to itemize or document travel money paid by other Ranger officers. As with back pay for Ranger prisoners, there was no obvious way to distribute the requested additional pay. The army said that in the past discharged troops received travel money inconsistently and when they did receive such money, it often reflected gratuities given by their officers without expectation of reimbursement. As Appy pointed out, the few times discharged troops got extra pay as travel money, it was for ten or thirteen days, not the twenty-six days Rogers was seeking. The claim was disallowed, but Rogers suffered no out-of-pocket loss.[19]

That left two items that the army disallowed. The larger one was nearly £1,000—almost $200,000 in today's money—that Rogers said he paid for firearms to provide to Rangers: £85 for guns given Ranger prisoners upon repatriation and immediately before their discharge in 1760 plus £870 for 497 guns to replace weapons lost or damaged during the war. The second piece of the claim clearly involved transactions dating back years, possibly to the start of the war. Nothing explains why Rogers waited until 1761 to raise this issue for the first time.

The army's disallowance of this claim was correct: Rangers were required by the terms of their enlistment to furnish their own weapons. Sometimes Rangers got a special allowance to buy weapons, sometimes the requirement was justified by their premium pay, but it was always a condition of enlistment.[20] Having agreed to compensation sufficiently generous to allow Rangers to furnish their own weapons, the army could not be expected to buy weapons for them a second time.

If Rangers or Ranger recruits lacked adequate or appropriate weapons, there was an obvious solution. As their paymaster, Rogers was able to deduct any advances given to Rangers from their subsequent pay, and he could easily do this with the cost of a new or replacement weapon. Such a system would have been easy to administer and would have imposed no serious hardship. Basic pay for a Ranger private was almost £4 per month. The guns at issue appear to have cost £1 to £2 each. Any Ranger who wanted or needed a new firearm could have it for about two weeks' pay, although obviously the Rangers would have preferred not to pay this expense and Rogers would have preferred not to charge it to a man if he thought he could get the army to pay.

If in doubt as to whether the army would pay him for guns he provided Rangers, Rogers could have asked a superior or other official. It defies belief that he would allow this expense to accumulate for years without making such an inquiry, unless he understood he was not entitled to reimbursement. If he believed he was entitled to reimbursement, he would surely have acted to collect the money promptly, as he did with other legitimate expenses. Assuming that Rogers actually had advanced personal funds to buy weapons for his troops, and was not trying to hoodwink the army, the obvious explanation for his long delay in asserting this claim is that he knew his claim was dubious and wanted to present the army with a *fait accompli*, hoping the army would be reluctant to deny reimbursement for such a large expense. Better to seek forgiveness than permission.

Rogers loudly protested denial of this claim, but his protest only made the correctness of the army position clearer. Backpedaling, Rogers said that most of the guns purchased were not to replace guns lost or damaged in service, but to furnish appropriate weapons to new recruits who showed up badly armed. Otherwise, Rogers argued, the recruits would have been ineffective. This argument ducks the fact that it was recruits' responsibility to show up properly armed. Rogers also said that his commanding officers, Loudoun and Abercromby, had told him to make sure his men were properly equipped, even if he had to buy guns himself. As Appy pointed out, this advice, if given, said nothing about who should pay for the weapons, the Rangers or the army, and Rogers never claimed he was told this was a reimbursable expense. Rogers' reference to Loudoun and Abercromby as commanding officers dates his claim for reimbursement for arms purchased for his troops back at least to 1758 and implies that he let at least three years pass without raising it.[21]

Rogers' pursuit of this claim wore on Amherst. He characterized it as "a most Extraordinary claim; no Allowance of this Sort ever having been made," given that Rangers were required "to find their own Arms." He refused to budge, the panel agreed, and the claim was disallowed.[22]

Rogers' persistence on this claim seems to show that, unlike almost all his other disallowed claims, this one involved real spending on his part. The amount is unclear. The nearly £1,000 he claimed to have spent over the years on weapons for Rangers was an estimate. The army did not need to study the estimate because it rejected the entire rationale for Rogers' claim. If the amount of pay owed to the 1755–56 Rangers is any indication, Rogers' "estimates" of what he was owed could be very generous to himself. His inability to recover this money, however, whatever the amount and even if the loss was his fault, was undoubtedly painful.[23]

One other item Rogers failed to get reimbursement for included an actual outlay: £162 for advances and pay to Stockbridge Indians who served on the 1760 campaign. About half this amount was pay Rogers claimed the army still owed to Indians. He wanted that money given to him to pay them. Army records showed the Indians had been paid. The remainder was money Rogers gave to Lieutenant Solomon, the principal Stockbridge recruiter, to advance to new Stockbridge recruits. Without disputing that Rogers had advanced this money, the army concluded that the Indians' final pay should have been docked and used to reimburse Rogers, and that Rogers was responsible for doing so. The army had paid the Indians the agreed-upon wage. Reimbursing advances would be overpaying.[24]

Again, Rogers fumed. He said he had told Amherst he was giving his own money to Solomon to advance to Indian recruits. This was true, but it did not address who was at fault for failing to recover the advance. Rogers said he asked Amherst not to dismiss the Indians until he returned from Detroit so that he could recover the advances from their final pay. This too was true, but Rogers' solution was unreasonable. Amherst could not be expected to keep an entire unneeded company of Rangers on duty at full pay for six months so that Rogers could recover less than £100 in advances. Rogers' clerk Burbeen was on the scene when the Indian Rangers were paid off and sent home. He could have had the advances withheld and given to Rogers. Appy characterized as "frivolous" the Rogers/Burbeen position that the army, not Burbeen, was responsible for failure to deduct the advances from the

Indians' final pay. Appy believed Burbeen was lazy or reluctant to withhold the money, hoping the army would have to give the Stockbridge Indians a windfall to make Rogers whole. Rogers may have lost money, but the amount was less than £100.[25]

Overall, the army's settlement with Rogers seems, with a few tweaks here and there, entirely fair and reasonable. Rogers received a small surplus of funds—payment for the snowshoes and some of the lump sum back pay awarded Ranger prisoners—and was made whole for legitimate expenditures. He came up short only for money spent on weapons and money advanced to recruit the 1760 Stockbridge Indians. Although these claims were denied, they cannot have exceeded £1,000, and likely were less. Either way, they were only a tiny fraction of the debt Rogers ran up in the early 1760s.

THERE is more than a scintilla of annoyance in the preamble to Amherst's warrant disposing of Rogers' claim. Appy had complained to Amherst about "the irregularity of [Rogers'] accounts." He accused Rogers of going "backwards and forwards several times" in his arguments and of committing multiple "blunder[s]" in presenting claims, making the process much more time-consuming. Amherst was exasperated. Accordingly, Appy drafted the warrant "in such terms as will obviate all future retrospects, which I apprehend is your [Amherst's] pleasure. . . ."[26]

Noting the total Rogers sought, the preamble asserts that "Sundry of these Charges cannot, with any degree of Justice, be placed to the Account of the Crown." It continues, "in Order that Major Rogers might be fully Satisfied, that he had no Claim, or little, to such of his Demands as are objected to, I have Caused his Accounts to be referred to three of His Majesty's Officers, who after a Strict Inspection & Revision of the Same, have pronounced his [Rogers'] Satisfaction for those Articles that are not allowed." The preamble concludes by saying that the payment of the allowed claims is in satisfaction "in full of all Claims, or Demands whatsoever, which he, the said Major Rogers, or any of the officers or men who served under his Command, in the Independent Companies of Rangers have, or may have, to this day Inclusive, against the Crown." Amherst's previously friendly relationship with Rogers developed a progressive chill following the settlement, as Rogers' financial difficulties deepened and he repeatedly turned to Amherst for help.[27]

   With the accounting completed, but with well short of what he had
hoped to receive, Rogers borrowed £3,430 from Bostonian Nathaniel
Wheelwright. The amount suggests the loan went to refinance borrow-
ings used to fund Rogers & Co., but the precise purpose is not
recorded.[20]

CHAPTER ELEVEN

MARRIAGE

Leaving New York after settling his army accounts, Rogers traveled to Boston, likely to accept that loan from Nathaniel Wheelwright, then to Portsmouth, New Hampshire, where he arrived on June 3, 1761. He was feted by his brothers in the Masonic lodge, to which he had belonged since 1756. The minister to the lodge, Reverend Arthur Browne, was also the Rector of the Anglican Queen's Chapel and one of Portsmouth's most prominent citizens. Less than a month later, an interlude crowded with business, family, and social obligations, Rogers wed one of Browne's daughters. He was twenty-nine; Betsy Browne was nineteen. The ceremony took place in her father's church on June 30, her twentieth birthday.[1]

The relationship was a terrible mistake, especially for Betsy. She later said she agreed to marry Rogers "solely in obedience to the Will of her parents, friends, &c."—a characterization consistent with the power parents of that era exercised over their children's choices of spouse, especially daughters'. Betsy also emphasized that Rogers was "a person at that time of some Character and distinction."[2] The match had an appeal for both Rogers and Reverend Browne. Browne was the patriarch of "one of the first families of New England's social capital," and the marriage brought Rogers instant respectability and social standing.

Rogers was "the army's most famous colonial fighter," and the match must have seemed a promising one to Browne. Rogers was already deeply in debt, a fact not yet well known, and Browne, more prominent than wealthy, was almost certainly unaware of his new son-in-law's finances.[3]

Rogers' twentieth-century biographers, apparently influenced by Rogers' letters to Betsy, conclude that the marriage was a love match, at least at the outset. Rogers' expressions of sentiment, which continued through the marriage, even when the two were barely on speaking terms, are formulaic and deserve no consideration. This was an age in which letter writers invariably signed off, "your humble obedient servant," even if chastising a subordinate or insulting an adversary. From very early in the marriage, Rogers displayed complete indifference to Betsy, which belied and even made a mockery of his expressions of affection.[4]

After a six-day honeymoon at her parents' house, Rogers left for South Carolina. He did not see Betsy for seventeen months. This set a pattern: long separations, brief reunions, Rogers always preoccupied. From South Carolina, Rogers appears to have written Betsy only three times. In November 1761, four months after his departure, he complains that he has had only one letter from her, although this appears to be his first to her. He assures her he is "a prisoner to Love," but the letter itself is mundane; he explains at length about a debt she apparently asked about, which he tells her he has paid, and says that he has authorized a Portsmouth friend to advance money on her behalf. He urges her to use this source to buy special items for herself and tells her he expects to be back over the winter. On January 2, 1762, he alerts Betsy that he will not be returning as soon as he had said. On May 17, 1762, he acknowledges her suggestion that he sell his South Carolina army commission and buy an equivalent commission closer to home, a possibility he had already raised with Amherst. He reports that he has asked Amherst for a leave to return north but has not heard back. If he cannot get the leave, he says, he will send for her to join him, warning her about the "scorching heat of summer" in South Carolina. Rogers concludes, "Nothing would give me more pleasure than to be settled in the manner that would be agreeable to Mrs. Rogers," and adds "I long to see you greatly."[5] He writes no other letters before his return six months later.

When Rogers did return north in October 1762, he did not hurry to Portsmouth for a reunion with Betsy but spent weeks attending to business in New York and Albany. This focus undoubtedly reflected the serious strain his finances were under, but also gives his expressions of sentiment a hollow ring.[6]

Returning to Portsmouth in November, the "prisoner to Love" soon was rebuked by his father-in-law for his neglect of Betsy and for his behavior when away from home. Attempting to raise money to satisfy creditors, he sold property in New Hampshire to Reverend Browne for £1,000 in December 1762.[7] He and Betsy continued to live with her parents. Business took Rogers to Newport, Boston, and elsewhere in the Northeast. Rumors reached Portsmouth about him spending extravagantly and living riotously. Absent almost a year and a half, he made one empty promise after another to Betsy about a reunion, with no apparent discussion of where they would live other than in her childhood home. She must have been perplexed about her marriage. Reverend Browne, who had just parted with £1,000 to help Rogers with his finances, exploded at the rumors of profligacy and immorality. In April 1763, he sued Rogers for the cost of his room and board while staying with the Brownes, the much greater cost of supporting Betsy for almost two years, and other miscellaneous expenses, a total of £2,590.[8] In a side letter, not part of the public filing, Browne accused Rogers of failing to support his wife and squandering his resources on "prodigality & ye Gratification of unlawful pleasures and Passions." Browne did not specify, but the transgressions likely included drinking, gambling, womanizing, and self-indulgent spending.[9]

It is difficult to exaggerate the anger Browne must have felt to have taken this drastic, public step. He and Rogers were well known, and the filing of legal charges so early in the marriage, even without the scandalous allegations Browne confined to his side letter, must have led to extensive gossip. The lawsuit surely reflected not merely a religious man's shocked anger but also a doting father's empathetic distress over his daughter's unhappiness with her husband and her marriage. Browne told Rogers that he brought the lawsuit "in order to relieve my Child from the tribulations and Distress that I had reason to apprehend she was under."[10]

Browne quickly made peace with Rogers, likely because in the spring of 1763 Rogers obtained a commission in a New York Independent Company, keeping him closer to home. He purchased a residence in Albany, where the company was stationed. He and Betsy moved to Albany and briefly seemed on the path to conventional married life. Browne declined to appear at the first hearing in his lawsuit and the case was dismissed.[11]

Rogers' brush with domesticity did not last long. In June 1763, Amherst ordered him to join an expedition to relieve Detroit, under siege by Indians as part of Pontiac's War. He could not leave Betsy alone in Albany, but he was under pressure to join the Detroit expedition, so he arranged for an escort to accompany Betsy back to her parents' house, where she lived for the next two and a half years.[12]

Betsy must have been furious at this unexpected reversion. Rogers plainly recognized how upset she was. Uncharacteristically, he wrote three letters in the month following his departure for Detroit. In the first, he begged her to "put on a Spirit of Resignation and be as contented as possible." In the second, he promised her he would be back in the fall but went on to alert her that he would then be going to England seeking a satisfactory appointment. He assured her, "I shall soon have it in my powar to make you [happy], both by my being with you and Cash enough to pay all." In the third letter, he called his separation from her "the greatest Hardship that I ever sufferd," and again promised financial stability: "I shall send you plenty [of cash]."[13]

We do not have Betsy's side of this correspondence but relations between the two were strained. Rogers seems to have written nothing further after July. When he did return east after the Detroit campaign six months later, it was four more months before he ventured to Portsmouth and the uncertain reception of his wife and in-laws.[14]

For most of 1764, Rogers, although back in New England, appears to have been on the move, ducking creditors and trying to raise money. He had occasional contact with Betsy but made no effort to move her from her parents' house and set her up on her own. In her 1778 petition for divorce, Betsy asserts that Rogers spent only "a few days" with her that entire year.[15]

In February 1765, Rogers sailed to England to try to revive his military career. Although he had mentioned this plan to Betsy in 1763, his departure in 1765 appears to have been without notice to her. His letter informing her that "I am going to England as fast as I possibly can to git whot Ever may offer" was written from aboard a ship about to cast off from Newport, Rhode Island, and did not reach her until after he was at sea. The letter oozes endearments. Rogers calls Betsy "My only Life" and "the only joy of my heart" and promises to "return to my own and dear Betsy as soon as I ever can." At the same time the context reflects the strained reality of the relationship. "Pray be contented I could not pay for a harpsichord," he writes, "or would have Sent you one but hope for Better times." He assures her "I have good Incouragements" and looks forward to being "in a better Cituation," but apologizes "I have but little money or would send you some." He does not appear to have written further to Betsy during his year-long sojourn.[16]

For once, Rogers' optimistic report of "good Incouragements" proved accurate. At the direct instruction of King George III, he secured an appointment as commander at Fort Michilimackinac on the Mackinac Straits in northern Michigan.

Rogers arrived back in the colonies in January 1766 and reached Portsmouth in March. Preparations for assuming the new post and the long trip there consumed six months. Betsy agreed to accompany Rogers to the new appointment, "desirous of doing her duty, and in hopes of winning him by gentleness and condescention."[17] Her experience of marriage cannot have given her cause to look forward to the experiment with enthusiasm.

MICHILIMACKINAC was a small, isolated outpost at the extreme northwestern edge of British North America. Its population, mostly military personnel and civilians engaged directly or indirectly in the fur trade, skewed heavily male. There were few luxuries and little in the way of culture. The environment seems to have brought out the worst in Rogers. In addition to constant conflict with his military and civilian superiors, and indebtedness to virtually everyone at the post, he was chronically unfaithful to Betsy. At Rogers' later court martial trial, the post's second in command, Captain Spiesmaker, testified that he had personal knowledge of Rogers' "Familiarity with the Non Commissioned Officers and Soldiers Wives."[18]

Betsy reported in her divorce petition that "she underwent every hardship, and endured every species of ill-treatment, which infidelity, uncleanness [presumably venereal disease], & drunken brutality could inflict from one bound by the tenderest & most sacred ties . . . ." While Rogers never had an opportunity to dispute Betsy's allegations, the claim of infidelity was corroborated by Spiesmaker. The claim of drunken brutality—not necessary for Betsy's divorce petition, which was granted on grounds of abandonment and infidelity, not abuse—was consistent with Rogers' known alcoholism. All of Betsy's divorce petition complaints are also corroborated by her prior consistent complaints to her brother-in-law that life with Rogers had left her "highly disgusted at the sight of men."[19]

Betsy became pregnant while at Michilimackinac. While this might suggest that life there with Rogers was not as bleak as she portrays, the pregnancy's timing makes this conclusion suspect. Arthur Rogers, named for Betsy's father, was born in late January or early February 1769, and most likely was conceived in late April or early May 1768. At that time, Rogers was in solitary confinement in heavy, painful leg irons, forbidden from contact with Betsy except for brief communications through a barred window. This period of near-total isolation began in February and lasted until late June or early July, when, en route to Montreal for his trial, the commander at Fort Niagara ordered the leg irons removed and allowed Betsy to join him. Although it is possible that Rogers' conditions of confinement were more relaxed in practice, he complained bitterly at his court martial that he was cut off completely from Betsy during this period, and Betsy herself complained to Thomas Gage, Rogers' ultimate commanding officer, about being denied contact with him.[20]

According to a journal kept by a surgeon's mate at Fort Michilimackinac, another officer there, Ensign Johnston, "used uncommon freedom with [her], common fame [common belief] says to the extent of carnal conversation with her," during Rogers' confinement.[21] Although this may seem uncharacteristic of Betsy, her circumstances make the report plausible.

It is impossible to know the paternity of Betsy's child. Rogers never disowned him, although he also never indicated any interest in him. The evidence argues that the child was not Rogers'.

Betsy accompanied Rogers as far as Fort Ontario on the way to his court martial in Montreal, then left in late July to return to New England to give birth to Arthur. She moved back in with her parents, in whose household she remained for the final ten years of the marriage. Rogers, released from custody following his acquittal on treason charges, returned to Portsmouth a year later, in July 1769, but, after a brief visit with the Brownes and the infant Arthur, and in the face of renewed creditor lawsuits, he departed almost immediately for England, hoping to repeat his 1765 success at salvaging his career. He would not do so and would not return to America for six years.[22]

In January 1770, Rogers wrote Betsy from London that he was preoccupied with recovering money from the army owed for his Michilimackinac service and could not return to America until he settled his accounts. He expressed hope that he would receive a knighthood for his past service. In February, he was imprisoned for unpaid debts, presumably bills he had run up in England rather than debts in America. Although Betsy likely found out about this event from American press reports, Rogers did not mention it. Instead, he told Betsy by mail in February 1770 that he expected his affairs, though not yet settled, to be resolved in a fortnight, and that he expected to sail for Portsmouth in March. "I am distressed that I have had only two letters from you since I left America," he added. "Why don't you write me oftener."[23]

Apparently, Betsy did write, and apparently she complained about his failure to return to America. The army still owed him £1,800 from Michilimackinac, Rogers explained in June 1770, and until this issue was settled he would remain in England, because he wanted to be able to provide her with the home of her own that she deserved. Betsy also apparently complained about rumors of his "Extravagant Living in London," an echo of the rumors that had so angered her father in 1763. A single mother still living with her parents, without resources of her own, Betsy must have found the hearsay maddening. Her accusation angered Rogers. He attributed the rumors to "Villenious" persons and told her to get off her "High Hors" about his supposed extravagance. The allegations likely were true; Rogers was living in the same expensive lodgings in the same fashionable London neighborhood he had lived in on his 1765 trip, and he was not known for otherwise depriving himself.[24]

After this dust-up, Rogers and Betsy seem to have had no further correspondence for almost four years. When Rogers next wrote, in March 1774, he addressed her frostily as "Mrs. Rogers." He complained that he had received an account of how she was doing from a mutual acquaintance but had heard nothing directly from her. During most of this period, Rogers was in debtors prison, a fact he did not share with her. Betsy complained to her brother-in-law that she had "received no satisfactory account from Major Rogers" about what he was up to in London. Replied her brother-in-law, "I don't wonder in the least at your resentment at his most impudent behavior & ill treatment of you."[25]

In the fall of 1774, a change in English bankruptcy law allowed Rogers to get out of debtors prison. He remained in England for another year, seeking without success to secure a government appointment. During this time, there is no evidence of communication between Rogers and Betsy.

Rogers arrived back in America in August 1775. He spent most of the next ten months crisscrossing the Northeast seeking to gather assets, exploring opportunities, and sounding out Patriot and Loyalist supporters about a role in the rapidly-escalating conflict between the colonies and the Crown. He met with Betsy and Arthur briefly in early December 1775 and briefly again in April 1776. In the first meeting, Betsy, whose parents had died, likely raised the subject of money. In his last extant letter to her, Rogers advises that he has no money to give her and that she "must do as well as you can till I Return." After the second meeting, he and Betsy never communicated again.[26]

Rogers declared as a Loyalist in June 1776 and began recruiting colonists to fight for the British. In January 1778, Betsy petitioned the New Hampshire legislature for divorce. Her petition mostly relates to his abandonment of her and failure to support her for most of the marriage, detailing the horror of her time spent at Michilimackinac. The petition adds a lurid detail. In their final meeting, Betsy says, "he was in a situation which, as her peace and safety forced her *then* to shun & fly from him—so Decency *now* forbids her to say anything more upon so indelicate a Subject." The implication, which Rogers' biographers all draw, is that he was showing obvious signs of venereal disease but no concern about infecting her.[27]

The New Hampshire legislature granted the divorce in February on grounds of abandonment and infidelity. Later in 1778, that body banned Rogers from returning to New Hampshire. In June 1778, Betsy married a sea captain, John Roche, to whom she remained married until his death in 1811. She died in 1813.[28]

Betsy was subjected to one injury and indignity after another throughout her seventeen-year marriage to Rogers. There is no evidence she got anything positive out of the relationship, and under even the most charitable interpretation Rogers was utterly feckless to the point of deliberate cruelty. The indignities Rogers subjected Betsy to would have driven any normal person to anger and despair. We hear very little directly from Betsy about her feelings regarding the marriage, but what we do hear rings true. Her divorce petition expresses years of pent-up anger supported by convincing detail. It cannot be dismissed as an exaggerated advocacy piece never subjected to rebuttal because it is consistent with complaints she confided to her brother-in-law years earlier. As far back as 1763, Betsy's "Distress" at the state of her marriage was obvious to her father, and the marriage did not improve thereafter.[29]

An early biographer expresses an accurate view of the marriage: "Nothing, indeed, is more significant of Rogers' real character" than his "habitual neglect of [Betsy], the calm indifference with which he forgot for months at a time his entire connection to her, and his failure to make any real provision for her separate maintenance."[30]

CHAPTER TWELVE

THE SOUTH, THE NORTHEAST, AND DETROIT AGAIN

AFTER his and Betsy's wedding and brief honeymoon, Rogers left for South Carolina on July 6, 1761. He was a captain in the British army now, with an annual salary of £560. Amherst, evidently based on Rogers' strength as a frontier fighter, assigned him to a company combating Cherokee Indians, but by the time Rogers arrived that campaign had ended. The Seven Years' War, over in North America, continued elsewhere. He spent most of his time recruiting troops for service in the Caribbean against the French.

Rogers hated South Carolina. He complained constantly about the heat and the mosquitoes. He apparently contracted malaria and endured repeated recurrences of fever and chills while he was there. The recruiting difficulties that had plagued his efforts to fill out Ranger ranks up north followed him south: many recruits were unfit, and desertion rates were high. The one bright spot in his tour of duty was his introduction to North Carolina Governor Arthur Dobbs. In October 1761, the position of Superintendent of Indian Affairs for the Southern District—the southern counterpart to the position Sir William Johnson held in the north—became vacant. Rogers sought the job. Dobbs had a key say in the appointment, and Rogers traveled to Wilmington, North Carolina, to meet him. He and Dobbs, who shared his enthusiasm about the Northwest Passage, hit it off and eagerly compared notes about that legendary subject. Dobbs recommended him to William Pitt for the Indian Affairs job. Rogers solicited Amherst's support as well, but he did not get the position.[1]

Perhaps spurred by his talks with Dobbs, Rogers began musing about the Northwest Passage and the fervor that would envelop its discoverer. He decided he was the person to command an expedition to notch that achievement. Such a position, which he imagined as prestigious and high paying, would take him beyond creditors' reach for years. And should he find the passage, he would bask in international acclaim and qualify for a £20,000 prize authorized by Parliament in 1744. By 1763, Rogers had shared this plan with Betsy and likely others. Entertaining the idea more as a daydream than a realistic enterprise, he nurtured it for more than a decade.[2]

By early 1762, Rogers was complaining to Amherst about his mundane military chores. On March 20, he wrote Amherst that with the Cherokee War over there was nothing to do in South Carolina; he was so sick with fever and ague he could barely walk. He asked for a transfer to one of the New York Independent Companies as he was "accustomed to the Northern Climates." On April 29, 1762, he wrote asking to be sent on the campaign against the Spanish in Cuba, disregarding that island's tropical nature. "The Southern Climate is very unhealthful," he complained. "I have had the Fever and Ague almost ever since I arrived in Charlestown." If not to Cuba, he suggested, how about somewhere north: "if permitted by Your Excellency should be glad to exchange [my present command] for an Independent Company elsewhere." Amherst sympathized, noted that Cuba has "a warmer Climate than that of South Carolina," and told him he was most useful where he was. Rogers persisted. On July 29, 1762, again citing his health, he asked for reassignment to a New York Independent Company. He felt "shut up in an oven and deprived of motion," he said. "I cannot live without a respite from this Climate."[3]

Amherst relented, albeit reluctantly and only partially. He told Rogers he would be happy to give him a northern appointment on "a proper occasion," but that such an appointment was not presently available, because "the Scene of Action will be to the Southward." "I could wish you would remain where you are," he wrote, "but if you think it absolutely Necessary for the recovery of your health to come to the Northward, you have my leave." This was not a reassignment, but time off from his South Carolina post.[4]

Rogers was back in New York by October. His principal concern seems to have been less his health than his finances. Before returning to Portsmouth, he traveled to Albany to meet with his fur-trading partner Askin to discuss Askin's efforts to recover money on his behalf from Rogers & Co. partner Cole. Askin advised that Cole had money owed to Rogers & Co. and agreed to dispatch his assistant James Gordon to track Cole down and collect the money. Gordon traveled 2,000 miles to buttonhole Cole. By March 1763 Rogers was able to meet with Cole, dissolve Rogers & Co., and receive his disappointing share of the assets: £975. While in Albany, Rogers borrowed £3,840 from Volkert Douw, likely to refinance fur-trading debts.[5]

The Albany trip had by no means solved his money problems. Rogers worried about his long-term status with the army. He proposed to Amherst that the army create a permanent force of one thousand Rangers to patrol the frontier and name him to command it. Amherst turned thumbs down: "In answer to your proposal for Raising a Corps of Rangers, I must acquaint you that Altho I have a very good Opinion of You, I Shall Readily Employ You when the Service will permit me, I have a very Despicable One of the Rangers In General and so far from thinking them of Use, I am fully Satisfied that Such a Corps will never answer the Ends proposed; and therefore while it Depends on me, the Crown Shall not be put to that Useless Expense."[6]

Rogers returned to Portsmouth. In early 1763, South Carolina merchants sued him there for £23. Rogers paid—in counterfeit money. The merchants' lawyer advised them that Rogers had a reputation for such dishonesty.[7] That the merchants pursued Rogers so aggressively for so small a debt suggests they must have been extremely angry at his behavior. That he cheated them so flagrantly when they caught up with him is a striking example of his willingness to flout the law.

Rogers had much larger financial matters on his mind. On the plus side, the New Hampshire legislature had appropriated funds to pay the 1755–56 Rangers, relieving that headache. He had raised cash by selling property to his father-in-law and settling with Cole. But he needed much more money. Bostonian Nathaniel Wheelwright, to whom Rogers owed

£3,430, was demanding payment. In March 1763 Rogers prevailed on his older brother James to pay this debt. Rogers never repaid James, who later sued him, unsuccessfully. Rogers' settlement with Cole took place in Newport; Wheelwright was in Boston. It was from these towns that rumors of Rogers' "prodigality" had reached Browne, prompting his lawsuit.

Extravagant spending while strapped for money is a pattern that recurred throughout Rogers' life.[8] An April 1763 example is illustrative. Portsmouth merchant William Pearson sued Rogers over unpaid bills for luxury goods bought earlier that year, including "1 fine hat" at £129. The total due was £478—almost Rogers' annual salary, owed a single merchant for a brief spending spree when Rogers was awash in debt. More suits followed demanding another £460.[9]

Rogers was so desperate he confided in Amherst, albeit misrepresenting the matter. In a letter no longer extant,[10] Rogers explained that he had loaned a large sum to a friend. The friend, unable to repay, had left Rogers without funds. "I cannot help Expressing my surprise at the largeness of the Sum which you have paid for One Man," a politely skeptical Amherst responded. "I am Extremely Sorry your Generosity should have Extended so far as to bring your own Affairs into Disrespectful Circumstances."[11] In other words, your explanation is hard to believe but, if true, does not reflect very well on your judgment.

Rogers really was writing to Amherst seeking to be appointed to command a fort on the western frontier. There, in addition to his army duties, he could trade in furs on the side and earn enough money to get out of debt. Amherst emphatically said no. "Altho I am really Sorry for your Circumstances and Should be glad to have it in my power to Alleviate them, I must Disapprove of the method you propose, by getting the Command of a Trading Post, for I have always thought it unbecoming an officer to be in any ways Concerned in Trade, nor could I think of allowing any such Practices while I have the Honor to Command."[12]

Amherst understood the seriousness of Rogers' problems. "From what I now Learn of Captain Rogers's Affairs, I fear, if his Creditors Lay Hold of him, they will treat him very Severely," he wrote to one of Rogers' fellow officers on May 8, 1763. "He Assured me, he had money Due to him, and Lands sufficient to Satisfy the Whole. If so, he ought to keep out of the Way, until he can Settle his Affairs, and when he has paid all his Debts, he will have his Half Pay to live on." Rogers' claim to Amherst that he had assets sufficient to cover his debts was untrue.[13]

Amherst's reference to "Half Pay" reflected another blow to Rogers' finances. In April 1763, he had succeeded, presumably with Amherst's approval, in selling his South Carolina commission and purchasing an equivalent captaincy in a New York Independent Company stationed at Albany. With this development, he was no longer on leave, but back on active duty. Less than a month later, however, the army disbanded Independent Companies. Rogers was involuntarily retired, entitled only to a retired captain's half pay.[14]

As a stopgap, Amherst in June 1763 assigned the decommissioned Rogers to join an expedition to relieve Detroit, under siege by Indians as part of Pontiac's War. The orders also accomplished Amherst's recommendation that Rogers should "keep out of the Way, until he can Settle his Affairs." The Detroit assignment landed Betsy back with her parents in Portsmouth. When Rogers returned from Detroit, he would be unemployed.[15]

In November 1763, Amherst was recalled to London. Thomas Gage replaced him as British commander for North America. Amherst had been Rogers' strongest supporter in the British army. Gage was a confirmed Rogers skeptic.[16]

The Detroit relief expedition's commander, Captain James Dalyell, had fought alongside Rogers at the Battle of Fort Anne and later was an aide to Amherst. En route to Detroit, Rogers recruited colonial troops to join the expedition. These men, whose ranks are variously reported as thirty-seven, twenty or fewer, or "a handful," apparently reported to Rogers. Dalyell's force totaled about three hundred.[17]

Pontiac's War had broken out in the spring of 1763. The lesser cause of the war was that England, as a matter of policy, had sharply reduced the volume of gifts distributed to western Indian tribes, to a value much lower than what the French had given when they controlled the frontier. The French had treated tribes as independent sovereignties, and both sides treated gifts as signs of respect, even tribute. England's economizing, apart from general parsimony in the wake of a very expensive war, reflected a desire to encourage Indian self-sufficiency. The Indians, feeling they were being treated wrongly as defeated peoples, took offense.

The bigger spur for Pontiac's War was British colonists' relentless western expansion, which threatened Indian lands and culture. Official British policy was pro-Indian. England tried to keep immigrant settlement east of the Appalachians. The Crown wanted to create Indian homelands further west that would be protected from European encroachment. But the fact that British garrisons now occupied western forts previously in French hands created a level of security for land-hungry colonists that had not existed before the French and Indian War, and England was never able to enforce its anti-expansionist policy.

Trying to roll back the European tide, Ottawa chief Pontiac stitched together an informal but impressive coalition of western tribes, which rose in a loosely coordinated revolt in the spring of 1763. By late summer, the Indians had overrun eight western forts, massacring their garrisons, leaving only Fort Detroit, Fort Pitt, and Fort Niagara in British hands. Led by Pontiac personally, the Indians had planned to take Fort Detroit by trickery, filtering into the fort with weapons concealed under blankets. The post's commander, Major Gladwin, tipped off about the plan, posted armed troops around the fort's perimeter, thwarting Pontiac's plan. Pontiac besieged the fort instead.[18]

The Dalyell expedition left Albany in June 1763, reaching Forts Niagara and then Detroit, on the way passing fallen outposts. Trailing behind came James Gordon, the Askin & Rogers employee who had tracked down Cole. Gordon left Albany in August 1763 with three boatloads of trade goods and 150 gallons of rum, concealed on instructions from Askin, who knew it was illegal to trade alcohol to Indians on orders from Amherst and Johnson.[19]

Rogers surely knew Gordon would be following him to Detroit with those goods. There is no evidence that Rogers knew about the contraband rum, but this was a topic one would have expected him to discuss with his partner Askin in Albany.

Gordon never got beyond Fort Niagara. Pontiac's War made civilian travel further west too risky. Even after the siege of Fort Detroit was lifted, hostilities continued deep into 1764, bringing the fur trade to a standstill. Gordon lingered at Fort Niagara until late November, sick much of the time, then returned to Albany and sold the trade goods at a loss. Discouraged about fur trading, he returned to Ireland. Askin & Rogers became insolvent and shut down in 1764. Askin continued in business individually, winning the forbearance of creditors, to whom he calculated he owed £7,000. He settled with them in 1771. He went on to success trading furs in the 1770s at Michilimackinac. The partnership's debts, however, dogged Rogers for the remainder of his time in North America.[20]

Upon his arrival in Detroit, Dalyell urged an immediate assault on the Indians. Post commander Gladwin, who outranked him, opposed the idea, deeming the Indians too numerous and too alert. Dalyell persisted; Gladwin acquiesced. After midnight on July 31, 1763, Dalyell marched his three-hundred-man force out of the fort and toward the Indian encampment. Less than two miles from the fort, Indians ambushed the column as it attempted to cross Parent's Creek over a wooden bridge, catching the British by surprise and putting them to flight. Dalyell was killed, his heart ripped out and thrust in the faces of captive British soldiers.[21]

Rogers played a useful subsidiary role in the battle. The road along which the British had advanced and then retreated was dotted with houses. Rogers seized one and, from within its walls, organized a few soldiers who kept up a steady fire, retarding the Indian advance and covering the British retreat. His action helped to avoid a complete rout, and British losses at the Battle of Bloody Run were relatively moderate: twenty-three killed and thirty-eight wounded.[22]

Despite the defeat, the Dalyell expedition had resupplied Fort Detroit, reinforcing its garrison with more than two hundred fresh troops. The siege continued, but by October it was clear the Indians would not prevail. Pontiac and Gladwin agreed to a truce. The war continued for nearly another year, but Fort Detroit was out of danger. Rogers and a body of expendable troops left Fort Detroit on November 17, 1763, arriving at Fort Niagara a week later.[23]

One of Rogers' early biographers asserts, without citation, that at Fort Niagara Rogers engaged in affairs "of no very creditable nature . . . using his uniform, his commission, and his reputation in furthering his business ventures." Rogers' trading with Mohawk and Delaware Indians incurred "the direct displeasure of Sir William Johnson at Albany."[24] Johnson may have learned about the contraband rum, and he certainly would have been sensitive to any underhanded trading with the Mohawks. No doubt by the end of 1763 he, like Gage, viewed Rogers with "displeasure."

CHAPTER THIRTEEN

THE LOST YEAR

ROGERS reached Albany in December 1763. He proceeded to New York, then to Connecticut, where he wrote to Gage, now North American military commander, reviving the proposal he had pitched without success to Gage's predecessor Amherst: Could the army create a thousand-man Ranger corps and name him its commander? This would be a timely project, Rogers argued, as Pontiac's War was continuing and there would almost certainly be a need to march against the western Indians during the 1764 campaign season. Rogers said he could have the Ranger corps ready by then.[1]

Returning to New York, Rogers was arrested for non-payment of a debt and imprisoned. The prison was near an army barracks housing multiple companies of the Scottish Highland regiment and other troops. Highlander private Robert Kirk had accompanied Rogers on the St. Francis raid. Rogers' imprisonment for so trifling an offense as debt outraged Kirk. He visited Rogers, and the two "concerted a scheme together for his escape." Other soldiers also met with Rogers, and muttering about the unjustness of his confinement caused security to be tightened at the jail.[2]

On the night of January 15, 1764, fifteen to twenty armed soldiers stormed the jail and freed all thirty-five prisoners. Rogers pretended to protest his unauthorized release by the mob but accepted a horse and money and galloped off. Alerted by the noise, a local resident organized fellow citizens and sailors to disperse soldiers milling about the jail. A fight broke out, shots were fired, and half a dozen persons were wounded. Most escaped prisoners were recaptured or returned on their own, but Rogers and four others remained at large. New York offered a bounty of £200—about $40,000 in today's money—for Rogers' capture and return.[3] He turned up in Connecticut.

The spectacle of army regulars rioting against local authorities and causing multiple significant injuries and the escape of five prisoners embarrassed General Gage. Witnesses reported the incident to him and to Sir William Johnson and let both men know that Rogers was the cause of it. With a bounty on his head, Rogers, unable to enter New York, had to conduct any business he did there through intermediaries.[4]

Rogers wrote to Gage on March 3, 1764, from Massachusetts. He began by complaining that he was due pay for the Detroit expedition, but quickly shifted to press for a far larger sum. Without explanation or documentation, Rogers claimed to have advanced "about Seventeen hundred pounds New York Currency" to troops accompanying him to Detroit. Pending a final accounting, Rogers asked for an advance of £656 against that "as the same sum is due to a certain Gentleman that I am desirous should be paid." His phrasing suggests he expected Gage to know exactly what and whom he was talking about.[5]

Rogers' claim to £1,700 in reimbursable expenses from the Detroit expedition was largely fabricated, an attempt to hoodwink the army. As Gage well knew, the troops who accompanied Rogers came from provincial units which were continuing to pay them. Amherst had not authorized Rogers to create a new Ranger force. Relatively few men had joined Rogers—estimates range from "a handful" to thirty-seven—and they served only six months. Even entitled to Ranger pay of not quite £4 per month—they were not, and there were no Ranger units at the time—the difference between that and their provincial pay cannot have been more than £2 apiece per month, a maximum of less than £500. There is no evidence that Rogers advanced any of this, or that he incurred any other reimbursable expenses on the expedition. Tellingly, Rogers never attempted to detail or document his supposed claim and dropped the matter once Gage said no.

As to Rogers' demand for pay to cover his trip to Detroit, Gage initially concluded he was entitled to nothing beyond his half-pay as a retired captain because he had volunteered. This was not an unreasonable conclusion. Rogers had no active rank in the British army. Gage, who undoubtedly knew about Rogers' role in Askin & Rogers and that firm's attempt to ship trade goods to Detroit, may have decided Rogers had commercial reasons for joining the expedition.

Rogers' March 3 letter was relatively neutral in tone. The next day, March 4, 1764, he wrote a less temperate letter hectoring Gage for failing to respond promptly to his proposal to raise a thousand-man Ranger corps: "I was in hopes before this time to have received your Excellencys Answer to the Memorial I wrote you from New Haven." He vowed to have the force at Albany "on the Shortest Notice." As an alternative, he asked that Gage "favor me with a Command at one of the Frontier Posts." Schooled by his experience with Amherst, Rogers did not advise Gage that he proposed to use the post to trade in furs. Rogers argued that he was entitled to special consideration for one of these appointments because of his past service, "and more especially as I have met with great Misfortune and Losses," including Amherst's refusal to reimburse him for money sent to "Prisoners in Canada." Rogers emphasized that his misfortunes had come about "not through my own Misconduct but purely through Bad Luck."[6]

Rogers then unloaded to Gage about his creditors in New York. "I heartily crave your Advice in my present Situation. . . . I am as sensible of my Serviceableness to the Nation as I am of my own misfortune by being in Debt, and hope that the Rabble Rout of a Jew and other Money Catchers will never harm the true Character of Major Rogers with any General in his Majesty's Service especially so worthy a Gentleman as General Gage." Rogers suggested he get a position in an anticipated campaign against the Delaware, a tribe with which he was "well acquainted," promising to "cut off that or any other Nation of Indians for you that may prove insolent." He ended by saying that he was sending his letters by Paul Burbeen, who would carry back any instructions from Gage. Rogers, still a wanted man with a price on his head there, could not go to New York himself.[7] Burbeen also carried a copy of Amherst's order to Rogers to join the expedition.[8]

Gage responded two weeks later. He had no military orders for Rogers. Now that he knew Amherst had ordered Rogers to join the Detroit expedition, he agreed that Rogers was due additional pay to reflect his active-duty status. Beyond that, Gage emphatically rejected Rogers' claim to be owed money with respect to provincial troops on the expedition. It is unlikely that Rogers actually paid anything to these troops and he did not press Gage further. Like Amherst, Gage rejected Rogers' request to command a Ranger corps or get a frontier post. "I am very well convinced of your abilities, and knowledge in that particular Service [Rangers]," Gage wrote, "but I do not know of any Rangers to be raised at present, nor of any Command to be given at any of the Frontier Posts." Units specifically designated as "Rangers" had been disbanded, but Gage's response was disingenuous. He was organizing a major campaign against the western Indians, and many colonial officers from the French and Indian War, including Israel Putnam, were to play a role in it. He could have found a spot for Rogers but preferred not to, telling Rogers, "Colonel Bradstreet will Command a Body of Troops this Spring, but [I] know not whether he will have occasion to employ you, or not." With respect to Rogers' plea for an advance to pay a "certain Gentleman," Gage was cutting: "in respect to your transactions in this place [New York], I have nothing to offer, I could wish to hear less of them."[9]

It is apparent from Gage's reference to "your transactions in this place" that he knew what those transactions were and who the "certain Gentleman" was. In Gage's view, the transactions reflected poorly on Rogers and were unrelated to his military service. In a later letter Gage attributed Rogers' debts of "some Thousands" to "Vanity and Gaming."[10]

Rogers had been in Albany and New York in December 1763. By February and March 1764, he had been to Connecticut, Massachusetts, and Concord, New Hampshire. He does not appear to have reunited with Betsy at Portsmouth until April or May. His laggard homecoming could only have reflected the degree of estrangement between Rogers and Betsy and the fact that he had no money and no professional prospects. Rogers seems to have remained in New England for most of the next year but seems to have spent scant time with Betsy and her parents—only a few days, according to her divorce petition. Of course, Rogers and Betsy had no "home" other than her parents' house.[11]

In June 1764, merchant George Boyd sued Rogers for passing English bills of exchange supposedly worth £500 but which Rogers knew to be worthless to satisfy debts of that amount owed Boyd. According to Boyd's writ, Rogers transacted "with wicked Intent to deceive & cheat the Plaintiff & diverse others." Rogers settled Boyd's suit by taking back the worthless bills of exchange.[12]

The reversals of 1763-64 blackened Rogers' reputation in the colonies. They showed him to be not merely financially irresponsible, but dishonest and defiant of the law. These events were widely known, and they informed the public assessment of his character. From 1764 forward, Rogers would be thought of as dishonest and unprincipled. As William L. Clements concluded, Rogers was "a weak moral character," whose "lack of a proper sense of honesty, his frequent indiscretions and sometimes his utter disregard for the opinions and orders of his superiors, led him to be regarded by his military associates with distrust."[13]

Reverend Browne had placed the properties he bought from Rogers in 1762 in Betsy's name. Rogers now prevailed on Betsy to mortgage these properties for £350 to help pay his debts. He also asked Abraham Douw, a long-time lender of his, to be patient about the repayment of money advanced to Askin & Rogers.[14]

In July 1764 came good financial news. In a program created by King George III to reward French and Indian War veterans, New Hampshire granted Rogers a three-thousand-acre tract in what is now southwestern Vermont. In September, Rogers sold 2,500 of those acres to four parties for a total of about £1,600. At about the same time, he bought 3,300 acres in New Burnett Township and another 3,300 acres in Draper Township from Joseph Blanchard for £250. A short while later, he bought five thousand acres in Charlestown, Massachusetts, for £1,500 Massachusetts pounds and 1,700 acres of a grant to Ranger lieutenant James Tute for £100. The value of the land that Rogers sold from his New Hampshire grant is approximately the same as the value of land that he purchased at about the same time, and appears to have been a real estate swap. This may have been an effort to diversify, or it may have been an attempt to make assets more difficult for creditors to find. Whatever the explanation, Rogers soon lost his grip on the real estate. In October 1764, he gave a mortgage on virtually all his real estate to Albany merchant Gysbert Fonda in partial satisfaction of debt totaling £5,670.[15]

The land grant's value—at least £2,000, assuming the tract Rogers retained had the same value as the tracts he sold—dwarfed the amount in dispute between Rogers and the army. The fact that Rogers immediately signed over all the properties he acquired in 1764 to satisfy a single pre-existing obligation and remained hopelessly in debt underscores the depth of his financial distress.

Apart from property transactions, there is little record of where Rogers was or what he was doing late in 1764 and early in 1765. He sailed for England in March 1765, intent on obtaining an appointment of significance in America. Betsy appears to have learned of his departure from a letter he wrote from on board the ship before it departed. She did not receive the letter until after he was gone.[16]

That same month, older brother James sued him for the £3,430 James had paid on Robert's behalf to Nathaniel Wheelwright. The sheriff's return of James' writ of attachment shows the "attachment" of the property that Robert had purchased in Charlestown, Massachusetts, but by March 1765 this property had already been mortgaged to Gysbert Fonda, and James does not appear to have recovered anything.[17]

ROGERS' accumulated debt in 1764 was stunning. Before he received his land grant in July 1764 and used it to satisfy one large debt in part, Rogers owed Albany merchant Gysbert Fonda £5,670. He owed Volkert Douw, who ultimately sued him in 1768, £3,840. He owed his brother James £3,430. He owed Portsmouth merchant William Pearson £478, and he owed another two creditors who sued him in New Hampshire £460. Having taken back the worthless bills of exchange, he still owed George Boyd £500. He owed the "certain Gentleman" in New York £656. These readily identifiable debts, all outstanding and unpaid at the same time, total £15,000, or about $3 million in today's money. They vastly exceed any amount Rogers could claim with any plausibility to be owed him by the army.

How did an army captain run up such crushing debt? In part the answer is poor decisions in business and insupportably extravagant living. Hinted at repeatedly and convincingly is an addiction to gambling. New York Chief Justice William Smith had known Rogers since the French and Indian War. After his army service, according to Smith, Rogers "gamed himself into Poverty." Gage reported in early 1766 that Rogers' "Thousands" in debts were due to "Vanity and Gaming." A British officer who testified about Rogers' reputation at his treason trial reported that he was known to be "a Gambler." Benjamin Roberts complained in 1769 that Rogers, in Montreal, "drinks and games as usual" while awaiting confirmation of his acquittal on treason charges. Gambling likely was one of the "unlawful Passions" that Rogers' father-in-law complained about. One of Rogers' recent biographers reports, without elaboration, that "gambling," for Rogers, was "a very costly addiction."[18] A gambling addiction is fully consistent with Rogers' personality and helps to explain his chronic indebtedness despite regular infusions of money, often in large amounts.

PART THREE

A SECOND CHANCE

CHAPTER FOURTEEN

A NEW LEASE
ON LIFE

IN EARLY 1765, Rogers appeared to be at a complete dead end. He was hopelessly in debt, had no employment or active command, and with Gage at the top of the American military hierarchy, he had little chance of obtaining the latter. Rogers' escape from obscurity, his revival of his fortunes through effective self-promotion, was a feat every bit as impressive as his escape from Indian pursuers at the Battle on Snowshoes or on the retreat from St. Francis.

Rogers was accompanied on his 1765 trip to London by a newly retained secretary, Nathaniel Potter, a Princeton-educated minister defrocked for serial adultery. A Boston newspaper described the pair as "the famous Major Rogers, and the infamous Parson Potter" and commented snarkily that they had gone to London to seek "peculiar Rewards." John Adams showed the same condescending bemusement, describing in his diary Rogers' and Potter's "Persecution in Boston, their flight to Rhode Island, their sufferings there; their Deliverance from Gaol." He went on to record their arrival in England "without Money," and speculated that the point of the trip was to allow Rogers to present copies of his soon-to-be-published books personally to the king.[1] In America, Rogers was no longer a subject of respect.

In England his status was different. Rogers was a household name; his "fame exceeded that of any other North American, Franklin and George Washington included." But London knew little about his finances. He may have arrived penniless, but he had the ability to borrow, if not to repay. He and Potter took up lodgings in the most expensive part of London.[2]

Rogers had come bearing letters of recommendation and letters of introduction from friends and supporters. He and Potter hit the drawing room and gentlemen's club circuits and soon were being introduced to persons of influence. The single most important of these was Charles Townshend, a Member of Parliament who was Paymaster General and a former First Lord of the Admiralty and Secretary of War. Townshend's brother Roger, an aide to Lord Amherst, died in combat during the 1759 campaign against Ticonderoga. Rogers had known Roger Townshend and undoubtedly emphasized this relationship to Charles, who became a valuable patron.[3]

Rogers and Potter also courted the press, which cheerfully broadcast Rogers' brief: in the late war, he "was the first Person in America who raised a Body of Troops at his own Expence, and headed them against the Indians. . . . His Regard for the Welfare of his Country however, utterly exhausted his private Fortune." He was retired on a captain's half-pay, while persons who had once been his subordinates now held active commands with higher ranks. He had come to London "to solicit some Preferment from the Ministry."[4] The injustice of Rogers' situation seemed to cry out for redress, although the reported cause of his distress was fiction.

One of Rogers' first tasks in London was to arrange for the publication of two books: his *Journals of Major Robert Rogers*, detailing his service during the French and Indian War, and *A Concise Account of North America*, a province-by-province and colony-by-colony travelogue of British North America. The books were printed and ready for sale by September 1765. Both were reviewed favorably and helped to boost Rogers' name recognition. The well-educated Potter is widely assumed to have contributed to polishing the prose.[5]

Whatever Potter's role, the *Journals* is a masterpiece of understated self-promotion. Brash, egotistical, and with an inflated sense of his own merit in real life, the Rogers of the *Journals* is modest, unassuming, and a faithful servant of king and country, quick to credit his brave officers and men for his own underplayed successes. He reports matter-of-factly the respect shown him by senior members of the British military hierarchy. He says that he "met with a very friendly reception" from Massachusetts Governor Shirley, then the North American military commander, when the two conferred in the spring of 1756. He quotes a 1757 letter from Captain Abercrombie, aide to General Abercromby, letting Rogers know that "all ranks of people here [in Albany] are pleased with your conduct, and your men's behavior." Abercrombie later became a severe critic of the Rangers. The Earl of Loudoun, Rogers lets us know, received him "in a very friendly manner" and expressed "entire confidence in your skill and knowledge."[6]

Rogers places special emphasis on the good opinion of the deceased war hero Lord Howe. Shortly after his arrival at the front, Howe "did us the honor to accompany us" on a scout, and then, "upon our return, expressed his good opinion of us very generously." Following the devastating defeat at the Battle on Snowshoes, Rogers "met with a very friendly reception from my Lord How, who advanced me cash to recruit the Rangers" needed to replace those fallen in battle. Shortly before Howe's death, Rogers "had a most agreeable interview" with him, and, on parting, Howe gave him "the strongest assurances of his friendship and influences in my behalf."[7] It is impossible to know if this meeting even occurred, but Rogers' message is clear: if the beloved Howe was such an ardent Rogers supporter, how could London power brokers fail to adopt the same view?

The *Journals* reports as fact Rogers' wildly exaggerated claims about his battlefield successes. After falling into the avoidable ambush in January 1757 in which he lost twenty men, Rogers says he killed more than one hundred attackers, nearly ten times the actual number and equal to the entire enemy force he faced. In the Battle on Snowshoes, in which nearly three quarters of his command was wiped out, he claims inaccurately that he was outnumbered four to one but nonetheless managed to kill 150 of the enemy and to wound an equal number, making it appear that the French and Indians suffered more severely than the Rangers. His description of the St. Francis raid is confined largely to a reproduction of his after-the-battle report to Amherst, which contains the false assertion that he killed "at least two hundred" Indians.[8] No one in London would have had any reason to doubt any of these claims.

Rogers also used the *Journals* to broadcast his theme that he exhausted his personal fortune in the service of his country and never received proper reimbursement. He complains that when the Earl of Loudoun, then the British military commander in North America, asked him to raise five new companies of Rangers in January 1758, he "was at the whole expense of raising the five companies" and "never got the least allowance for it." Rogers never raised this complaint at the time, and it is complete fiction. Loudoun's order plainly authorized Rogers to draw government funds to pay recruits advances to be deducted from their later pay. A little known document, a "Receipt" dated January 24, 1758, shows that Rogers and his recruiting officers received more than £1,400 in government funds, enough to advance a month's pay to nearly every man he was authorized to recruit. Rogers also claims that he advanced "a thousand [Spanish] dollars" to a recruiting captain who later died, leaving Rogers unable to recover the money. Another little known document, a record of a court martial proceeding, shows that Rogers himself commenced the proceeding to recover the debt and was awarded £42 from the deceased captain's estate.[9]

Equally remarkable is Rogers' treatment in the *Journals* of his old grievance, pay for the thirty troops who stayed with him at Fort Edward over the winter of 1755–56. This issue was resolved in 1763, when the New Hampshire legislature appropriated funds to pay these troops. When Rogers asked Amherst in 1760 for help with this pay issue, he put the amount due at £406. When he sought money for these troops in his 1761 account settlement, he claimed they were owed £615. New Hampshire settled the claims in 1763 for £235. Now, in 1765, the amount ballooned to an improbably precise "828 pounds, 3 shillings, 3 pence sterling," not counting legal fees, all of which, says Rogers, "I paid out of my private fortune." What is more, he concludes, without any reference to the 1763 New Hampshire appropriation, "for all of [this] I have not at any time since received one shilling consideration."[10] Virtually no one in London would have recognized this claim as invented.

Finally, Rogers complains that he "entirely lost" about £400 in personal funds stolen when his convoy was ambushed en route to Crown Point in early 1760.[11] As Rogers knew perfectly well, after initial resistance Amherst authorized the full reimbursement of these lost funds.

Concise Account is a brief, readable, and enthusiastic overview of the Canadian provinces and American colonies, much of it based on Rogers' personal experience. He sketches the history of each jurisdiction, its form of government, inhabitants' dominant religions, and its principal products and industries. Rogers constantly stresses the land's bounteousness, the abundance of fish and game, and especially the soil's fertility. Quebec, he writes, "may be justly denominated a healthy, fruitful, and pleasant country." The Lower Coos, Rogers' rendezvous spot on his retreat from St. Francis, "for its beauty and fertility, may be deservedly styled the garden of New England." The Connecticut River Valley is "pleasant and fertile." Rhode Island, "for its beauty and fertility . . . [i]s exceeded perhaps by no spot in New England." New York is "very pleasant and fertile"; Long Island has "excellent soil"; the Delaware Valley lands "are excellent, and scarce ever fail to reward the husbandman in a plentiful manner"; land along the Susquehanna is "exceedingly fruitful and easy to cultivate"; Virginia produces an abundance of "excellent tobacco"; western North Carolina is "most fruitful and pleasant."[12] It is difficult to imagine a London reader who would not wish to see this land in person.

Rogers reserves special enthusiasm for the upper St. Lawrence River Valley and the Great Lakes, the region now comprising the province of Ontario and the states of Ohio, Indiana, Illinois, Michigan, Wisconsin, and Minnesota. All these lands lay west of the existing provinces and colonies and were in the very early stages of settlement by Europeans. Of the land south of Lake Superior, where Rogers had extensive holdings, he writes that he does not "see any reason why this should not become a rich and valuable country, should it ever be inhabited by a civilized people." The Lake Michigan area is "capable of rich improvements," and its speedy settlement "is even of national importance." The land south of Lake Erie, present-day Ohio, "if peopled, and improved to advantage, would equal any of the British colonies on the sea coasts." The entire St. Lawrence basin west of Quebec has "a prospect in future, not only of a flourishing province, but a rich and great kingdom, exceeding in Europe, and exceeded by few, if any, in the fertility of its soil." "[T]here is no part of North America," he writes, that is "better worth settling, improving, and defending than this."[13]

Rogers' vision for the future of what was then the American frontier was entirely accurate. His enthusiasm for settlement, improvement, and development, however, put him on a collision course with British policy in the mid-1760s. England was not, at the time, interested in the rapid development of the frontier. It feared that land-hungry farmers and avaricious traders would come into constant conflict with the western Indians, provoking endless border wars. England preferred to see frontier interactions between Indians and Europeans heavily regulated to protect the Indians from exploitation, with large regions entirely off-limits to European development.

Concise Account ends with a lengthy section on the "Customs, Manners, &c of the Indians." Rogers paints a sensitive, well-informed, and largely positive portrait of Indians, whom many fellow colonists dismissed as savages. Although he notes their weakness for alcohol—a weakness he freely exploited in his trading activities—and although he chides Indian males for a tendency toward idleness, which he attributes to a view that work is degrading, Rogers emphasizes that "Indians do not want for natural good sense and ingenuity, many of them discovering a great capacity for any art or science, liberal or mechanical." They are physically fit and rarely deformed. Mothers "take great care of their children, and are extremely fond of them," and Indians respect their elders. They exhibit little in the way of avarice or ambition, and their society has little division between rich and poor.[14] Rogers presents a highly favorable description of the Ottawa chief Pontiac, whom Rogers says he met on his 1760 expedition to Detroit, before the outbreak of Pontiac's War. Rogers attributes to Pontiac "great strength of judgment and a thirst after knowledge," and reports that he would be happy to live in peace and acknowledge British sovereignty, but only if he was treated with "respect and honor."[15]

Pontiac was the subject of a third work Rogers published during his 1765 sojourn to England, a play entitled *Ponteach*. Unlike the *Journals* and *Concise Account*, *Ponteach* was thoroughly panned by critics. Rogers' role in writing the play is unclear. Although he was widely thought to be the author, or one of the authors, the play was printed without an author credit. It is clear, however, that Rogers was responsible for the publication of *Ponteach*; his publisher Millan, who also published the *Journals* and *Concise Account*, sued Rogers in 1772, during his second trip to London, for failing to pay him for publishing the play.[16]

While readying the *Journals* and *Concise Account* for publication, Rogers prepared a detailed proposal for an expedition to discover the Northwest Passage. Such a passage, if it existed, would greatly reduce travel time between England and Asia and promote trade between the regions. Rogers was encouraged to prepare the proposal by his new patron Charles Townshend, himself a Northwest Passage enthusiast. Townshend had previously been a member of the Lords of Trade and Plantations and, in that capacity, had supported earlier seaborne expeditions to find the Northwest Passage.[17]

Rogers' undated proposal, likely completed in August 1765, is "Humbly Submitted to the Wisdom of the Kings most Excellent

Majesty and his Ministers." It begins with a recital of Rogers' qualifica-
tions to command the expedition: his "Knowledge of the Country, his
Capacity for making Discovery, his Strength of Constitution . . . , his
Talent for Conciliating the Friendship of the Indians." These qualifica-
tions were true enough. Somewhat more dubious was his assertion that,
from his superior officers during the French and Indian War, "he has
not the least Doubt that he shall be able to obtain the fullest Testimonies
of his Character and Capacity for the Executing of all that he has the
Honour to propose." Amherst and others might have supported Rogers
to lead an expedition of exploration, but, as his proposal itself makes
clear, Johnson and Gage were unlikely to, and Rogers knew it. Johnson
and Gage were in America, however, and not easy to consult.[18]

Rogers assures his audience that "he has obtained a Moral certainty"
about "the real Existence of a North West Passage." This is said to be
based on his interrogation of Indians about rivers flowing to the Pacific
Ocean or Hudson Bay, but although Rogers had heard in Detroit about
a river flowing to a bay connected to the Pacific, there is no evidence
that Indians, who were not interested in ocean exploration, had told him
anything about a Northwest Passage. The notion that the bay Rogers
had heard about also connected, directly or indirectly, to Hudson Bay
or otherwise to the North Atlantic seems to have been Rogers' addition
or a surmise he had heard from North Carolina Governor Dobbs.
Rogers points out that even if the expedition were to establish that there
is no Northwest Passage, this clarification would be of great value because it would "put an End to Repeated, Hazardous and Expensive attempts for the Discovery by Sea."[19]

Rogers proposes that the expedition, to the extent possible, follow
water routes by canoe, portaging between waterways or constructing
new canoes as needed. As to the route, he is extremely vague: the expedition is to proceed from the Great Lakes to the headwaters of the Mississippi and from there seek a river called Ourigan by Indians. This
presumably means the River of the West, and both names presumably
refer to what we know as the Columbia. The Ourigan was believed to
flow into a bay that projected northeastward into the American continent from the Pacific. The proposal does not indicate where the expedition is to look for the Ourigan. The information Rogers learned in
Detroit was inconsistent, placing the Ourigan's headwaters in at least
three locations hundreds of miles apart. Rogers later suggested two even
more far-flung routes in completely different directions, by which one

might reach the Ourigan. The proposal does not address this dilemma, but recommends finding the Ourigan, following it to the bay connected to the Pacific, and exploring that bay to find the Northwest Passage.[20]

Rogers then pivots to a related suggestion. "Should the Design be patronized, Major Rogers thinks it would be Expedient and absolutely necessary, to Subserve this proposal that he should be appointed Governor Commandant of His Majesty's Garrison at Michilimackinac and its Dependencies on the Great Lakes." Considering his estimated three-year absence on the Northwest Passage expedition, he should have a Deputy Governor Commandant "on whose Diligence, Steadfastness and Integrity he can rely." Rogers asks "that the General Commanding in Chief in North America [Gage] & Sir William Johnson have Orders to give him their assistance in their respective Departments as Occasion may require." Rogers seems to envision appointments for himself and his deputy that are political as well as military ("Governor" and "Commandant" and "Deputy Governor Commandant"), independent of Gage and Johnson. In a burst of audacity, Rogers requests that the two senior British officials in North America be ordered to give their assistance to him.[21] He promises to transmit to the government an "Authentic Account" of the expedition upon its completion.[22]

Rogers next detours to his favorite topic: injustices done him. He has undergone great fatigues, he writes, and suffered numerous wounds, in the service of his country. Despite this, he has "been exposed to the [illegible] Consequences of Expensive Law Suits, merely on Account of the Services, by which he has been reduced, and indeed Ruined, in his private Fortune without any other Reward than the Slender Subsistence arising from a Captain's Half pay."[23]

Rogers then details a budget for the expedition. He proposes daily compensation rates for twenty-eight officers, sergeants, surgeons, and assistants, and for two hundred privates. He asks for eight hundred traps for fur-bearing creatures to help the expedition be self-supporting and a generous allowance for gifts for Indians. With the costs of provisions and ammunition, as well as his own compensation, left to be filled in, the cost of the three-year expedition exceeds £32,000, more than $6 million in today's money.[24]

Rogers' proposal is extremely vague about the expedition's route and silent about distances and other geographical obstacles. When he was later forced to supply these details, his plan's impracticality became clear. Even in its original form, however, the proposal would have raised serious questions in the mind of a careful reader. As a simple expedition of exploration intended to expand knowledge of the North American continent west of the existing frontier, it was unfocused, premature, and unnecessarily large and expensive. As an expedition with the specific objective of discovering, or disproving the existence of, the Northwest Passage, it was ill-conceived and had limited chance of success.

For a simple expedition of exploration, the primary problem with Rogers' proposal is that he had very little information about what lay to the west of the Great Lakes, and the information that he had was conflicting and plainly unreliable. This made it impossible to focus on goals that would incrementally advance England's geographic knowledge of North America. Rogers is sometimes portrayed as a forerunner of Lewis and Clark, someone who, properly supported, might have anticipated their discoveries. Although Lewis and Clark's expedition almost forty years later is widely and properly seen as a leap into the unknown, Lewis and Clark had substantial, reasonably accurate information about most of their route up the Missouri River to its headwaters. This information was sufficient to allow them, for example, to plan to winter at Mandan Indian villages. The single missing piece for their expedition was how to cross the Rocky Mountains and find a west-flowing river that would take them to the Pacific. This was a significant and daunting gap, and their success was far from assured, but it was a specific, defined challenge.

Rogers, by contrast, was almost completely in the dark about the land he intended to explore. Rumors about a west-flowing "River of the West" or "Ourigan River" variously placed its source just on the far side of a divide north of the headwaters of the Mississippi; in the Lake of the Woods, one hundred miles north of that; or in Lake Winnipeg, another two to three hundred miles northwest. These were vast distances, the routes they dictated were incompatible and could not be covered in a single expedition, and Rogers clearly had no idea where to begin exploring.

Any exploration of lands west of British holdings in North America, of course, had value in adding to what they knew about the continent. In 1765, however, it was not clear who even owned these lands: from the Mississippi to the Rocky Mountains Spain, not England, had ownership rights, although the northern boundary of Spain's holdings was vague. Exploration of the lands did not have an urgency or obvious value that required immediate attention, nor did it require a 230-man expedition lasting three years. It could be done in increments with a commitment of far fewer resources.

An expedition of the size and duration Rogers proposed could only be justified—and in Rogers' mind was justified—as a means of finding the Northwest Passage. It would not be fair to criticize Rogers for his faith in that geographical Holy Grail's existence. Many of his contemporaries shared this erroneous belief. But an overland expedition by foot and canoe was not a reasonable means of discovering it. In addition to the paucity of information to guide the search, the Northwest Passage was imagined to be a water route for ocean-going vessels to pass between the North Atlantic and the Pacific. Indeed, to be awarded the prize of £20,000 for discovering the Northwest Passage, a claimant needed to sail an ocean-going vessel through it. Even if Rogers' overland expedition, carrying canoes or building new ones as it went, could reach the bay supposedly thrusting inland from the Pacific, and even if this bay connected, directly or indirectly, to the North Atlantic, it was unlikely that Rogers, proceeding by foot or by canoe, could discover, map, and pass through this extensive waterway. The logical way to conduct this exploration was by ocean-going vessel. By 1765, the eastern portion of this task—searching Hudson Bay for an outlet to the west—had been undertaken without success. The western portion—sailing the Pacific coast north from present-day Seattle, searching for an outlet to the east—was about to begin. Rogers' overland approach was highly unlikely to add information about the passage that could not be gleaned more comprehensively and accurately from seaborne expeditions. He noted that seaborne expeditions were expensive and hazardous, but so was his proposal.

Rogers' expedition never attracted sufficient support. The proposal was read by the Lords of Trade and Plantations—the body to which Townshend had once belonged—on September 6, 1765. The Lords said they viewed the proposal with favor, but, because it involved a commitment of a substantial body of uniformed troops, referred it to the War Department, which took no action. King George III himself reviewed the proposal and referred it to his Privy Council for consideration on October 2, 1765, but the Privy Council deferred consideration until the next day and never followed up. The issue appears to have been costs. England was struggling with French and Indian War debts, the colonies were objecting to having the costs imposed on them through additional taxation, and a large new expense for an expedition of discovery, value uncertain, was not appealing. Rogers' proposal languished.[25]

Townshend asked Rogers to prepare a less costly version, promised to promote it, and opined that approval of some form of the proposal was likely. To cement Townshend's commitment to the project, Rogers sold him a portion of the land he had acquired from the Chippewas in 1761 on the south shore of Lake Superior for £200.[26] By the time Rogers left England, however, no action had occurred.

The Northwest Passage proposal itself died a quiet death, but it raised Rogers' visibility in official London. Along with the *Journals* and *Concise Account*, the proposal gave Rogers an aura of vision, talent, energy, and enterprise that he burnished through effective networking. He parlayed his moment into concrete rewards. The king read the Northwest Passage proposal and, although he declined to order its implementation, he was moved by Rogers' description of his financial straits. Rogers had been promoting this theme with the press, in the *Journals*, and undoubtedly with persons of influence. The king ordered that Rogers be appointed to command at Fort Michilimackinac, the outpost Rogers mentioned in his proposal. The monarch also ordered that Rogers' claims for reimbursement by the army be reconsidered, and that he be advanced £500 in anticipation of the favorable outcome expected to emerge from that re-examination.[27]

On September 16, 1765, Secretary of War Barrington wrote to Gage instructing him to give Rogers command at Michilimackinac "or some other outpost among the Indians" and a position in an American regiment that would "put him on a comfortable footing." The next day, Barrington said Gage should order a re-examination of Rogers' reimbursement claims, noting that Rogers had represented that he was broke and encumbered by debt owing to unreimbursed expenditures on public service that he could document thoroughly. Secretary of State Seymour Conway wrote to Gage on October 12, 1765, directing him to "immediately appoint Major Rogers to have the Command at the Fort of Michilimackinac" and recommending that he have some role in Indian Affairs, subordinate to Sir William Johnson. Conway too ordered a review of Rogers' army expense claims.[28]

These directives got Rogers an audience with the king on October 16, 1765. Rogers kissed the monarch's hand and presented him with copies of the *Journals* and *Concise Account*. The king formally advised Rogers of his appointment as commander at Fort Michilimackinac and of the royal order that his claims for reimbursement from the army be re-examined.[29]

Rogers did not get everything he wanted. He was not appointed governor at Michilimackinac. He was clearly subordinate to Gage and Johnson, and his role in Indian Affairs was left to their discretion. His
Northwest Passage proposal was not approved. But he had achieved a
stunning reversal of fortune. The king himself had ordered his appointment to command at Michilimackinac and the re-examination of his
expenses. Even Rogers' army and administrative superiors dared not
quarrel with these Royal orders. He and Potter were completely "re-
born" by the king's actions.[30]

CHAPTER FIFTEEN

RETURN
TO AMERICA

ROGERS arrived in New York on January 6, 1766. The senior British officials in North America, Thomas Gage, military commander, and Sir William Johnson, Superintendent of Indian Affairs for the Northern Department, had read rumors in the press about Rogers' lobbying in London but were largely unaware of his success until he presented letters to them from Secretary of War Barrington and Secretary of State Conway. Rogers personally gave copies to Gage in New York and posted copies to Johnson at Johnson Hall in the Mohawk River Valley, promising that a courtesy copy of the recently published *Journals* would follow shortly.[1]

Gage and Johnson were aghast. Neither considered Rogers qualified to command at Michilimackinac, and both viewed him as untrustworthy and difficult to control. But the orders came directly from the king, and Gage assured Barrington and Conway that he would comply after appropriate consultation with Johnson about how to structure Rogers' responsibilities.[2] That caveat gave the men room to maneuver, and they set about trying to use it.

Gage's and Johnson's antipathy toward Rogers, as expressed in their private correspondence, was extraordinary, especially in comparison to

their measured tone in official correspondence. Gage vented his frustration in a letter to Johnson dated January 13, 1766, and marked "Private." Advising Johnson of his instructions from Barrington and
Conway, Gage wrote, "I wish something could be hit upon to employ
him where he might do less Mischief." He characterized Rogers as
"wild, vain, of little understanding, and of as little Principle," adding
that Rogers had "Cunning, No Modesty or veracity and sticks at [i.e., is
deterred by] Nothing." Gage predicted that "[w]here Capt. Howard
[the departing Michilimackinac commander] has charged you Hundreds, This Man will charge Thousands, unless prevented by all the
Checks you can think of to bind him by." He told Johnson to "Send me
your Advice in what manner he may best be tied up by Instructions and
prevent[ed from] doing Mischief and imposing upon you." Gage
lamented that Rogers had "squandered" his money "in Vanity and
Gaming" and remained "some Thousands in Debt here [New York]."
Presumably, Gage worried that staggering debts would undermine
Rogers' judgment and effectiveness.[3]

Johnson responded in kind with a long letter, also marked "Private,"
on January 25, 1766. "I must own it Surprised Me a good deal, to find
the papers for some time past filled with Govr. Rojers and his Great Appointments," he began. Johnson recounted his history with Rogers: he
was a man of action in the early years of the war, when such men were
few, and a talented Ranger whom Johnson had helped to promote, but
he "soon became puffed up with pride and folly from the extravigant
encomiums & notice of some of the Provinces," which "spoiled a good
Ranger." In Johnson's view, Rogers "was fitt for nothing else," especially
not "for a large Command," as "he has neither Understanding, education, or principles. . . ." For these reasons, Johnson was "astonished that
the Government could have thought of Such an Employment for him,
but as it is so, I am of Your opinion he should be tied up in such a manner as may best prevent him from doing Mischeif. . . ."[4]

Besides generally having qualms about Rogers' "principles," Johnson
worried that Rogers "has been concerned in trade" and would continue
to be. As commander at Michilimackinac, "he will have it in his power
to confine the trade in a great degree to himself and friends;—neither
can I think he would stick at saying anything to the Indians, to effect
any of his purposes." Agreeing with Gage, Johnson wished that Rogers
could have been bought off with a high-paying job of limited scope,
hampering his capacity to do harm.[5]

But Johnson and Gage had orders from the king and his ministers. Accordingly, Johnson proposed to "lay before you such articles, as may in some measure, tye up his hands." Gage should "point out [to Rogers] from whom he is to take his orders respecting Indian affairs, the channel through which his reports are to be transmitted, and to limit his expenses to pipes, tobacco, and a little liquor, unless he may be ordered to meet any body of Indians; but not of himself, to incur any other expenses, or to assemble or treat with the Indians."[6]

Gage's and Johnson's concerns about Rogers arose from a complex context. England had taken full control of the northwestern frontier posts in 1761. In short order came Pontiac's War, a violent, bloody affair that put the British on the defensive. Only now was England beginning to implement a frontier policy, a process in which Johnson had a major role. He was building a staff of deputies to be stationed at major frontier posts that were to have parallel military and civil command structures, with military officers reporting to Gage and Indian Affairs personnel answering to Johnson. Johnson had a history of working closely with Gage, but to ensure consistency, each had to be in control of his sphere. The last thing either man wanted was a loose cannon at a remote post, especially one with a personal business agenda.[7]

On January 30, 1766, Johnson wrote to Gage, this time with a tone less of anger at Rogers than of sadness at the diminished fortunes that made him so unpredictable. "I have known Major Rogers ever since 1755, and should be glad the Government had made a better or more adapted appointment for him," Johnson wrote. "I hope he will act a proper part, prove of service to the public and extricate himself out of his difficulties, and deserve a better character than the public has for some time bestowed upon him, the particulars and causes of which you are so well acquainted with." Gage had never liked Rogers, but Johnson had, and here he showed distress at the woes of one he once respected. At the same time, Johnson made clear that he believed Rogers had only himself to blame for his "difficulties." A reference to the "particulars and causes of" Rogers' poor public reputation, "which you are so well acquainted with," plainly invoked events of 1764, when Rogers, imprisoned for debt in New York, broke out and became a fugitive under circumstances that Gage "could wish to hear less of." Johnson went on: "I am sorry to say, [Rogers] does not appear much esteemed, for it gives me a sensible pain to find a useful active man, suffering under the disadvantages of distress, and a bad name." Apparently, however, he thought better of expressing strong sympathy for Rogers to Gage, who had none, and he did not include this section in the final letter he sent.[8]

Gage responded to Johnson's letters on February 3, 1766. He said that, as Johnson had advised, he would instruct Rogers to get his military orders from Gage in New York. "He will be referred to you for all Orders respecting your Department. I shall only appoint him Commandant of the Garrison; and think it best, that he should not be called Superintendent of Indians, for many Reasons; which will occur to you." He asked Johnson to report to him if Rogers engaged in "bad Management," promising if need be to remove him to a post "where he can do less Mischief."[9]

Gage's written instructions to Rogers appear to have been designed to hem him in, as he and Johnson had agreed, but they were more ambiguous than Gage intended. He told Rogers to follow the instructions of the king, Gage, and "any other of your Superior Officers, according to the Rules and Discipline of War." He was to report frequently to the Commandant at Detroit, "under whose immediate Command you are." With respect to expenses, "I can't recommend too strongly to you, the strictest Oeconomy in the small Expenses that may unavoidably be incurred at this Post now put under your Command, but nothing New or Chargeable, must upon any Account, be undertaken by you, of your own head." This admonition clearly reflected Johnson's recommendation to bar Rogers from incurring any major expense on his own authority, but it appeared in instructions on his military duties, not his role in Indian affairs. With respect to "Intercourse with the Savages," Gage told Rogers to take his orders from Johnson. "[U]pon this Subject, you are to pay the Strictest Attention and Obedience [to Johnson]." Rogers is to make regular reports to Johnson on all matters relating to Indians. Gage gave Rogers a copy of his own general orders to "Officers Commanding Posts, relative to their Treatment of Indians." These orders provided, among other things, that "Presents are not to be made to Indians but on Occasions which shall render such measures unavoidable."[10]

Johnson's written instructions to Rogers, bland and generic, admonished him to keep the peace with the Indians, assure them of Johnson's "Friendship and good Offices," "avoid giving any Umbrage to the Indians," and "prevent any Quarrels from arising between them & the Soldiery or Traders." Johnson did not address issues that later became controversial, such as gifts to Indians and restrictions on trading, including wintering in Indian villages. Perhaps believing that Gage had done so, Johnson did not expressly prohibit Rogers in writing from incurring any significant expense relating to Indian affairs on his own initiative. He did have a conversation with Rogers at the conclusion of their meeting at Johnson Hall in June 1766 in which Rogers expressed a desire for "Some Latitude in the Article of Ex[penses for Indian gifts]." Johnson disagreed and instead "gave him such Verbal Orders as I apprehended [would have] been a Sufficient Caution to him to Avoid" such expenses.[11] But this restriction was not in writing, and while Gage instructed Rogers in writing to incur no expenses solely on his own authority, it was not clear whether this restriction applied to Indian affairs or only to military matters.

Rogers' request for discretion in the matter of Indian gifts suggests he had already conceived the idea of a large council with Indians in the Michilimackinac region as a means of cementing his relationships with them. Johnson's refusal to give him latitude in the matter of gifts notwithstanding, Rogers began planning the council immediately upon his arrival in Michilimackinac.

Johnson gave Rogers no explicit instructions about the regulation of trading with the Indians, perhaps because he believed government policy was well-established and well-understood. As early as 1761, Johnson's deputy Croghan had urged a policy of strict government oversight of the fur trade to avoid "Irregularitys" that might cause "his Majesty's Indian Interest in Gineral [to] Suffer." Johnson and Amherst endorsed such a policy,[12] under which trading was restricted to government posts under government supervision. Traders were prohibited from following the French practice of traveling to Indian villages to trade on their own, nor could they winter over in Indian villages to obtain furs.

As Johnson explained to Gage, at least two factors underpinned this policy. Most fur traders on the northwestern frontier were French, and, although the war was over, they remained hostile to the British and often incited Indians against the British. Unrestricted fur trading created a security issue and a related economic issue. French fur traders had a huge head start over British counterparts, and if they were not restricted, British traders would never catch up. The British also believed that unscrupulous traders—more likely British than French—would exploit the Indians, creating tensions that would fuel chronic border warfare—the "Irregularitys" that Croghan had warned about.[13] Gage supported strict supervision of fur trading and used the same rationale in explaining it to Secretary of State Conway.[14]

Traders and Indians disliked the British restrictions. Indians trading at Michilimackinac and other remote posts generally lived far from these commercial hubs. The inconvenience of having to travel to trade reduced trading volume. Johnson and Gage both recognized this, guessing the reduction might be as much as a half, but believed the benefits outweighed the cost.[15] Traders constantly pressed British officials to ease up.

In the fall of 1765, Michilimackinac commander Captain Howard bowed to this pressure. Howard relaxed trading restrictions and licensed a limited number of traders, mostly British, to travel to Indian villages to trade, as well as to winter in villages. Complaints from traders denied licenses reached Johnson, who recognized that selective application of restrictions was wrong. He advocated uniform strict enforcement rather than general relaxation of constraints.[16] Complaints about favoritism reached London, but Gage took the same position as Johnson: favoritism was unacceptable; the correct solution was strict enforcement across the board.[17]

Rogers could hardly have been unaware of the controversy, or of the government's official position. But as a fur trade investor he generally sympathized with traders and Indians. He took refuge in Johnson's admonitions to "avoid giving any Umbrage to the Indians" and to "prevent any quarrels from arising" between Indians and traders. The ambiguity of his written instructions, coupled with distance from his superiors, set the stage for a clash.

BESIDES ordering Gage to appoint Rogers commander at Michilimackinac and give him an appropriate role in Indian affairs there, Barrington and Conway had ordered Gage to again scrutinize Rogers' reimbursement claims. In his first communication to Barrington about his orders, Gage protested that he knew of no basis for Rogers' claim. He nonetheless promised to conduct an inquiry. Gage asked Rogers to put his claims and proof in writing, then appointed a commission of officers to examine Rogers' claims and make a recommendation.[18]

A similar panel appointed by Amherst in 1761 had been generally sympathetic to Rogers. Although the reviewers supported Amherst on most major issues, they agreed with Rogers on some key claims, and Amherst adopted their more generous recommendations. We know little about the 1766 panel appointed by Gage. Rogers' biographers have generally assumed them to have been under Gage's thumb, told directly or given to understand that Rogers was to get nothing. Biographers have treated the 1766 review as a charade undertaken with a foregone conclusion imposed by Gage.[19] This view is mistaken.

The new panel did recommend denying most of Roger's claims, finding in his favor on only one comparatively small item. That was Rogers' claim for somewhat more than £300 in additional pay for Rangers disbanded in October 1760 at the end of hostilities with the French, while Rogers was in Detroit. The commissioners believed this claim had not previously been presented. The recommendation to allow it may have been, as one biographer put it, "a sop to prove [the] fairness" of the review.[20] After all, the king himself had ordered the review, and had advanced Rogers £500 against amounts expected to be found justified. To award him nothing would seem like a direct affront to the king.

But something remarkable happened. Secretary of War Barrington, in ordering the review, apparently believed Rogers was owed a substantial sum. Now, presented with the commission's recommendation, Barrington rejected it, not because it awarded Rogers too little, but because it awarded him too much. When ordering a re-examination of Rogers' accounts, Barrington had not known the details of Amherst's 1761 settlement and the specifics of Rogers' current claims. Rogers had assured the secretary of war he was owed thousands of pounds and could document his claims. Barrington had since retrieved and studied Amherst's warrant, with its detailed recitation of the review process and itemized account of claims accepted and rejected and a cogent explanation for each decision. Comparing the 1761 settlement with Rogers' current claim, Barrington was appalled; every claim Rogers was presenting in 1766 was one he had submitted to Amherst in 1761 and had had rejected. Even the claim Gage's commission had recommended accepting had been presented to and rejected by Amherst; the 1766 commission had not had at hand the details of Amherst's 1761 warrant. Barrington felt Rogers had deliberately misled him.[21]

Barrington was undoubtedly struck by the meticulousness, fairness, and intended finality of Amherst's review; Rogers had been given multiple opportunities to present arguments that had passed through at least three rounds of review—by Amherst's secretary Appy, by Amherst, and by a sympathetic three-officer panel—and Amherst had been flexible in reversing himself to Rogers' benefit when urged to do so. Every decision had been explained, and the preamble to the warrant even recited that Rogers himself agreed the settlement was full and fair and that it resolved all his claims against the army. In 1766, Amherst was back in London, and Barrington may well have consulted him regarding Rogers' allegations of unfair treatment.

To Gage, Barrington was devastatingly blunt: Rogers was not *entitled* to anything. Any award to him would be at the "Bounty" of the government, a discretionary award not for amounts due, but for past service. Passing the buck, Barrington left it to Gage to decide whether such an award was appropriate, but he made clear his personal view: "it appears rather irregular, and necessarily throws a shadow on the claims made by Major Rogers" that these claims had all been presented to and rejected by Amherst.[22] It was not Rogers' chronic antagonist Gage, but the initially sympathetic Secretary of War himself, who sent Rogers away empty-handed in 1766.

Rogers kept the king's £500 advance. Deaf to Barrington's anger at having been deceived, Rogers wrote Gage in July 1767, noting that Barrington had given Gage complete discretion to make an award for past service, and urging Gage, in light of "the many Difficulties and Hardships that I have struggled with," to "Recommend my Case to his Majesty's Bounty."[23] Within a short while, Rogers' plea became moot.

Two months after arriving in New York, Rogers belatedly made his way to Portsmouth. In all of 1764, when he was in New England continuously, Rogers had spent only "a few days" with Betsy. Apart from alerting her after his departure that he was leaving for England in March 1765, he does not appear to have corresponded with her during that calendar year. His 1766 homecoming can only have been tense and awkward, but Betsy agreed to accompany Rogers when he took up his new post at Michilimackinac.[24] She said later that she did so "against the remonstrances of many of her friends." There is evidence that her father counseled her to go, but Betsy did not make this claim. Her explanation shows a complete lack of enthusiasm and seems intended to address the unspoken question "What in the world were you thinking?" She says she was "desirous of doing her duty, and in hopes of winning him by gentleness and condescention." These hopes would be cruelly dashed.[25]

Preparations for the long journey consumed nearly two months. During this time, Rogers traveled to Boston to meet with French and Indian War colleagues Jonathan Carver and James Tute. London had been cold to his proposal for a Northwest Passage expedition owing to cost, but his patron Charles Townshend had promised to push for a cheaper alternative. Carver had served in provincial regiments and fought alongside Rogers during the war. He was now a mapmaker and surveyor with a keen interest in western exploration. Rogers asked him to participate in an expedition of discovery to depart from Michilimackinac as soon as possible.[26]

In his contemporaneous journal, Carver recorded that Rogers said he had presented his proposal for a Northwest Passage expedition to the Board of Trade in London. Carver assumed the proposal would be approved, and, because Rogers had just returned from England, Carver believed in his "pretended power and authority." Whether or not Rogers told Carver in Boston that the expedition had official approval, he did so several months later in writing at Michilimackinac. Carver signed on to be principal cartographer.[27] Rogers also recruited James Tute, longtime Ranger officer, survivor of the Battle on Snowshoes, and a landowner from whom Rogers had purchased property. Rogers hired Tute as the military commander of the expedition.[28]

Rogers and Betsy left Portsmouth for New York in late April 1766, arriving in early May. Late May and early June found them meeting with Sir William Johnson at Johnson Hall, where Johnson gave Rogers his instructions with respect to Indian affairs. They proceeded to Oswego, then Fort Niagara, Detroit, and Michilimackinac, arriving in early August. Tute and Carver, traveling separately, arrived a short while later.[29]

WHILE Rogers was wending his way to Michilimackinac, a drama was unfolding behind him. In late April 1766, a French cargo vessel made an unscheduled stop in New York harbor, allegedly for emergency repairs. A passenger aboard was carrying letters for addressees in the colonies. The letters found their way to General Gage. One was addressed to Rogers. Gage became suspicious. Why would a newly appointed British officer be in correspondence with the French? Gage opened the letter, made a copy which he had certified, and re-sealed it.[30]

Signed "Maryland" in a feeble attempt at disguise, the letter asked Rogers to respond "without signing you [sic] name" in care of a "Mr. Hopkins," who was plainly the letter's author. Joseph Hopkins, of Maryland, had been a captain of a provincial unit during the French and Indian War. He had served with Rogers on the expedition to relieve the siege of Detroit during Pontiac's War. Thereafter, unhappy with his treatment by the British army, he had defected to the French. "This is the third time I've wrote you since our last meeting in New York," Hopkins began. "As I promised, you were remembered in my Conversations with the Minister of the King I now Serve, [and] I have reason to think you would have a reasonable gracious Reception." Hopkins added that "untill my Affairs are entirely finished, and the promises which were made me amply accomplished, I cannot think of persuading or enticeing you on." Hopkins and Rogers, apparently, had discussed the possibility of Rogers joining the French service, as Hopkins had, and Hopkins was endeavoring to keep this prospect alive, although he thought acting on it premature. "[Y]ou know the injustices we have suffered particularly yourself," he reminded Rogers, "nor is it in the power of England to recompense you for the disgraces you underwent for having Served them too faithfully." While waiting for the moment to be right, Hopkins, aware of Rogers' new appointment, urged him to "Seize every opportunity of ingratiating yourself in the favor of the Indians where you are placed Governor."[31]

From Rogers' possible change of loyalties Hopkins turned to the general state of affairs in North America. He assured Rogers that "although Detached from the British Interest intirely & Absolutely, believe me always North American, and ready to render the Continent and my Country men all [my] Services." He insisted "there can be no Obstacle to their being a free and independent People," and predicted that in the event of an independence movement "there are Powers [i.e., the French] who might think themselves happy in being of the number of your Allies and Friends."[32]

Hopkins concluded by asking Rogers to remember him to his many Indian friends. "[I]f you have an Interview with Pondiac [Pontiac] take him by the hand for me, and make known to him, I serve his Father the King of France." He also asked Rogers to remember him to various European friends on the frontier, including Reaume, whom Rogers later appointed interpreter for the Tute-Carver expedition.[33]

Rogers, on his way to Michilimackinac, had by this time left New York for Johnson Hall. Gage sent the letter to Johnson to give to Rogers there. Without telling Johnson he had read the letter, Gage wrote him mysteriously that, "for very Particular Reasons, which I can't now mention," Johnson should "give the strongest Orders to your Interpreters and Commissarys to watch Major Rogers's Transactions with the Indians and that they send you Information if he holds any bad Conversations with them." Noting that Rogers spoke no Indian languages, Gage cautioned Johnson to be particularly alert if Rogers bypassed the Indian Affairs department and used a French interpreter to hold discussions with Indians. Such conversations, Gage predicted, were likely to begin in Detroit, "particularly with Pondiac." He told Johnson, "Your People should keep their Instructions secret and not divulge what you write them on this Subject." Johnson, his curiosity piqued by Gage's mysterious tone, unsealed the Hopkins letter and copied it. Not realizing that Gage had done the same, he wrote to Gage that he had made "a very extraordinary & alarming Discovery not to be mentioned at this time."[34]

Realizing that Johnson must have looked at the Hopkins letter and knew what was afoot, Gage explained himself more fully. He had opened and copied *all* the letters Hopkins had sent, he told Johnson, not just the one to Rogers, although the letter to Rogers was the only one referring to prior correspondence. Any recipients confronted with their letter from Hopkins, Gage reasoned, would deny any relationship with him and say the letter was unsolicited. Better to have all the letters delivered and see what happened next. Any reply would have to come through New York, and Gage could intercept it. Of Rogers, he said, "If his intentions are honest, he would show the letter immediately which would clear him. If he liked the proposal, his Answer wou'd come, and I should get it."[35]

By the time Johnson received the first letter from Gage, Rogers had left Johnson Hall for Michilimackinac. Taking his cue from Gage's second letter, Johnson forwarded the Hopkins letter to Rogers there, with a cover letter inquiring innocently if the letter he was enclosing "brought him any agreeable news from Europe." Rogers acknowledged receipt of the letter but said nothing of its contents, which Johnson took as conclusive evidence of Rogers' complicity with Hopkins. "As you justifiably observed in a former letter," he wrote Gage, "there is the utmost reason to think the contents were agreeable, otherwise I imagine [Rogers] would have at least said something upon it."[36]

But the case remained ambiguous. Rogers had not actually responded to Hopkins. Johnson and Gage no doubt looked on with alarm as Rogers aggressively sought to ingratiate himself with the Indians at Michilimackinac, as Hopkins had urged. Rogers' subsequent proposal for a province of Michilimackinac took on a sinister cast. If Rogers were granted the unchecked powers he sought, he would be able to align the entire vast province with France. But the Hopkins letter, while alarming, was vague; there were no reports of "bad conversations" with Indians, Rogers does not appear to have met with Pontiac in Detroit, and the impetus behind Rogers' actions as commander at Michilimackinac was not clear. Gage and Johnson did not have sufficient evidence to act. They could only watch and worry.

CHAPTER SIXTEEN

MICHILIMACKINAC

MICHILIMACKINAC was the westernmost French fort in North America and, following the French and Indian War, the westernmost English outpost. Strings of small civilian trading posts stretched further west as far as the forks of the Saskatchewan River in the present-day province of Saskatchewan, but Michilimackinac was the last military and commercial center within the area of European settlement. It lay astride the straits of Mackinac, linking Lake Huron and Lake Michigan, and it lay close to the passage from Lake Huron to Lake Superior. It was thus the strategic gateway to the northwest of colonial America.

To the Indians, Michilimackinac, "the place of the turtle," was the location from which life emerged and had great symbolic cultural value. The dominant local tribes were the Ottawa and the Chippewa, but Michilimackinac was also a trading and gathering place for tribes much further to the west.

Within days of reaching Michilimackinac in August 1766, Rogers met with the community's merchants and traders. The delegation's spokesman read Rogers a letter expressing "particular Satisfaction, that you are appointed our Governor," because he had arrived "at a Time that many of the Indian Nations, almost worn out with repeated Solicitations for Traders, are on the Eve of Discontent." The Indians resented having to travel to the fort to trade, preferred to have traders come to them, and were on the verge of exiting the English orbit. The merchants and traders expected Rogers to end all this: "our Hopes from you, Sir, to reconcile Matters, and put the Trade upon a proper Footing, are very sanguine."[1]

Rogers did not disappoint. He immediately rescinded regulations restricting fur trading to the fort, allowing all traders to travel to Indian villages to do business and to winter at villages if desired. This blanket relaxation remained in effect throughout Rogers' tenure at Michilimackinac.

The change was a flagrant act of insubordination. Regulation of trade with the Indians was up to Sir William Johnson, and Gage had placed Rogers under Johnson's direction for such matters, ordering that he "pay the Strictest Attention and Obedience" to Johnson. Johnson's rules governing fur trading may have been widely unpopular, and Rogers may have agreed with those who disliked them, but they were Johnson's rules, and Rogers was duty-bound to enforce them. Even if Rogers could plausibly claim uncertainty about what regulations he was to enforce, he was to give Johnson "notice of every thing you shall think worthy of his knowledge, relative to the Conduct and Temper of the Savages." Rogers acted unilaterally, without prior or subsequent notice to Johnson, who found out about Rogers' action months later through a letter from his son-in-law in Montreal. The letter was dated October 16, 1766. In it, Daniel Claus wrote that "[b]y the last account from Michilimackina, Major Rogers was arrived there, and immediately without hesitation, gave a general permit to all Traders to go wintering."[2]

This news no doubt infuriated Johnson. He would have been even more furious to learn that Rogers breezily characterized his action as "consistent with the Instructions I have" from Sir William Johnson. Rogers even credited Johnson for the policy change. Johnson's "Judgment and extensive Knowledge in Indian Affairs," Rogers affirmed, allowed the source of traders' grievances to "speedily be removed."[3]

Neither Johnson nor Gage acted to censure Rogers, overrule him, or reinstate the old regulations, even though this overreaching was exactly what they had feared. Why? For one thing, by the time they found out what Rogers had done, his new rules had been in effect for months, and it would take weeks or months for orders to reach Rogers to reverse himself. Traders would already have set out for villages and could not be recalled until spring at the earliest. Rogers, as he plainly intended, had presented Johnson and Gage with a knotty *fait accompli*.

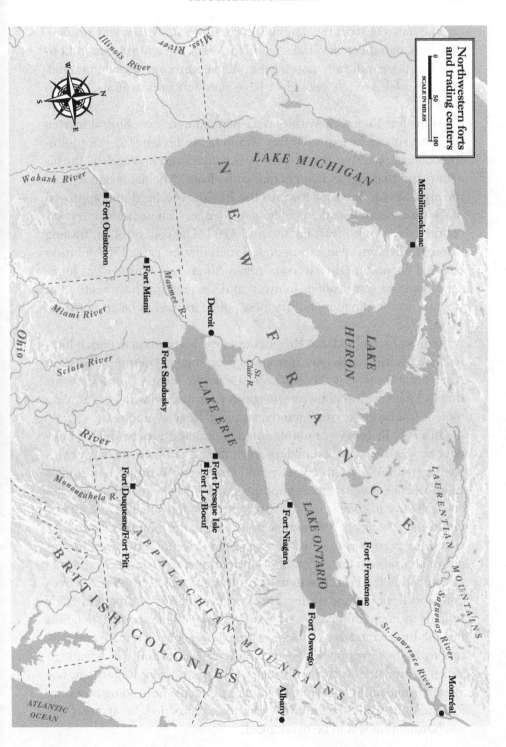

Northwestern forts and trading centers

SCALE IN MILES
0   50   100

Illinois River

Miss. River

LAKE MICHIGAN

NEW FRANCE

Michilimackinac

Wabash River

Fort Ouiatenon

Fort Miami

Maumee R.

Miami River

Detroit

Sciato River

Ohio

St. Clair R.

LAKE HURON

Fort Sandusky

LAKE ERIE

River

Monongahela R.

Fort Presque Isle
Fort Le Boeuf

Fort Duquesne/Fort Pitt

Fort Niagara

LAKE ONTARIO

Fort Frontenac

LAURENTIAN MOUNTAINS

Saguenay River

APPALACHIAN MOUNTAINS

BRITISH COLONIES

Fort Oswego

St. Lawrence River

Montreal

Albany

ATLANTIC OCEAN

The status of strict regulation of fur trading, moreover, was ambiguous. Although the policy had reigned for years, the government in London had never officially approved it. The constraints were unpopular, and critics felt strongly enough to have hired lobbyists to attack them in London.

At the fort Rogers' new rules were popular and successful, at least in the short run, as he expected they would be. In his letter alerting Johnson, Claus noted that Rogers was "vastly liked and applauded" for his action and that "[t]he Traders that came from [Michilimackinac] told me also that his behavior towards the Indians was liked and approved of by them, as well as the people of the place." These positive reports continued through 1766 and into mid-1767. The volume of fur trading through Michilimackinac rebounded such that by early 1767 Johnson believed the post merited its own Indian Affairs "commissary," as Johnson's deputies were called. Johnson and Gage might have seethed at Rogers' insubordination, but the new policy seemed to be an improvement.[4]

Johnson had fretted that Rogers would use his position to enrich himself and his friends. Rogers appears to have engaged in some trading at Michilimackinac, but there is no evidence he favored himself or his friends.[5] Johnson was not wrong to suspect self-interest as Rogers' driving motive, but he underestimated the scope of Rogers' ambition.

In 1766, Rogers was not interested in building a successful fur business, he was interested in building an empire of immense scope, encompassing multiple present-day states and provinces. According to historian Keith Widder, Rogers' "most important goal at Michilimackinac in 1766 and 1767 was to convince the British government to create a new colony out of the 'District of Michilimackinac' and name him its governor." A robust fur trade was the engine that would drive this endeavor, but his personal success in fur trading was only peripheral. Rogers believed passionately that the French system of fur trading, which emphasized freedom and flexibility for traders and lavish regular government gifts for Indians to maintain peace and good will, was the correct model, and that the British model of strict government oversight of trading and parsimony in the distribution of gifts was short-sighted and self-defeating.[6] When he unilaterally turned British policy on its head, Rogers was not after personal profit but trying to create a profitable fur-trading economy to sustain his would-be empire. If his plan succeeded, he assumed his insubordination would be overlooked.

JAMES TUTE and Jonathan Carver arrived in Michilimackinac within a few weeks of Rogers. Anxious to make progress before winter, Rogers dispatched them almost immediately on their expedition of discovery. Carver went first. Rogers' written orders to him, dated September 12, 1766, recited that it is "for the good of his Majesty's Service to have some good Surveys of the Interior parts of North America." For that purpose, wrote Rogers, "I do by Virtue of the Authority given me appoint you" to conduct such surveys. Carver is to be paid "eight Shillings Sterling per Day (untill Discharged)"—about £150 a year. He was "directed to set out from this Post immediately" and proceed ultimately "to the Falls of St. Antoine's"—present-day Minneapolis—making "an exact Plan of the Country" on the way. Carver was to report to Rogers in the spring, and then, "Should you receive Orders from me to march further to the Westward, with any other Detachment that I may send this fall or winter, you are to do it."[7]

Rogers had already planned a follow-on detachment led by former Ranger officer Tute, and he drafted orders for it the same day. Tute did not leave Michilimackinac until Carver had gone, but his orders identify the full scope and purpose of what was to become a joint expedition. Tute, said Rogers, was to be "Commanding a Party for the Discovery of the North West Passage from the Atlantic into the Pacific Ocean, if any such Passage there be, or for the Discovery of the Great River Ourigan that falls into the Pacific Ocean about the Latitude Fifty." He was to carry presents for Indians, whom he was authorized to employ for assistance, and was also given a secretary and second-in-command James Stanley Goddard, and a fourth-in-command and interpreter, a Mr. Reaume. Together with third-in-command Carver, these men were to comprise a council that would make all decisions for the expedition.[8]

Tute was to proceed to the Falls of St. Anthony, link up with Carver, and winter in that region. Come spring, Tute was to head northwest, arriving at Fort des Prairies at the Forks of the Saskatchewan, where he was to winter again. The Forks of the Saskatchewan River, in present-day Saskatchewan, are several hundred miles west of Lake Winnipeg and nearly one thousand miles northwest of the Falls of St. Anthony. A series of tiny French trading posts stretched from the western edge of Lake Superior to Fort des Prairies. Rogers promised to send additional supplies to meet the expedition at Fort des Prairies. Only the following spring, the third year of the expedition, was Tute to leave Fort des Prairies, the westernmost outpost of European advance, head west by northwest, and begin the search for the River Ourigan.[9]

In addition to their exploratory mandate, Rogers gave Tute and Carver a second mission. By the time he dispatched them, Rogers had committed to staging an immense Indian council in the early summer of 1767. Tute and Carver were to advertise this council as they traveled, invite Indians to attend it, and give them gifts as an inducement to attend.

Rogers advised Tute that he had authority to draw bills on Rogers "for the purchase of Goods and Merchandise of Traders that you may meet, or for the Payment of Indians that you may employ for carrying on the Expedition." "[S]uch Drafts at a Small sight," Rogers assured him, "shall meet with due Honor."[10]

Like Carver, Tute was to be paid "Eight Shillings Sterling Per day." So was Goddard, whom Rogers appointed the same day secretary of the expedition "by Virtue of the Power and Authority to me given." In addition to his pay, Rogers advised Tute, "you are entitled if you discover a North West Passage from the Atlantic to the Pacific Ocean Twenty Thousand Pounds Sterling to be paid to the Detachment." Even the simple discovery of the River Ourigan would entitle him to an award "according to the Value of the Discovery."[11]

For the second time in barely a month, Rogers engaged in brazen insubordination. No money had been approved for the expedition, and Rogers had no information to suggest that it would be. Gage's orders were clear: he was to incur no significant expense without his military superiors' approval. Rogers did not have the "power" or the "authority" to give Carver, Tute, and Goddard orders. He had committed the army to salary costs of at least £450 a year, for at least three years, together with the substantial costs of supplies. In the short run, Rogers may have funded some of these costs on his personal credit, but in the long run they could only be paid—and were paid—by the government. By the time the bills came due, Rogers' personal credit was worthless.

Rogers likewise lacked authority to award prize money for finding the Northwest Passage or the River Ourigan. The official prize offered for the discovery of the Northwest Passage identified it as a "passage for vessels by sea, between the Atlantic and Pacific Oceans," and required the claimant, as proof of discovery, to have navigated from one ocean to the other, a condition Tute and Carver were in no position to satisfy.[12]

Rogers hoped his unauthorized actions would be ratified after the fact. Either news would arrive from London that his expedition had been approved and funding for it allocated, or Tute's and Carver's discoveries would prove so valuable that the army could not help but embrace them. Either event would help advance Rogers' broader purpose, the creation of a province of Michilimackinac, envisioning the province as he did not only as economically productive, but as a launching point for western exploration.

Rogers did not breathe a word about the Tute-Carver expedition to Gage or, apparently, anyone else in authority. Gage and Johnson appear to have learned about the undertaking only after the expedition's return a year later.[13]

In his 1765 proposal to the Board of Trade, Rogers had been extremely vague about where to find the supposed River Ourigan. He recommended starting at the Mississippi's headwaters, then searching for the Ourigan somewhere to the northwest.[14] In Detroit in 1760, where Rogers had first heard about the River Ourigan, then called River of the West, Indian reports about the river's origin were conflicting and ranged from northern Minnesota to Lake Winnipeg. In his 1765 proposal, Rogers did not advocate a particular alternative. He believed, however, that, once found, the River Ourigan would be seen to empty into a bay penetrating northeastward into the North American continent. The bay connected to the Pacific Ocean to the southwest and was believed to connect to Hudson Bay to the northeast. Rogers maintained this assumption in his instructions to Tute in 1766.

Now, however, he was much more specific about the River Ourigan. He had the search begin at the Forks of the Saskatchewan, far to the northwest of the headwaters of the Mississippi and far to the northwest of any previously rumored origin of the river. To find the river, Rogers instructed Tute to leave the Forks of the Saskatchewan and "Travel West, bearing to the North West," attempting to "fall in with the great River Ourigan, which rises in several Branches between the Latitudes of Fifty Six and Forty Eight." By instructing Tute to head northwest from the Forks of the Saskatchewan, Rogers had him searching the more northerly portion of this range. From its apparently multiple points of origin, the River Ourigan "runs Westward for near three hundred Leagues [nine hundred miles]," until it was joined in succession by a river entering from the south and another entering from the north. This confluence of rivers was said to be "an Inhabited Country, [of] Great

Riches," including quantities of gold three days' journey up the river joining from the north. From the confluence, the river, now "much larger," traveled another four hundred leagues (1,200 miles) until it "discharges itself into an Arm or Bay of the Sea, at near the Latitude of Fifty Four." This would be roughly the north-south midpoint of present-day British Columbia. The bay was "supposed to have a Communication with the Hudson Bay, about the Latitude of Fifty nine," which would have placed it roughly at the present-day border between British Columbia and the Yukon Territory.[15]

It is not clear where Rogers obtained this new and seemingly precise information about the course of the River Ourigan and its connection to Hudson Bay. By 1766, Rogers also had new and specific warnings. "You must take great care not to be deceived by the Rivers Missisure [Missouri]," he told Tute, "or by the River that falls into Hudson's Bay, or by other Rivers that empty into the Gulph of Californie," as these would not lead to the bay connecting the Pacific to Hudson Bay.[16] Years later, Rogers reversed himself and concluded that the quickest way to the critical bay would be to follow the Missouri to its headwaters, cross the Continental Divide, and find a west-flowing river.

Even assuming that Rogers' information had been accurate, Tute and Carver could not possibly have carried out their orders, and the mission, had they actually attempted it, would have ended in ruin. The distances to be covered were far greater than the expedition could possibly manage. From the Falls of St. Anthony to the Forks of the Saskatchewan was almost one thousand miles, and the difficulties in making even the first leg of the journey proved insurmountable. From the Forks of the Saskatchewan, the ostensible River Ourigan still lay hundreds of miles west, and then, by Rogers' own estimate, the expedition would need to follow the nonexistent river for a full two thousand miles more, with no assurance of its navigability. This entire distance was far beyond the westernmost European trading post, and nothing was known about it. Given the northern latitudes at which the expedition would be traveling—54° and higher—they would have only a short season for travel before winter set in. The best they could hope for would be to reach the bay into which the River Ourigan emptied by the end of year three, leaving exploration of the supposed connection to Hudson Bay, hundreds of miles further north, for year four. And then what? The expedition would have exhausted its supplies, with no means of obtaining more, and it could survive only by hunting. Whether or not they discovered the Northwest

Passage, they would face a return journey exceeding three thousand miles whichever path they chose, whether the way they came (against the current for two thousand miles on the River Ourigan) or on a grand circuit by canoe via Hudson Bay, which was subject to violent storms that made travel even by ocean-going ship highly hazardous. Rogers had drawn up a plan that, even if executed successfully, would leave his men in a highly vulnerable situation with no obvious exit strategy.

Although Rogers was much more specific about the location and course of the River Ourigan than in 1765, his information was still sketchy. The Saskatchewan River flows east. The expedition would need to get beyond its headwaters to begin searching for a west-flowing river, and for each of the Saskatchewan's major branches this was hundreds of miles west of the Forks. As Rogers warned, they would still be at risk of picking a waterway that took them the wrong way. How were they to know if they made such a mistake? If they failed to find the River Ourigan reasonably quickly, they would be trapped by winter in a totally unknown wilderness.

The expedition did not have anywhere close to the manpower needed. Rogers' 1765 proposal had called for a force of more than two hundred. In 1766, the mission was entrusted to the four individuals Rogers had appointed, plus such miscellaneous assistants and Indian guides and porters as they could cobble together. Once past Fort des Prairies, the expedition would be beyond European settlement and on its own, needing manpower to carry the supplies and trade goods necessary to keep going. A force so small would be far too vulnerable to disease, starvation, exposure, injury, or Indian attack to succeed.

The Tute-Carver expedition was also woefully underfunded. It needed an enormous flow of supplies and presents for Indians, and while Rogers provided the initial stock and promised at least one resupply mission, the speed with which the expedition was bound to go through supplies, even if able to make purchases on Rogers' personal credit, boded poorly. Credit would be worthless beyond Fort des Prairies. Rogers apparently recommended that the expedition trap or trade for furs to fund itself at least partly, but it needed all the trade goods it could carry to barter for food and other necessities and to distribute gifts to Indians, leaving nothing to trade for furs, and it lacked time and manpower to engage in trapping. In any event, any furs the expedition might acquire would be valuable only while the expedition was within close proximity to trading posts.

The long-term problems the Tute-Carver expedition would have faced proved to be irrelevant, because the expedition aborted after less than a year without even coming close to its first major objective, Fort des Prairies. Carver and Tute, traveling separately, reached the vicinity of the Falls of St. Anthony in late 1766. Carver elected to winter in a Sioux village on or near the Minnesota River to the west of the Falls, while Tute wintered at Prairie du Chien, an Indian trading settlement also frequented by European traders on the Mississippi River to the south of the Falls. In the spring, Carver joined Tute at Prairie du Chien and the two purchased supplies and trade goods, relying in part on Rogers' credit. Unhappily, much of the trade goods they acquired went to gifts to Indians passing through to induce them to attend Rogers' grand council. As the expedition headed toward Fort des Prairies, it quickly became apparent that their supplies and trade goods were inadequate for the long journey. In his initial orders, Rogers said he intended to ship supplies to Fort des Prairies over the summer of 1767. By letter dated June 10, 1767, and sent by messenger to Tute, he confirmed this plan, saying that he had appointed agents "to keep that passage open from Lake Wennepeck [Winnipeg] to Lake Superior" and was sending "Ten Canoes" along that route. With this information in hand, Tute, to restock, decided to detour to Lake Superior and intercept the supply canoes. The party arrived in late July, "near mutiny from lack of provisions." Supplies trickled in, but not in the quantity expected, and with the last canoe came a letter of explanation from Rogers.[17]

In early 1767, Tute, in a letter entrusted to a party traveling to Michilimackinac, had apparently predicted to Rogers that he would be able to send a supply of furs to help defray expedition costs. He had been unable to do so. To buy supplies and gifts for Indians, he had drawn bills on Rogers' credit, as Rogers had authorized him to do. These steps angered Rogers: "it is very bad to me that you did not send me in the Peltrys that you promised me last Spring," Rogers wrote, "and am astonished at your heavy Drafts on me." Given what Tute said he had spent, Rogers said, "you must have now Goods enough with you to Compleat your Expedition," adding that he would be sending fewer supplies than he had promised to make up for Tute's ruinous "Extravagance." He concluded by directing Tute to "push on your Journey with all speed and be more prudent than you have hitherto been."[18]

Rogers was experiencing a credit crunch of his own arising out of the enormous council of Indians, at which he had distributed lavish gifts he had bought on credit. The explanation for Rogers' pique was irrelevant to the explorers, however, because the letter's insulting tone aside, Rogers presented the expedition with a dilemma. They did not have goods and supplies enough to "push on" to Fort des Prairies, much less continue beyond. The expedition's "council" voted unanimously to cut their losses and return to Michilimackinac.[19]

The explorers arrived at the fort in late August 1767 and were immediately dismayed to learn that their effort had been unauthorized and that there was no money to pay them for a year's labor. They appealed to Gage in December 1767, but Gage, apparently learning about the expedition for the first time, angrily declared that Rogers had had no authority to engage them.

ROGERS' mandate from Johnson was to promote peace and good will with the Indians in the Michilimackinac vicinity—but he was to do so within the bounds of the strict parsimony the government imposed on gifts to Indians. This economizing contrasted dramatically with French practice, and many Indians resented it. Rogers considered the policy shortsighted and counterproductive.

Beginning in the fall of 1766, Rogers courted Indians, traveling to their villages and receiving them as visitors at the fort. He was extremely popular with them. Until the spring of 1767, he had great success fostering good relations with the Indians without incurring excessive expense.[20]

The crowning event in Rogers' campaign to cement friendship with the Indians was an enormous conference, or council, with regional tribes that he scheduled to be held at Michilimackinac in early July 1767. Invitations to the conference flowed in the fall of 1766 and the spring of 1767. Tute and Carver were instructed to spread word of the conference as they traveled through the territory now organized as the states of Michigan, Wisconsin, and Minnesota. One purpose of the conference was to broker peace between the Sioux and the Chippewa, whose ongoing state of war was creating regional tensions and threatening the fur trade. Rogers also wanted to showcase and reinforce a broad spirit of peace and amity on the frontier under his leadership.[21]

The council drew representatives of a dozen or more Indian nations. Estimates of participants ran into the thousands. It was the largest assembly of Indians ever seen at Michilimackinac. The event apparently was a great success, seeming as it did to reconcile the Sioux and the

Chippewa, as well as other warring parties, and enhancing Rogers' personal prestige.[22]

This extravagant display came at huge cost. Rogers began dispensing gifts in connection with invitations to the council in early 1767. The first voucher he submitted for reimbursement for gifts purchased on his personal credit, for something more than £400, exceeded the outlay incurred for Indian gifts at Michilimackinac for the entire preceding year.[23] Apprised of this, Gage told Johnson to tell Benjamin Roberts, newly-appointed Indian Affairs commissary at Michilimackinac, to instruct Rogers "to incur no more expense, and that you [Johnson] will answer to no More Draughts from him." Gage was not being petty. He was under enormous pressure from London to control Indian Affairs expenses, and had previously instructed Johnson to rein in expenses across the board.[24]

Roberts, as instructed, told Rogers to incur no further expenses and warned him that no further drafts would be honored, but Roberts arrived in Michilimackinac only in late June 1767, too late to do any good. The Indians had already gathered, the presents for them had been purchased, and there was no way for Rogers to turn back. Rogers' first voucher for somewhat more than £400 proved to be only the tip of the iceberg. Months later, when the bills were tallied, they came to more than £5,000—more than $1 million in today's money.[25] Rogers purchased most of the gifts on his personal credit, and as it became apparent that reimbursement might not be forthcoming, his credit dried up. He was forced to importune local traders and merchants to contribute an additional £400 to defray conference costs.[26] The "heavy drafts" that Rogers complained about to Tute had gone in part to goods distributed to Indians to encourage them to attend the Michilimackinac council. This was why Tute and Carver had insufficient supplies and trade goods to complete their march to the Forks of the Saskatchewan without resupply. As Rogers had grimly predicted to Tute, he was financially ruined.

Johnson and Gage were furious. Rogers was authorized to meet with Indian leaders and give them small gifts, but his superiors had contemplated nothing on the scale of the July 1767 council, and an event of this size plainly required consultation with and approval by Johnson. There did not appear to be any need for the council other than to make participants feel good. Johnson considered the negotiation of peace between the Sioux and the Chippewa a "pretense," such a peace being something "with which we have very little to do, in good policy or bad." Johnson never would have authorized the expenditures. The expenditures were certified by officers at Michilimackinac as "absolutely necessary," but Johnson later reported that "some of them as Signified by letters to me" had a "contrary" opinion, implying that they had been pressured by Rogers.[27] Rogers plainly knew he had exceeded his authority, but, as in the past, he assumed the army would reimburse him for lack of a better alternative. He was wrong, and he was never made whole for the Indian council expenses.

Johnson accused Rogers of self-interest in staging the council. Writing to the Earl of Hillsborough on August 17, 1768, he cited the £5,000 cost, then complained that peace between the Sioux and the Chippewa, "had it been attended with success, would have been only interesting to a very few French, and others that had goods in that part of the country." Johnson presumably included Rogers among these "others," because he was engaged in trading in the affected region or because development of his Chippewa lands, recently discovered to contain rich copper deposits, would be impeded by inter-tribal conflict. "[B]ut the contrary has happened," Johnson observed, "and [the Sioux and Chippewa] are more violent than ever against one another."[28]

Once again, Johnson underestimated Rogers' ambition. Whatever his personal interests, the true prize was the governorship of a vast new province of Michilimackinac. The key to the economic viability of that independent entity was a successful fur trade, which demanded peace with the Indians. (The other requirement was the removal of restrictions on traders, which Rogers had accomplished.) Rogers believed in purchasing peace in part with lavish gifts. He expected such a program not just to benefit "a very few French," but to cause the fur trade to grow exponentially, justifying the creation of a new province. The Indian council's success highlighted his starring role in brokering and maintaining peace on the frontier.

CHAPTER SEVENTEEN

THE MICHILIMACKINAC PROPOSAL

W HEN he left England in late 1765, bearing Barrington's and Conway's orders to Gage to appoint him commander at Fort Michilimackinac, Rogers undoubtedly anticipated that he would have considerable freedom in his new position. The orders, after all, came at the direction of the king, a sign of royal favor that no doubt would protect him from too much interference or oversight from Gage or Johnson.

Gage's and Johnson's instructions made clear he had had been too optimistic, and Rogers quickly saw that he had fundamental disagreements with policies he was expected to implement. Acting behind Gage's and Johnson's backs, he set in motion policies he believed appropriate. He hoped to see orders arrive from London giving him additional authority ratifying some of those actions, but, in the long run, he needed complete independence from Gage and Johnson.

In his 1765 Northwest Passage proposal, Rogers had recommended the creation of a province of Michilimackinac, with himself as governor, reporting directly to London and bypassing Gage and Johnson. The sole purpose of the recommendation was to enhance the chances of success of his Northwest Passage expedition. High cost had tabled that project, and no one had bothered to study independently the proposal to establish a new province. Rogers now revived and fleshed out that proposal as a stand-alone enterprise. His Michilimackinac journal contains a draft of the proposal, which he reorganized and edited lightly, then submitted in final form to the Earl of Dartmouth and the Board of Trade in a memorial dated May 24, 1767.[1]

The proposal was "breathtaking in scope."[2] It rested on Rogers' commitment to French-style fur trading with its freedom of movement for traders and regular, generous government gifts to Indians. Rogers had largely "completed the reconstruction of the French fur-trading system," without Gage and Johnson realizing how far he had gone.[3] In his memorial, Rogers outlined eloquently the French system's logic, emphasizing Indians' strong desire to have traders travel to them.

The heart of Rogers' proposal was an analysis of the potential for commerce in the region surrounding Fort Michilimackinac. He estimated in detail the prospective annual consumption of trade goods by Indians who could be reached from the fort. Using this information, he gauged the theoretical total value, before trader profits, of the region's fur trade. Permitting traders to travel to Indian villages and winter in them to collect furs, he said, would demand one hundred canoe loads of trade goods. He pegged those goods' value, at Albany and Quebec prices, including transport and other costs, at more than £60,000. The value of furs received in exchange would greatly exceed this sum. Given British policy, however, restricting traders to doing business at the fort and requiring Indians with furs to travel to the fort, Rogers calculated that trade at Michilimackinac would amount to only £6,000 in trade goods.[4] The volume of furs acquired would plunge a corresponding 90 percent.

Rogers railed at that policy—which, of course, he had declined to enforce. Most Indians, he argued, lived too far from the fort to be expected to leave their families and villages on a months-long annual trip to trade furs. England's competitors, the French and Spanish, would exploit the situation by traveling to Indian villages to siphon off trade. The result would be disaster all around. The French and Spanish could not supply all the Indians' needs, and their trade goods were generally inferior to those of the British, so the Indians would suffer. British profits would decline, and Crown policy would drive the Indians into the hands of England's "most dangerous and implacable enemies," creating a security risk on the frontier.[5]

Apart from the economic cost of what Rogers believed to be Britain's short-sighted trade policy for the colonial west, Rogers argued that allowing traders—and ultimately Rangers—to travel widely through Indian territory and garrison ever more remote trading posts would greatly expand Britain's knowledge of the North American continent. Obliquely invoking the Northwest Passage, he mused, "who can say what valuable Discoveries may at one time or other be made by this means?" The presence of British traders and troops would also prevent European rivals from gaining a foothold on the American frontier.[6]

Aware that his proposal clashed with existing policy but wishing not to be seen as advocating total reversal of that policy, Rogers carefully built his case. He noted that Forts Pitt, Niagara, Detroit, and other western outposts had large Indian populations in their vicinities. Confining trade to those forts and keeping that trade under government supervision was completely workable, he acknowledged. But Michilimackinac was unique because the regional Indian population was much more distant and dispersed. Tight government regulation of trade would hobble development of the region's enormous potential. Moreover, a pro-active program of trade and exploration to the west of Michilimackinac would serve as an early warning system of potential encroachments on British interests by other European powers. Michilimackinac "[i]s or ought to be a Barrier to all who come Westerly, North Westerly, or South Westerly to the Pacific Ocean. It is or ought to be a Beacon from which a most extensive and hitherto unknown Territory is watched and observed. It is or ought to be a Store House fraught with all manner of Necessary's for the constant supply of Innumerable Bands, Tribes, and Nations of Savages."[7]

Rogers posed rhetorical questions. Is it in Great Britain's interest to keep the territories it won in the last war? Is it in Great Britain's interest to secure and increase the fur trade? Is not Michilimackinac central to this trade? Would it not greatly contribute to the security of the trade to create a civil government for Michilimackinac? Would it not also contribute to this goal to garrison Michilimackinac with Rangers? Should not French traders be expelled from the region as inimical to British interests? "If the above Queries be answered in the affirmative, as they surely must," he wrote, "the following Plan seems absolutely necessary."[8]

Rogers called for Michilimackinac and its "Dependencies" to be established as a Crown province and given a civil government with a governor, a lieutenant governor, and a council of twelve, selected from the province's leading merchants, empowered to enact all necessary laws, subject only to the king's approval. The governor should also be the military commander and the agent for the region's Indians, and in all these functions he and the council should report directly to the king and his ministers in London, not to any intermediate North American authority. The proposal, in short, would remove Rogers—obviously the intended governor—from Gage's and Johnson's oversight. The governor should be allocated a liberal annual sum of money, directly from London, to be spent on presents for Indians, subject to no review by any other North American authority. Regular army troops garrisoning the province should be supplemented, even replaced, by Rangers reporting to the governor. These troops could be deployed as a peace-keeping force at distant trading posts and to prevent encroachments by the French or the Spanish. Rogers argued the Rangers' functions could not be entrusted to regulars. Because they are unfamiliar with Indians, regulars, in times of unrest, would be likely to be surprised and massacred, as they were during Pontiac's War. In times of peace, regulars garrisoning remote trading posts would be prone to corruption and to tyrannizing resident traders. The problems of corruption and tyranny, Rogers concludes, are best solved by vesting all levers of power in the governor.[9]

The proposed province would be immense, encompassing all or most of the present-day states of Michigan, Wisconsin, Minnesota, and North and South Dakota, and large portions of the present-day provinces of Ontario, Manitoba, and Saskatchewan.[10]

Commentators agree that Rogers' proposal for the province of Michilimackinac was "unrealistic," "needed more fleshing out," and was "far from a well-considered plan of government."[11] Clements, writing more than a century ago, was scathing. Thinking wrongly that Rogers never submitted the proposal to London, he wrote, "[T]his is fortunate, for it was a selfish motive that led [Rogers] to propose it for himself." "His scheme," Clements argued, "was a wild one for the conditions and times, and both his Government and trade plans were creations of a disordered brain."[12]

Johnson, who found out about the proposal after the fact, angrily critiqued it to the Earl of Shelburne, then Secretary of State. The proposal, said Johnson, was full of "falsehoods and absurdities," written by "a needy man, of bad circumstances, and worse principles." The sole point of the proposal, Johnson argued, was to put Rogers in power "to carry on an extensive trade where he pleases." Johnson acknowledged that "[i]n time, we may be form [*sic*] several governments even, with the consent of the Indians, but it is certain, that unless they are framed, and their power executed, by the most disinterested persons, they will totally defeat their intentions."[13]

Johnson scoffed at the notion that a "council of twelve," elected by merchants and traders, would act in anything but individual members' self-interest. He also attacked the idea of Rangers garrisoning the province. Turning Rogers' argument about the likely corruption and tyranny of regular troops against him, Johnson argued that the New York Independent Companies, formed after the French and Indian War ended, had "degenerated in America through the avarice of their captains." He predicted a similar result with Rangers: "Rangers, under an interested needy man, in a remote corner without check or control, will be in a short space of time, reduced to a handfull of faggots, or at least a few sufficient to be employed in trade for him, at the charge of the Crown."[14]

Johnson probably need not have worried about Rogers' proposal being accepted. In December 1767, Rogers was under suspicion of treason and about to be arrested, as Shelburne knew. But Johnson, burned once, was taking no chances. His savaging of Rogers' proposal, however, was mostly *ad hominem* attack and did not address its serious structural flaws.

Rogers likely exaggerated the Michilimackinac region's potential for trading in furs. In his Michilimackinac journal, he began to tally a sum representing the actual monetary value of fur trading in the region, but the spaces for numbers are blank because he apparently lacked sufficient data. Instead, in the proposal he gave the Board of Trade, he only adds up the possible cost of goods bought to trade for furs.[15] This estimate, £60,000, increased by allowing for robust trader profit, suggested a yearly possible value for furs acquired through Michilimackinac of £100,000 or more. In 1770, however, the actual value of furs exported from all of British North America was only £91,000, only a small portion of which was from the Michilimackinac region.[16]

Rogers undoubtedly was correct that more aggressive policies could significantly increase fur trading volumes at Michilimackinac, as Gage and Johnson conceded. The question was at what cost in money and in policy objectives. If Rogers' Indian Council of 1767 is any indication, he considered £5,000 an appropriate annual outlay on Indian gifts. The force of frontier Rangers he proposed—and which Amherst and Gage

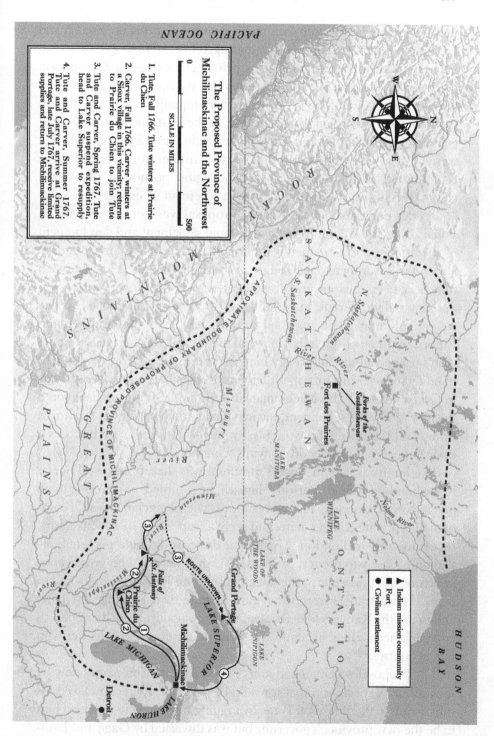

The Proposed Province of
Michilimackinac and the Northwest

SCALE IN MILES

0   500

1. Tute, Fall 1766. Tute winters at Prairie
   du Chien

2. Carver, Fall 1766. Carver winters at
   a Sioux village in this vicinity; returns
   to Prairie du Chien to join Tute

3. Tute and Carver, Spring 1767. Tute
   and Carver suspend expedition,
   head to Lake Superior to resupply

4. Tute and Carver, Summer 1767.
   Tute and Carver arrive at Grand
   Portage, late July 1767, receive limited
   supplies and return to Michilimackinac

rejected—would have been extremely expensive. During the French and Indian War, pay for Ranger privates ranged from £45 to £55 per year, far more than that of regular army privates.[17] A one-hundred-person company of Rangers, with officers, would cost more than £5,000 per year. Rogers contemplated two to three companies, likely more. The cost of civil government would include, at the least, the salaries of government officials and their staff. The fur trade these large expenditures were to promote, while important for the frontier and critical for the economy of Michilimackinac, was a negligible portion of the overall colonial economy, constituting less than 3 percent of exports.[18]

Besides being expensive, Rogers' proposal was not particularly visionary. England was not interested in rapid settlement and development of the frontier and remained committed to attempting to prevent, or at least retard, European encroachments on Indian lands. This approach may have been quixotic and obviously doomed, but Rogers' vision was not materially different. Fur trading was the only economic activity he wanted to stimulate; he imagined an Eden in which Indian trappers and European traders lived in harmony in an unspoiled wilderness. The region's true economic future lay in agriculture, mining, and, eventually, manufacturing—in short, in settlement. Rogers had acknowledged this in *Concise Account*. In his Michilimackinac proposal, however, he ignored the inevitability of settlement, the inevitable problems settlement would bring, and the unsuitability of his "council of twelve" merchants as a body to govern a rapidly diversifying economy.

The foremost flaw in Rogers' proposal was that it placed all power in the hands of a single person—himself, he assumed—answering to no one in North America. The Governor of Michilimackinac would command his private Ranger army and serve as supervisor of Indian affairs, reporting only to London. Michilimackinac would be a personal fief tied only loosely to the rest of British North America. This governance structure was particularly alarming considering Rogers' militant call to expel French traders from the region, despite their long history there, and to use the Rangers to defend aggressively against French or Spanish encroachments. This structure was a recipe for disaster no matter who was in control.

The proposal was matched in its disconnection from reality only by the author's expectation that it would be adopted. Rogers prefaced his submission to the Board of Trade by arguing that the king intended him to be the new province's governor but was thwarted by Gage and Johnson. He enclosed Conway's letter to Gage outlining the appointment (but not Barrington's letter doing the same), as well as the written instructions given him by Gage and Johnson, declaring: "your Lordships will plainly perceive that his Majesty's Royal Pleasure and Instructions toward your Memorialist are in some Respects not all comply'd with." The limitations placed on him by Gage and Johnson "never [were] meant nor intended by his Majesty & Ministers."[19] This grossly mischaracterized Barrington's and Conway's instructions. Those orders made clear that Gage had discretion in framing Rogers' powers and duties and emphasized that Rogers was to be subordinate to Johnson on matters of Indian policy.

Rogers' submission of his proposal to the Board of Trade without notice to Gage or Johnson was a flagrant and provocative breach of protocol. Rogers was an army captain notorious for debt, dishonesty, and insubordination. Gage was a major general, and Johnson a civilian official of equivalent rank. Gage was military commander for all of North America. Johnson, one of the most capable officials in North America, had been in office for more than a decade, and his knowledge of the frontier and of Indian ways matched or exceeded Rogers'. For Rogers to assume that ministers in London would promote Rogers over these men's heads to a position of unchecked power and authority, commanding a private army perhaps supplemented by thousands of Indian auxiliaries was preposterous.

ROGERS thought his tenure at Michilimackinac had started out promisingly. His deregulatory decisions had completely transformed fur trading in the region and won him Indians' good will. He had high hopes for Tute's and Carver's explorations. But by summer 1767, things had come unstuck. The Tute-Carver expedition was in trouble. London had not authorized that venture, and Rogers had no way of paying for the expedition—or for the recent, fabulously expensive Indian council. Financially, he was ruined. Perhaps in reaction to these setbacks, he allowed several disputes with individuals to curdle into bitter feuds.

The first involved Benjamin Roberts, whom Johnson had appointed Indian Affairs commissary at Michilimackinac. Roberts arrived in late June 1767 as hundreds, perhaps thousands, of Indians were enjoying Rogers' grand council. Rogers was about to distribute among his native guests a lavish array of gifts that he had purchased on credit. Roberts, as instructed, directed that Rogers was to incur no more Indian expenses and that the government would not reimburse him for any further such outlays. Roberts and Rogers were set up to clash. Before dispatching Roberts to Michilimackinac, Johnson shared the Hopkins letter with him, poisoning Roberts' view of Rogers. For his part, Rogers bristled at Roberts' title as commissary. Rogers believed Johnson already had an Indian Affairs representative at Michilimackinac—himself. Gage deliberately had declined to give Rogers an Indian Affairs position, intending for Michilimackinac eventually to have a commissary who would control Rogers. Rogers considered this a trampling on his rights. In his orders to Carver, Tute, and Goddard, he had described himself as "Superintendant to Sir William Johnson for the Western Indians." Rogers told Roberts he did not recognize his authority.[20]

Rogers let traders do whatever was necessary to facilitate the fur trade, including distributing alcohol, even if officially discouraged or outright illegal. In early August 1767 Roberts complained to Johnson that Rogers, to curry favor with Indians, was allowing free flow of rum to them.[21] On August 20, acting on a tip, Roberts seized forty kegs of rum smuggled out of the fort without documentation and hidden on a nearby island. He presumably believed the rum was meant for Indians and had been removed from the fort with Rogers' knowledge. Rogers insisted that the rum be returned to an army storehouse under his supervision. Roberts wanted the kegs under *his* supervision. A face-off ensued. Rogers shouted that he was in command; Roberts shouted back, "I have as much command as you" and "am not under your command at all." Rogers called him "impertinent," and Roberts told him to "be damned." Rogers ordered Roberts to his quarters. When Roberts refused, Rogers called for guards. Roberts still refused to go. Rogers had him carried to his quarters and confined under guard.[22] Tempers cooled with time, and Roberts was released, but a new dispute broke out almost immediately. Roberts asked Rogers to let an Indian department blacksmith use the army's forge. Rogers allowed access for a few days but then told Roberts to get his own forge. Roberts demanded that Rogers provide one. Rogers refused. Again, the two fell to shouting, and Roberts again landed in in his quarters confined under guard. This time, Rogers ordered Roberts expelled from Michilimackinac. Roberts claimed to fear for his life, later testifying that during this period someone had fired two shots at him. When transport arrived, Rogers had Roberts sent to

Detroit, telling Spiesmaker and Gage that Roberts had "grossly insulted me" and was trying to "make Muteny under my Command."[23]

Amid Rogers' dustups with Roberts, he fell out with Nathaniel Potter, his secretary. Whatever the original issue, Potter quit and announced he was going to London. Rogers owed him £55; Potter demanded payment. Rogers, as usual broke and deep in debt, refused. £55—about $10,000 in today's money—was a significant sum. Angry talk escalated into blows. Potter accused Rogers of assaulting him, stealing valuables, and threatening to refuse to allow him to go to London. This dispute made allies of Potter and Roberts, with fateful consequences for Rogers.[24]

Also that August, Tute and Carver returned to Michilimackinac, immediately quarreling with Rogers for lying to them about his authority and failing to pay for their expedition, including their salaries. As summer turned to fall, tensions ran high at Michilimackinac.

ELIZABETH ROGERS charged that Rogers subjected her to "drunken brutality," among other injuries, during their time at Michilimackinac. It is difficult not to suspect that alcoholism was at least part of the explanation for Rogers' extreme, even bizarre, behavior as commandant there.

Rogers engaged in at least three flagrant acts of insubordination that he cannot have expected to go undetected: his reversal of existing British policy on regulation of the fur trade, the Tute-Carver expedition, and the Indian council, all carried out without so much as notice to his superiors.

The visions that drove Rogers—the nonexistent Northwest Passage and the delusional province of Michilimackinac—were grandiose and unrealistic. Sending a tiny band of undersupplied explorers on foot and by canoe nearly to the Yukon and back to find the Northwest Passage was not an act of responsible leadership. Proposing himself as the unchecked ruler of a vast empire protected by a private army was not a serious proposal for governance.

To this must be added the violent quarrels with Roberts and Potter, and his appalling mistreatment of Betsy. There is something unhinged about Rogers' tenure as commander at Michilimackinac. And if alcohol is at least part of the explanation for this, it is fair to wonder whether alcohol may have figured earlier in Rogers' erratic, impulsive behavior.

Whatever the explanation, Gage had had enough. Gage likely did not even know yet about the Tute-Carver expedition, but when he learned about the Indian council expenses, he exploded. This was precisely the profligacy he had worried about when he first received his orders to appoint Rogers to the post, and it constituted a clear violation of his written orders to Rogers. Writing to Johnson on September 21, 1767, Gage said, "With respect to [Rogers], I could devise no better means to stop his proceedings, and put an immediate end to all the mischiefs he may create, than to remove him immediately from his command. I have therefore done this, and ordered him to meet Mr. Croghan at Detroit." At Detroit, Croghan would hand Rogers Gage's letter dismissing him and forbidding him to return to Michilimackinac. Regarding the bills for the Indian council, "pretended to have been incurred on a trifling affair, undertaken solely by his own authority, contrary to the orders given him by you as well as by me," Gage's letter would "acquaint him that they are protested, and will not be paid."[25]

A new crisis intervened, however, and made this action unnecessary.

CHAPTER EIGHTEEN

ARRESTED
FOR TREASON

Dislike of Rogers drove Benjamin Roberts and Nathaniel Potter into each other's arms. Although Rogers had threatened to refuse to give Potter permission to return to London, he eventually relented. Rogers remained unable to repay the money he owed Potter, however, and Potter continued to stew about this and other grievances. Shortly before departing for London, Potter sought out Roberts to denounce Rogers. His falling out with Rogers, Potter confided, was not simply a dispute over a debt. Rogers "wanted to engage him in some bad Affairs, and had Villainous designs in his head." According to Roberts, Rogers showed Potter the Hopkins letter, which Roberts already knew about. In later testimony, after Potter's death, Roberts claimed that Potter told him Rogers had replied to Hopkins and had shown Potter a second letter from Hopkins acknowledging Rogers' reply and agreeing to the plan Rogers proposed in that response. The plan was for Rogers to go down the Mississippi in the spring of 1768 to join the French in New Orleans. Potter advised Roberts to look out for himself, as he imagined Rogers had designs against him.[1]

Roberts remained undecided about Potter's denunciation. He believed Rogers guilty of treasonous plans based on his knowledge of the Hopkins letter, but he told Potter to his face that "he was of a bad Character" and that Roberts "could not believe him." Plainly Roberts suspected others would not believe Potter either. Rogers was in command at the fort, and the second-in-command, Spiesmaker, had consistently carried out Rogers' orders, including during the earlier dispute between Rogers and Roberts. Michilimackinac was hundreds of miles from the nearest British fort, Detroit, which had an officer who outranked Rogers and could intervene, but that avenue of relief was uncertain. Roberts was also uncertain about his own authority, including whether he could even disclose his knowledge of the Hopkins letter; Johnson had told him to keep the Hopkins letter in confidence. After Potter's departure, Roberts, continuing to feud with Rogers, accused him, without detail, of conspiring to commit treason. He even made a written accusation to Spiesmaker, urging him to arrest Rogers and seize his papers, which, Roberts said, would prove his accusations of treason. Spiesmaker took no action; however, Roberts did not press the matter, and most people at the post likely had no idea what he was talking about. After Rogers ordered him removed from Michilimackinac and sent to Detroit, Roberts went to Spiesmaker to tell him about his conversation with Potter. Potter was already gone, and Spiesmaker, knowing about the enmity between Rogers and Roberts, resolved only to be "more upon his Guard."[2]

Potter brought everything to a head. En route to London, he denounced Rogers to the British governor in Montreal, Guy Carleton, and on September 29, 1767, gave a sworn statement detailing his allegations. Potter began by saying that Rogers "was much dissatisfied with his Situation" at Michilimackinac "and expressed a distant design of taking some extraordinary methods to better it." In July, Rogers had a "Private Conversation" with Potter in which he discussed his plans. He told Potter he was "resolved to apply to the Government of England, to do something to better his Situation; and that he wished they wou'd Erect the Country about Michilimackinac into a separate Province, and make him Governor of it, with a Command of three Companies of Rangers, Independent of Sir William Johnson, or of the Commander in Chief of the Forces in America; that this would satisfy him and make him easy, and nothing else wou'd."[3]

Knowing that Potter was returning to England, Rogers asked him to lobby there for this proposal and let him know promptly if he succeeded.

"[I]f he did not meet with Success," according to Potter, "he would immediately upon receiving notice of his disappointment, quit his Post and retire to the French towards the Missisipi, and enter into the Service of the French." Rogers, according to Potter, disclosed that he "had a Letter from one Hopkins," who was in the French service, and that "Hopkins had offered him great Encouragement if he would embrace the French Interest, and stir up the Indians against the English." He advised Potter to join in this plan, "as it would be much for his Interest."[4]

Potter expressed "Surprize and Indignation at this proposal, as being contrary to his Duty and Conscience," prompting Rogers to call him a "fool." Rogers said he intended to proceed anyway, adding that "he would not go empty handed," but would seize for himself "all the Goods he could, both from Traders and others, by right or wrong he cared not how."[5]

When Potter made clear he would not participate, Rogers "flew into a violent passion," swore he would not pay Potter anything he owed him, and threatened to kill him if he revealed Rogers' plan. Potter told Rogers he "apprehended himself to be bound in Conscience, and by the Duty which he owed his Country, to give Intelligence of it to proper Persons, in order to prevent it's taking place." This caused Rogers to take up an Indian spear and threaten to kill Potter on the spot if he did not swear to keep the conversation secret. Eventually, Rogers allowed him to return to his lodgings.[6]

These events, according to Potter's statement, occurred in July. Potter remained at the fort another month, leaving August 29. He told no one about Rogers' treasonous plan until, shortly before his departure, he disclosed Rogers' plan to Roberts. This would place his discussion with Roberts shortly after Roberts' angry and very public argument with Rogers over the rum moved improperly from the fort.[7]

Governor Carleton sent the transcript of Potter's statement to Secretary of State Shelburne in London on October 9, 1767, and to Gage on October 13, with similar cover letters to each. Oddities and improbabilities dotted Potter's statement. Carleton flagged one: "it appears so very surprising that Major Rogers, after a confidential Avowal of no less than the Crime of high Treason, should Quarrel with the Person to whom he had entrusted so dangerous a Secret, and let him quietly slip through his Fingers." Emphasizing that he knew both Potter and Rogers only by reputation, Carleton allowed that Potter was a person of "bad Character" who "may be actuated by views of self-interest and motives of revenge." But it was easy to be suspicious of Rogers, Carleton said, because of "his General Character, and the very great Distress his Extravagancies have involved him in." Carleton concluded: "Unhappy is it for Major Rogers that his character does not stand in so fair a Light, as to render excusable a total Neglect of Mr. Potter's Information." Carleton also forwarded the Potter transcript to Johnson and Gage.[8]

To Gage, Johnson predicted that Rogers, "a weak vain man," would now fly to the Indians. To the Earl of Shelburne, Johnson sent a copy of the material he had received from Carleton, apparently not realizing that Carleton had already sent it to Shelburne. Johnson also enclosed a copy of the Hopkins letter and filled Shelburne in on his relationship with Rogers. When Rogers was appointed to his present position, Johnson advised Shelburne, he "took care by the advice of General Gage, to give him very little powers with regard to Ind'n management or expenses there, the General and myself well knowing the man, the heavy debts he had incurred, and reasonably concluding he ought not be entrusted with much authority." Gage, Johnson added, had already moved to relieve Rogers of his command for other abuses when the Potter information came to light.[9]

Shelburne understood. Writing to Gage on December 19, 1767, he reported that Potter died en route to London, but that he had personally interviewed two traders from Michilimackinac, Baxter and Bostwick, who accompanied Potter on the voyage. The traders reported to Shelburne that Rogers was in debt to everyone at the post, expressed fear of Rogers' defecting to the French, and were particularly alarmed at Rogers' apparent plan to "debauch the Garrison in Michilimackinac, in which they feared he would have too much success." Bostwick had been at Michilimackinac in 1763, when, during Pontiac's War, Indians had captured the fort by ruse, massacred twenty members of the garrison, and plundered many traders, including Bostwick. Shelburne concluded to Gage that the charge against Rogers "is of a very serious Nature" and that it "deserves the strictest Enquiry, and, if proved, a very exemplary Punishment."[10]

Gage did not wait for orders from London. Based on the Potter declaration, he ordered Rogers arrested on October 19, 1767. The order took more than six weeks to reach Michilimackinac. Spiesmaker, to whom Gage had addressed his order to have Rogers arrested for "holding Dangerous and Traitorous Conferences with His Majesty's Enemies," executed the order on December 6, 1767, and had Rogers confined to his quarters under guard. Rogers, who assumed Roberts was behind his arrest, immediately wrote Gage to complain. Recognizing that the allegations in the arrest order could only refer to his relationship with Hopkins, he acknowledged receiving a letter from Hopkins but denied responding. He volunteered that Hopkins had approached him in London in 1765 to broach the idea of his entering French service, but that Rogers had rebuffed the proposal in the presence of Sir Jeffery Amherst's brother.[11] In that setting, one could hardly expect him to do otherwise.

The conditions of Rogers' initial confinement to his quarters were relatively benign, but Rogers seemed inclined to test boundaries. He left his quarters to greet Indians visiting the fort until Spiesmaker forbade that. He held parties for soldiers' wives at his quarters, which Spiesmaker also forbade. These dictates angered Rogers, who told Lieutenant Christie, now the fort's second-in-command, that "he would be revenged of him Captain Spiesmaker to the last Verge of Life." Spiesmaker, previously very supportive of Rogers, now ordered that "no one should be admitted to [Rogers] without [Spiesmaker's] permission in writing."[12]

In late January 1768, a much more alarming development occurred. A French trader named Ainsse privately warned Spiesmaker that he was in danger because Rogers, assisted by his orderly Fullerton, was planning to take the fort's officers prisoner and escape. Rogers, said Ainsse, was seeking to enlist Ainsse in the plot. Seeing Spiesmaker's skepticism, Ainsse offered to set up a meeting with Fullerton to discuss the plan while Spiesmaker eavesdropped from concealment. Accompanied by a French-speaking witness named Frobisher—the parley was expected to be in French—Spiesmaker went to Ainsse's house and heard Fullerton confirm to Ainsse that Rogers intended to join Captain Hopkins, whom he believed to be in New Orleans, and that to facilitate his escape he wanted Ainsse to arrange for Indians to seize Spiesmaker and Christie outside the fort and hold them hostage until Rogers was released. Ainsse asked Fullerton whether he fully understood the consequences of participating in this plan. Fullerton answered, "Hell Yes," saying he would run away to the Indians if the plot was discovered. He admonished Ainsse to keep the matter secret.[13]

To reinforce the evidence, Spiesmaker told Ainsse to go to Rogers and ask Rogers what reward he could expect for his assistance. Ainsse returned with a note from Rogers dated February 4, 1768: "I promise to pay Mr. Joseph Anse Annualy one hundred pounds Sterling for Five

Years Successively to carry me to Mr. Hopkins." Spiesmaker and Christie confronted Fullerton the next day. Fullerton "fell on his knees, begged [Spiesmaker to] intercede with the General [presumably Gage] for his Life, and promised to make a fair Confession; then [Spiesmaker] took all [Fullerton] said in Writing, upon Oath."[14]

The allegations against Rogers were entirely believable. He had engineered a jailbreak in New York in 1764. Everyone attested to his close friendships with Indians living in the vicinity of the fort. Fullerton assured Ainsse that Rogers believed most of the garrison sympathized with him, making the capture of Spiesmaker and Christie enough to secure his release. Spiesmaker ordered Rogers removed from his house, placed in the guardhouse in heavy irons, and forbade him visitors, including Betsy.[15]

Rogers remained in close confinement for months. The boat to take him to Detroit did not arrive until May and did not depart until month's end. Rogers, still in irons, was placed in the hold; Betsy had separate quarters. Armed Ottawa and Chippewa warriors gathered at the fort to protest Rogers' removal. The garrison was put under arms, and two armed boats accompanied the boat rowing Rogers out to the Detroit-bound vessel, but there was no violence.[16]

In Detroit, Rogers was confined in irons in a cell for two weeks, then transferred to a boat bound for Montreal. Only at Fort Niagara, in late June or early July, were Rogers' irons removed and Betsy allowed to stay with him. The reunion with Betsy did not last long. In Oswego, Betsy, pregnant either by Rogers or, more likely, Ensign Johnston, left to return to her parents in Portsmouth. Rogers was taken on to Montreal for his trial for treason.[17]

CHAPTER NINETEEN

THE TRIAL

Rogers' court-martial for treason, which began in Montreal on October 19, 1768, was a complete fiasco. The army's case proved at trial to be much thinner than anticipated, with much evidence of suspicious activity but scant proof of criminality. Rogers, apparently permitted counsel who could advise him but who was not allowed to address the court, was effective, even eloquent, in his own defense. He proclaimed his unswerving loyalty to the crown, established bias on the part of key witnesses for the prosecution, argued that he had been improperly denied access to documents that would have further established his innocence, and complained bitterly that the terms of his confinement were cruel and unnecessary.

The army's warrant charged Rogers in three articles. Article 1 charged him with forming "Designs of a Traitorous and Dangerous nature of deserting to the French, after plundering the Traders and others of His Majesty's Subjects, and Stirring up the Indians against His Majesty and His Government." Article 2 charged him with "holding a Correspondence with His Majesty's Enemies." Article 3 charged him with "Disobedience of his Orders and Instructions during his Command at Michilimackinac in having undertaken expensive Schemes and projects" which were "Conformable to the Council [sic] given in a letter to him" by Hopkins.[1]

The only evidence supporting the charge that Rogers planned to plunder traders and others at Michilimackinac was the Potter declaration. Apart from weak implications that might be drawn from the Hopkins letter itself, the Potter declaration was also the only evidence supporting the charge that Rogers intended to stir up the Indians against the British. Potter, however, was dead, and Rogers argued that because he had not had the opportunity to cross-examine Potter, the statement, as a legal matter, should be disregarded. The tribunal admitted the declaration, but Rogers made a telling point about the weight it should be given. Taking no chances, he introduced evidence of Potter's reputation for dishonesty and of his declared extreme animosity toward Rogers.[2]

Even on its own, Potter's declaration seemed dubious, at least in part. As Carleton had pointed out, it was improbable that Rogers would have made so clear and complete a confession of planned treason and then allowed Potter to leave Michilimackinac and broadcast this confession to the world. Given Potter's reputation, his supposed "Indignation" with Rogers for proposing a plan so contrary to "Duty and Conscience" and his profession to Rogers that he felt duty-bound to report him seem exaggerated and improbable. And something does not ring true about the circumstances in which Rogers disclosed his treasonous plan to Potter. The primary purpose of the "Private Conversation" Rogers had with Potter was to ask Potter to lobby on behalf of his Michilimackinac province proposal in London, not to join him in defecting to the French. Rogers clearly wanted to hear London's response before doing anything, so there was no reason, in July 1767, for him to disclose in detail to Potter what he would do if his proposal was rejected. And there was no reason for Rogers to insist so strenuously that Potter agree to assist his plan to defect if matters came to that. Potter would be in London at that point, and his support or lack thereof would be irrelevant.[3]

Is it at least fair to infer that Potter must have had *some* conversation with Rogers about the Hopkins letter because he could not otherwise have known about it? Not really. Roberts had read the Hopkins letter, which Johnson showed him. Roberts was dying to discuss his knowledge of the letter, and he and Potter were aligned in their enmity toward Rogers. Roberts could easily have shared the details of the Hopkins letter with Potter, and Potter could easily have tailored his statement to include these details, knowing they would be corroborated by the Hopkins letter.

The army called Roberts as a witness to bolster the Potter declaration by showing that Potter had given him substantially the same account he later gave in Montreal, but Roberts plainly had no personal knowledge of the relevant facts, and his evidence was only as reliable as Potter. Roberts' account of what Potter told him also differed in important respects from Potter's own account. Potter never claimed, as Roberts did, that Rogers had shown him the Hopkins letter, only that Rogers told him about the letter. Roberts testified that Potter told him he had seen the letter. Roberts testified further that Potter told him Rogers had shown him a second, far more incriminating, letter, in which Hopkins acknowledged receipt of a letter from Rogers agreeing to defect and confirmed a plan for Rogers to come down the Mississippi to New Orleans in the spring of 1768. There was no other evidence of Rogers responding to Hopkins or of this second, highly damning letter from Hopkins to Rogers. The antagonism between Rogers and Roberts was well known; Rogers called a witness to confirm Roberts' ill opinion of him, and the tribunal could easily have concluded that Roberts simply invented the additional Hopkins-Rogers correspondence.[4]

The weakness of the Potter and Roberts evidence meant that the lurid story of Rogers' post-arrest plan to have Indian co-conspirators attack and seize Spiesmaker and Christie, free Rogers, and help him flee to the French in New Orleans was critical to proving Articles 1 and 2 of the charging warrant. That story, however, seemed far less powerful in court.

Fullerton recanted much of his prior testimony. He now acknowledged only that Rogers had asked him to reach out to Ainsse to serve as an intermediary between Rogers and the Indians to effectuate Rogers' escape. Fullerton denied agreeing to assist in this plan, and he said nothing about Rogers' intention to desert to the French. In fact, as Fullerton understood it, Rogers simply "wished to get out of the hands of those among who he was, in order to go and deliver himself to General Gage at New York." To the extent he had said anything more in his statement to Spiesmaker and Christie, Fullerton now said he had been "threatened" by these officers, who "made him Sign" a statement they prepared that he did not understand.[5]

Fullerton then produced a remarkable certification dated May 26, 1768, after his own and Rogers' arrest. The certification, signed by four officers of his regiment, including Spiesmaker and Christie, attested that "no Soldier bore a better Character until his Acquaintance with Major Rogers, by whose insinuating behavior" Fullerton was induced to assist Rogers, "which we verily believe proceeded entirely from his Ignorance and blind Attachment to [Rogers]." The signers asked General Gage to "take these things into his Consideration, and take pity upon [Fullerton]." This certification seemed to support Fullerton's credibility, and hence the reliability of his recantation. The tribunal refused to admit into evidence the statement Fullerton had given to Spiesmaker and Christie in February 1768, admitting only his more limited direct testimony at the trial.[6]

Apart from Fullerton's testimony to the tribunal, Spiesmaker testified to the conversation he overheard between Fullerton and Ainsse, stating that he "clearly heard" Fullerton say that Rogers "intended to joyn Captain Hopkins, whom he supposed to be then at New Orleans" and then "requested [Ainsse] to make an interest with the Indians to take Captain Spiesmaker, and Lieutenant Christie Prisoners" to secure Rogers' release. This testimony is odd, because the conversation between Ainsse and Fullerton must have been in French, Ainsse speaking no English, and Spiesmaker brought Frobisher, a French-speaking witness, to eavesdrop on the meeting. How could Spiesmaker have "clearly" understood what Fullerton said? Frobisher gave a general corroboration of Spiesmaker's account, including that the plan was for Rogers to "get possession of the Garrison" and then "go to join Captain Hopkins supposed to be at New Orleans," but he acknowledged only a hazy recollection of the event.[7]

Ainsse then testified, further muddying the waters. Although he said he came to understand that Rogers wanted to go to New Orleans to join Hopkins, and that his role was to "gain the Indians to assist in freeing him" by seizing Spiesmaker and Christie, Ainsse volunteered that in the beginning "he could not rightly understand" Rogers, because Ainsse could not speak English and Rogers' French was poor. Ainsse also testified that after the first conversation with Fullerton monitored by Spiesmaker and Frobisher, Spiesmaker told him "he had lost much of what was said" because "the Wind was so high." Ainsse had to arrange a second meeting with Fullerton, which Spiesmaker and Frobisher also listened to, until Spiesmaker was satisfied he had heard enough.[8]

Then there was the note Ainsse claimed to have received from Rogers promising to pay him £100 a year for five years. According to Ainsse, Rogers initially objected to giving him the note, then, because of language problems, made several unsuccessful attempts to write it out before getting it right. Although Ainsse testified that Spiesmaker had compared the signature on the note to examples in Rogers' hand and declared the note genuine, Spiesmaker made no mention of this, and the army made no attempt to prove the note's genuineness. Rogers insisted the note was a forgery. The note itself seems suspect. Ainsse's task was not "to carry [Rogers] to Mr. Hopkins," but only to arrange for Indians to release him from custody. If Rogers really intended to defect to the French in New Orleans, his note would be worthless to Ainsse in Michilimackinac, making the entire transaction a charade.[9]

Rogers aggressively attacked Ainsse's character, calling two witnesses who said that in the 1763 attack on the fort, Ainsse had helped Indians plunder certain traders' stores. One of these witnesses, Bostwick, gave vivid testimony about Ainsse motioning an Indian to kill him. Only the intervention of another Indian friendly to Bostwick saved his life. Although this testimony seemed credible, and undoubtedly prejudiced a tribunal of British officers against the Frenchman Ainsse, it remained unclear what motive Ainsse would have to implicate Rogers falsely, especially when it seemed beyond dispute that Rogers had sought him out in the first place to enlist the Indians to free him.[10]

Collectively, the testimony of Spiesmaker, Frobisher, Ainsse, and Fullerton, for all its problems, established convincingly that, following his arrest, Rogers conspired to escape from custody by enlisting Indians to seize Spiesmaker, Christie, and perhaps others and hold them hostage until Rogers got away. Even Rogers made only a half-hearted effort to deny this. Although he argued, implausibly, that "the utmost extent of my Offense" was to have "some Romantic Conversation between Mrs. Rogers and me, merely to pass away time during my Confinement, and never intended to be put in Execution," he made a better point when he argued that any evidence of a plan to escape needed to be seen in context. Such evidence related to "my Conduct in the Tumult of my grief and Resentment for the usage I received in being Confined when Conscious of my Innocence."[11]

The more important issue is that the warrant does not charge Rogers with attempting or conspiring to escape from custody. The escape plan, even if proven to have existed, would be relevant to the actual charge only if it were pursuant to a plan to desert to the French, or to plunder traders and others, or to stir up Indians against the British. The army presented no credible evidence of the latter two plans, so Rogers could be convicted under Article 1 of the warrant only if he had a preexisting plan to desert to the French and his plan to escape from custody after his arrest was part of that plan.

Here, the evidence was closer. Although Fullerton recanted his testimony on this point, Ainsse, Spiesmaker, and Frobisher stated that Rogers' plan of escape was to flee to the French in New Orleans after the Indians procured his release. It is difficult to believe that all three witnesses fabricated this testimony. Even if the testimony is credited, however, it does not, by itself, show a pre-existing plan to defect to the French. Rogers may have had no such plan, but he could reasonably have feared conviction on a false charge of treason and concluded that he had no alternative but to turn to the French.

Assuming the court-martial panel discounted Potter's testimony, as it should have, this meant that Rogers' guilt or innocence on both Article 1 and Article 2 of the Warrant turned on a single question: What weight should be given to the Hopkins letter and Rogers' conduct following the receipt of it? Did these pieces of evidence show a pre-existing plan to engage in treason? Rogers argued at trial that "I abhorred the Scheme, and never entertained a thought about answering that Letter." This argument is seriously undermined by Rogers' failure to bring the Hopkins letter to the attention of anyone in authority. Hopkins was a representative of the French government who had consulted French ministers about Rogers and then invited a British officer commanding an important post in a vulnerable frontier region to defect. Rogers must have recognized the seriousness of the matter and recognized that a responsible officer in his position would bring the Hopkins letter to the attention of Gage or Johnson or both, if only to alert them to French attempts to undermine British security.[12]

Rogers knew that his failure to alert his superiors was the most damning piece of evidence against him, but he had an answer: he *did* send the letter to Gage with his comments, but it got lost in the mail. He called a witness, Garson Levy, who testified that a boat carrying mail from Michilimackinac to Detroit sank in the fall of 1766, and that he had heard that there was correspondence from Rogers to Gage aboard that vessel. He elicited from a second witness, Ensign Robert Johnston, a claim that Rogers had told him he sent the Hopkins letter to Gage on a boat that sank, but this conversation occurred after Rogers' arrest and after it was apparent that the Hopkins letter was central to the government's case. For good measure, Rogers claimed that Potter wrote his cover letter to Gage transmitting the Hopkins letter and would, if still alive, have corroborated his testimony.[13]

This claim, impossible to disprove, was too convenient to be believable. Rogers raised it for the first time well after his arrest and confinement, when he knew how crucial the letter was and had had time to think about how to explain his response to it. In his letter to Gage immediately after his arrest, he acknowledged receiving the letter and said he had not responded but made no claim to have forwarded it to Gage so that Gage would know of the French attempt at meddling.

The most likely explanation of what Rogers did with the Hopkins letter is that he pocketed it for future reference. Rogers' first choice plainly was to have London give him the governorship of Michilimackinac, with the broad authority he proposed. In that event, he could simply let whatever discussions he had had with Hopkins lapse. Rather than disclosing the Hopkins letter to Gage or Johnson, he likely kept quiet about it. Even if he had disclosed and repudiated the letter promptly, its contents suggested earlier conversations and raised questions about Rogers' loyalty, or at least his judgment. And Rogers likely wanted to keep his options open. The believable portion of the Potter declaration is the portion discussing Rogers' intense frustration at being subordinate to Gage and Johnson, his desperate desire for the Michilimackinac governorship, and his willingness to consider extreme alternatives if thwarted. Rogers would not have wanted to close off one such alternative by disclosing the Hopkins letter.

If that is what happened—and the credible evidence did not establish anything more—it was still too little to sustain a finding that Rogers entered a treasonous conspiracy. Rogers may have shown poor judgment and a dangerous willingness to at least entertain the possibility of treason, but the evidence did not show an actual agreement between Rogers and Hopkins or any other representative of France, or any action prior to his arrest to reach such an agreement. This meant he had to be acquitted on Articles 1 and 2 of the warrant.

That left Article 3, which charged Rogers with unauthorized expenditures. This should have been the easiest article to understand, and the army's evidence turned out to be stronger on this than on the first two articles, but the army's presentation on Article 3 was half-hearted, and Rogers was able to raise doubts where there should have been none.

The first unauthorized expenditure was the Tute-Carver expedition. Rogers gamely argued that his patron Townshend had assured him that a less expensive proposal for an expedition of discovery than the original "would be highly agreeable to His Majesty." After Rogers reached

Michilimackinac, Townshend and numerous other friends and supporters in England reiterated that the discoveries he proposed were highly
desirable, and "it was by Virtue of these Recommendations that I proceeded in the manner I did." This defense did not address head-on the
fact that the expedition, desirable or not, had not been authorized, but
it created ambiguity about Rogers' motives.[14]

The largest item of unauthorized spending was the cost of the Indian
council of June-July 1767. Rogers' biggest obstacle to showing that this
expense was authorized was Gage's written instruction to him to incur
no major expense on his own authority. Rogers deflected this argument
by countering, disingenuously, that "[t]his part of the Instructions is Re-
strictive to the Garrison only, and not to the Management of Indian Affairs." Johnson had also placed limits on Rogers' spending authority for
Indian gifts every bit as strict as Gage's, but he had done so orally, not
in writing. Before the trial, Johnson wrote to Deputy Judge Advocate
Cramahe describing those restrictions, but Johnson did not testify at trial
and his letter on its own was not admissible, so the tribunal was left without evidence of Johnson's instructions.[15]

That left Gage's standing order to post commanders regarding Indian matters, which he had given to Rogers and which provided that
"[p]resents are not to be made to Indians but on Occasions which shall
render such measures unavoidable." Without quite addressing the "unavoidable" standard, Rogers called two witnesses, an interpreter at the
fort and a trader, who testified the presents were "necessary" to prevent
Indian nations from diverting their trade to the French or the Spanish.
Anyone connected with the fur trade could be expected to applaud the
government's distribution of gifts to Indians, because it would help increase their volume of business at government expense. As a result, this
testimony likely carried little weight. Rogers, however, had a trump card
to play. He produced certifications from the fort's officers, including
Captain Spiesmaker, made immediately after the Indian council. At
that point, Rogers knew that the Indian Department had threatened
to pay no more bills for gifts for Indians, but he was unaware of the
trouble brewing over the Hopkins letter. The certifications stated that
the presents Rogers gave to the Indians "were Absolutely necessary."
Without them, "an Indian War must have taken place in this Country
instead of a Peace," and the peace was "greatly to the Advantage of
His Majesty's Interest, and to those of his Subjects Trading to this
Country."[16]

This claim was preposterous. England was at peace with the Indians in mid-1767, and there was no imminent threat of hostilities. Warfare among the Indians themselves was a long-running feature of frontier life and tended to be localized and episodic, offering no threat to general stability and security. One of Rogers' own witnesses testified that under the French, who had maintained a thriving fur trade at Michilimackinac and who were known to be far more generous than the British, the annual cost of Indian presents ranged from £1,000 to £3,000. Rogers' spending in fewer than eleven months was almost double the higher amount. Rogers' first claim for reimbursement for the cost of Indian gifts, for about £430 in early 1767, was already more than the entire expenditure for the prior year.[17]

Johnson had written to Gage before the trial that some of the officers who made this implausible certification had sent him letters saying they had "contrary" opinions, intimating that Rogers had pressured them. But Johnson did not testify, and the army did not attempt to impeach the certification. To do so would have been awkward, showing several of the fort's officers, including one of the army's main witnesses, to have thoughtlessly signed certifications they believed false. Left with the uncontested statement that Rogers' spending had been "absolutely necessary," the tribunal acquitted Rogers on Article 3, as well as on Articles 1 and 2, and had an entirely reasonable basis for doing so. The tribunal may also have recognized that on Article 3 the army had a completely independent and adequate remedy that did not require a court-martial conviction: it could reject Rogers' claim for the unauthorized expenses.[18]

Despite the acquittal, Rogers was not at liberty. The king needed to confirm the court-martial verdict. Immediately following the verdict, Rogers remained confined to his quarters. In February 1769, an order from Gage reached Montreal allowing Rogers freedom to move about the city, but he could not leave town. During this interlude, he and Roberts, who was then also in Montreal, had an angry confrontation in the street in which one or both men challenged the other to a duel and Rogers, according to Roberts, put his hand in Roberts' face. Rogers remained convinced that Roberts had put Potter up to giving his declaration, which Rogers considered perjurious, to pressure Rogers to repay the money he owed Potter. Before any duel could take place, Montreal authorities called Rogers in, told him he would be returned to confinement unless he swore not to duel with Roberts, and warned him not to insult Roberts.[19]

The king's order on the court-martial verdict reached Montreal in June 1769. He approved the verdict of acquittal, but added that "it appears to His Majesty, that there was great reason to suspect the said Major Rogers Entertaining an improper and dangerous Correspondence, which Suspicion the account afterwards given of his mediating an Escape tended to confirm."[20]

Rogers had been acquitted but not exonerated. To an extent that Rogers failed to appreciate, the trial left his career in ruins. Rogers had effectively impugned such witnesses as Roberts, Potter, and Ainsse, and he had drawn out the intense animosity that witnesses like Roberts, Potter, Spiesmaker, and Christie harbored toward him. Even viewed in the light most favorable to Rogers, however, the trial revealed conduct that, whether treasonous or criminal, was dangerous and inexcusable coming from a British officer. Rogers had shown contempt for his superiors and defiantly refused to take orders from them. He had at least toyed with defecting to the French if England could not satisfy him. He had planned to recruit Indians of dubious loyalty to anyone but himself to take and hold fellow officers hostage to procure his unlawful escape. Even if he intended these officers no harm, the plan carried an enormous risk. Such a man could not be trusted in a responsible military or civil post.

That Rogers' career was over was clear to Gage. Upon receiving the king's order confirming Rogers' acquittal, he wrote to Secretary of War Barrington that "unless His Majesty should be also of opinion, that he ought again to take upon him the Command of the Said Fort; I cannot Answer it, after Maturely considering all that has happened, to reinstate Major Rogers in the actual Command of Missilimakinac, or any other Post in the Indian Country." Neither the king nor Barrington disagreed.[21]

Rogers left Montreal in June 1769 and went to New York. Gage gave him permission to go to London, as well as a note confirming he had not been paid his Michilimackinac salary or reimbursed for the expenses of his confinement in Montreal. He went to Portsmouth in early July for a brief reunion with Betsy, her parents, and infant Arthur. Even before he arrived, a major creditor, expecting him to return there eventually, had sued him for almost £4,000. Expecting this to be only the first of many creditor lawsuits, Rogers left almost immediately for London, hoping, unrealistically, to repeat the enormous success he had had there in 1765.[22]

PART FOUR

FINAL DECLINE

CHAPTER TWENTY

LONDON,
1769–1775

ROGERS arrived in London in September 1769. As in 1765, he had no money. As in 1765, he took quarters in the most expensive part of town. His most important patron, Charles Townshend, had died in the fall of 1767. Rogers set out seeking candidates to enlist in his latest campaign to support a claim for rewards for past service and appointment to a position of responsibility.[1]

Initially, he seemed to meet with success. An ally secured him an audience with George III in November 1769. The monarch had formally expressed his reservations about Rogers in his ruling on the court-martial verdict; upholding the acquittal, he nonetheless found "great reason to suspect" that Rogers had entertained "an improper and dangerous correspondence" with a French agent. Undaunted and encouraged, no doubt, by the fact of being granted an audience, Rogers decided to present aggressive demands. Directly during his audience or indirectly through intermediaries, he asked to be made a baronet, with an annual allowance of £600. He wanted payment of all his Michilimackinac bills, including the expenses of the Indian council. He wanted the governorship of Michilimackinac, presumably with the free rein he proposed in his memorial for the creation of the new province.[2]

The request to be made a baronet with an allowance of £600 a year was likely based on the reward Johnson received following his victory at Lake George in 1755. That victory, though not decisive, was Britain's first in the French and Indian War. It led to the capture of the French commanding officer, and involved thousands of combatants, many times as many as the largest of Rogers' battles, which were defeats. In 1759 Johnson had gone on to triumph at Fort Niagara, the greatest British victory to that point in the war. He had recruited a large Mohawk contingent, which had induced France's Iroquois allies to defect rather than fight their Mohawk relatives, and he used the Mohawks to assist in trouncing a French relief force, forcing the fort to surrender. Rogers had accomplished nothing even remotely comparable. Nothing came of his request for a knighthood and a generous annuity.

Back in North America, Rogers' antagonist Roberts was experiencing his own decline in fortune. Johnson had supported Roberts in his feud with Rogers, but, speaking in confidence with Gage, he characterized Roberts as a man who had "no money & few friends." Gage, no fan of Rogers, conceded that Roberts was as much at fault as Rogers for the bad blood. In March 1769, Johnson advised Roberts that the position of commissary was being eliminated due to the "Expence & difficulties attending it." Roberts was let go, whether in a genuine budget-tightening or because Johnson recognized that Roberts was not an effective administrator.[3]

Roberts was planning to visit London to seek a new appointment, but rumors about Rogers, persistent and credible, reached him in America before he left. The news that Rogers was seeking a knighthood and the Michilimackinac governorship, and speculation that he would succeed, drove Roberts half-mad with anger and frustration. Rogers may well have been behind the chatter. To Betsy, Rogers wrote in January 1770 that he was being considered for a "Knight Hood," and he likely intimated as much to others.[4]

Rogers was deluding himself. Neither knighthood nor appointment materialized. Payment of his Michilimackinac salary and reimbursement for the costs of his confinement at Montreal, which Gage had not disputed, were delayed. In February 1770, Rogers was imprisoned briefly for debt, then released on the bond of friends. Presumably the debts related to living expenses Rogers could not pay. Without telling Betsy about his imprisonment, Rogers wrote her in February 1770, complaining about her failure to write him more frequently. He told her he would be able to wind up his affairs and sail for America in March.[5]

That prediction was overly optimistic. Even the uncontroversial portion of Rogers' claim for payment, for back pay and confinement costs, was not resolved until June 1770. Resolution of his other expenses, primarily from the Indian council, remained up in the air. Treasury referred the matter to Gage. Gage agreed the expenses had been properly documented, but argued that they "greatly exceeded [Rogers'] Powers in expending such considerable Sums." He urged Treasury to deny reimbursement for fear of creating a precedent that would encourage other officers to overspend. Treasury agreed and, in late 1770, denied Rogers further financial award. This left him with crippling debts to traders at Michilimackinac. In the short run, Rogers was beyond the reach of these creditors, but the debts made a hasty return to America unadvisable.[6]

On June 4, 1770, Rogers told Betsy he had obtained the king's warrant for £3,000 in back pay and confinement costs, but a full settlement was dragging on and he did not want to return until he had achieved it. On July 20, 1770, still waiting, he again pleaded that he needed to secure all the money to which he was entitled so he could buy her the home she deserved. She likely put little faith in Rogers' promises.[7]

Apparently Betsy had complained about talk that he was living the high life in London. Rogers' July 20 letter included a protest that "It is impossible for any man on Earth to be more Industrious than I have been since I have arrived in London." He attributed the reports that reached Betsy to "Villenious" gossips.[8]

Rogers' July 20, 1770, letter was at least his fifth to Betsy during his latest London foray. Thereafter, correspondence between them appears to have stopped for almost four years. Rogers had nothing further to report except more disappointments, more empty promises, and more excuses. Nor did he want to disclose his multiple imprisonments for debt, the final one quite lengthy. Betsy, coping unsupported with a young child and aging parents, was over him.

Rogers' professional fortunes were as disheartening as the state of his marriage. His audience with the king in late 1769 had led to nothing. London friends and supporters lacked Charles Townshend's clout or, given Rogers' reputation, were unwilling to risk overtly backing him. In April 1771, he was again arrested for debt, his property seized and sold at auction to satisfy bills. One wonders what had happened to the £3,000 he had received less than a year earlier. Johnson's son-in-law Daniel Claus reported that Rogers "is in jail again at last found out and despised by his former Patrons." Claus added that Rogers' arch-enemy

Roberts, with his "Chariot & keeping a house & Lady in the Country" seemed headed for the same fate—debtors prison.[9]

Rogers prepared a series of increasingly unrealistic, increasingly desperate attempts for financial relief. In May 1771, he petitioned the Board of Trade to grant him a large tract of land near Lake Champlain that he promised to occupy and improve.[10] In June 1771, he sent a petition to the Privy Council detailing his "Services, sufferings, and losses" and seeking an award of more than £12,000.[11] In November 1771, he importuned Secretary of State Hillsborough to give him an unspecified sum in consideration of his service to the crown.[12] In February 1772, he petitioned Treasury to support an application to the House of Commons for a discretionary financial award for past service.[13] In a bizarre request to Sir William Johnson, Rogers argued that prior to Roberts' arrival at Michilimackinac he had performed the same functions that Roberts later did, in addition to his duties as commanding officer. As a result, Rogers reasoned, he was entitled to be appointed retroactively to the post of Indian Affairs Commissary at Michilimackinac and awarded back pay.[14] None of these petitions succeeded.

Rogers maintained his interest in the Northwest Passage, and in February 1772 he sent a revised proposal to the king and his ministers for a Northwest Passage expedition. Rogers began by invoking his 1765 proposal and subsequent inaction on it. Since that time, he said, he had learned much, leading him to two conclusions. The new information "tend[ed] to assure, evince, and almost positively establish the Existence of a Navigable Passage by the North West from the Atlantic into the great Pacific Ocean," discovery of which "is only practicable by Land." Second, "the expense of the first proposal, may be reduced to a very moderate sum."[15]

In year one, the expedition would travel from Schenectady to the Great Lakes, then winter by the Falls of St. Anthony at present-day Minneapolis. This was not novel, and it would put the expedition in the same place as the Tute-Carver expedition at the end of year one. In year two, instead of heading northwest to the Forks of the Saskatchewan to begin an overland search for the River Ourigan, the expedition would head due west by foot and canoe to the Missouri River, a much shorter distance. In 1767, Rogers had warned Tute and Carver not to be duped by the Missouri, but he had changed his mind. The expedition would follow the Missouri to its headwaters, cross the Continental Divide, and portage "about thirty miles to the River Ourigan." The explorers would follow the river to a new body of water, "the Straits of Amian," leading to the bay Rogers had always posited as the link between the Pacific, to the bay's southwest, and Hudson Bay, to its northeast. Here Rogers proposed that the expedition winter and gather supplies for a third year's travel.[16]

In year three, the expedition was to follow the bay to the northeast, presumably by canoe, exploring "every Inlet, Nook or Bay," until it found a connection to Hudson Bay. Rogers seemed still to believe that the connection to Hudson Bay lay roughly in the latitude of northern British Columbia or the southern Yukon Territory, a trip of many hundreds of miles likely taking until the end of year three. As with Rogers' plan for the Tute-Carver expedition, the question became: Now what? Rogers' new answer was as unsatisfactory his old answer. One option was for all or part of the expedition to winter where the bay leading to the Pacific joined Hudson Bay, "ready the Ensuing Season to navigate or pilot through the ship or vessel which may be dispatched to pass through into the great Pacific Ocean." This idea nodded to the requirement that a party seeking to claim the £20,000 prize for the discovery of the Northwest Passage needed to traverse it by ship, but it raised more questions than it answered. Who was to dispatch this ship to Hudson Bay, and when? How was the vessel's crew to find the waiting members of the expedition? And if that meeting occurred at the outlet west from Hudson Bay into the bay leading to the Pacific, the crew of the ship dispatched to the rendezvous would have discovered the Northwest Passage on its own, and the Rogers expedition would have proven unnecessary and irrelevant.[17]

Rogers recognized that wintering at a supposed western outlet of Hudson Bay might be impossible because of hostile Indians or lack of provisions. Or the expedition might fail to find a Northwest Passage. In any of these events, the return to civilization by the route taken would be long and daunting. Rogers proposed an alternative worse than the problem it aimed to solve. He suggested that, as winter neared, the expedition proceed northwesterly, between Japan and the North Pole, to Kamchatka, then on to Siberia, cross from east to west, and proceed through Europe to England.[18]

Rogers justified his proposal to explore by land and canoe by saying that it would allow the expedition to avoid polar winds that swept Hudson Bay from the north, preventing oceangoing ships from finding an outlet from the west side of Hudson Bay to the Pacific. Of course, the

ship Rogers proposed sending to Hudson Bay to meet the explorers
would have to contend with these same winds to find them, as would
any future ships using the Northwest Passage. And the hazards his land-
based expedition encountered would easily eclipse those faced by ocean-
going vessels.[19]

Rogers included a detailed budget. Even with the expedition roster
slashed from more than two hundred to fifty-five, personnel costs, now
including Rogers' salary of more than £1,000 per year, remained substantial, not to mention equipment, supplies, and goodwill presents for
Indians. The revised proposal might come in a third less than he had
estimated in 1765, but the return trip via Siberia would add at least a
year to the trip, eating up those savings.[20]

The Missouri River portion of Rogers' 1772 proposal can be seen as
prefiguring Lewis and Clark, but also raised a new issue. The northern
boundaries of Spain's holdings in North America were hazy in 1772,
but those Spanish lands clearly included the Missouri River to its headwaters. This territory had few Europeans, Spanish or otherwise, and
Spain might have had to struggle to defend it, but the Spanish certainly
would have protested, and might have even resisted, a British expedition.
This made government backing for the project problematic.

IN OCTOBER 1772, Rogers, "in despair and drinking heavily," was
imprisoned for debt for a third time and confined for almost two years.
His creditors in 1772 included his British publisher Millan, to whom he
owed money for producing *Ponteach* in 1765. Millan and other creditors
were seeking £1,400. Rogers' imprisonments in London appear to have
been unrelated to his North American debts. There is no evidence that
American creditors pursued him to London. The sums at issue there
were far smaller than those in America and seem to have involved bills
dating to 1765 and debts incurred in 1769 and later. Rogers had been
awarded £3,000 in mid-1770. None of this went to Betsy, so Rogers
should have been able to cover the £1,400 in debt that landed him
prison in 1772, but by then he must have run through the £3,000.[21]

Rogers' long stay in debtors prison largely leaves an informational
blank in his story. Two events stand out. In June 1773, Rogers prepared
another petition to the Privy Council, of which Sir Jeffery Amherst was
now a member. Rogers acknowledged he was petitioning from "Close
Confinement in Fleet prison." He claimed falsely that he was there

"Merely and entirely on Account" of his army service in America. He complained that his confinement had left him "greatly injured in his Health." The petition asked for a land grant of "Sixty Miles Square of Your Majesty's Common Lands," which Rogers promised to subject "to such Modes of Cultivation Population or other Terms of Improvements as may be thought necessary." It was ignored.[22]

In 1774, still in prison, Rogers got wind that Gage was in London and had his former superior served with a lawsuit for trespass, damages, and false imprisonment arising from Rogers' arrest and confinement in Michilimackinac. He sought £20,000 in damages. Gage returned to America without restraint shortly after being served, and Rogers' suit, an obvious publicity stunt, lapsed.[23]

Betsy's parents both died in early 1773. She and Rogers do not appear to have corresponded about this. In March 1774, Rogers sent her a letter, the first she preserved since 1770, addressed to "Mrs. Rogers." Rogers acknowledged a visit from a mutual friend named Parker, who updated him on news from Portsmouth. He concluded the letter testily that he "should have been happy instead of a Verble accont to have had a letter from you."[24]

In June 1774, a new British bankruptcy law facilitated Rogers' release. By signing over to the government whatever property he had, he got his debts discharged and in August 1774 was freed. Two factors kept him in London nearly another year: his quest for money and his need to rehabilitate himself professionally. He successfully petitioned to have his captain's half-pay retirement salary reinstated, bringing him a yearly income of £280. He continued to petition unsuccessfully for a military or governmental position.[25]

Freed from Fleet Prison, Rogers reconciled with Jonathan Carver, who was in London and who remained interested in North American exploration. Carver, initially infuriated at Rogers for telling him his 1766–1767 expedition was authorized, had since petitioned the British government successfully to have the expenses of that expedition, including his salary, paid. Having been reimbursed, Carver was less bitter about Rogers' deceptions, and even conceded that Rogers might have had valid cause to think he was authorized to dispatch the expedition. Carver knew a Member of Parliament, Richard Whitworth, who was eager for an expedition of discovery across western North America following a route like the one Rogers pitched in 1772. Rogers agreed to team with Carver, work with Whitworth, and try to make the expedition a reality.[26]

In early 1775, Rogers drafted a series of documents for Whitworth. These included a memorandum explaining the expedition and its route and contrasting his proposal with a Northwest Passage hunt undertaken exclusively by sea. He advised Whitworth on how to pitch the government, urging him to make sure the expedition would be independent of the military command in North America and of the Department of Indian Affairs. Rogers drafted orders to himself as expedition leader and a lengthy list of needed equipment and supplies. The plan was for Rogers to lay groundwork in America, while in London Whitworth secured Crown approval and funding. If all went well, the expedition would set out in the spring of 1776.[27]

In late May 1775, Rogers, having given up on employment opportunities in London but holding out hope for the Whitworth expedition, resolved to return to America.[28]

AMERICA AGAIN,
1775–1776

ROGERS landed in Baltimore in August 1775, several months into the American colonies' rebellion. He made his way to Philadelphia, where the Pennsylvania Committee of Safety took him into custody as a British military officer, albeit retired. He remained in Philadelphia until late September. As a condition of his release, he gave an undertaking "that I will not bear arms against the American United Colonies, in any manner whatever, during the present contest between them and Great Britain; and I will not in that time, attempt to give intelligence to General Gage, the British Ministerys or any other person or persons, of any matter relating to America." In exchange, the Committee of Safety gave him a certificate addressed "to all persons to whom these presents may appear" recommending that Rogers be "permitted to pass where his business may lead him, without any hindrance or molestation."[1]

In Philadelphia, Rogers met with John Adams and Samuel Adams. According to John Adams' diary, Rogers predicted that "we shall have hot Work, next Spring." He told the Adams cousins an experienced hand like him "would sell well next Spring" and concluded: "if you want me, next Spring for any Service, you know where I am, send for me."[2]

A short while later, Rogers wrote his patron Richard Whitworth in London. Patriot sentiment in Philadelphia had quickly made clear to Rogers how badly he had misjudged doings in the colonies. "I am exceedingly chagrin'd at my present Situation," he wrote. The expedition he and Whitworth had hoped to launch in 1776 was clearly impossible, "as the present times will not permit it to be carried on unless affairs were Settled between the Mother Country and her Colonies." If present circumstances persisted, "every man [in the expedition] wou'd be made prisoners."[3]

From Philadelphia, Rogers traveled to New York, where he stopped to visit New York Chief Justice William Smith, whom he had known from the French and Indian War. Smith described him as "pennyless," a condition he ascribed to Rogers' having "gamed himself into Poverty." Rogers now wanted to satisfy creditors while still preserving "a Farm or two for his own subsistence." Smith, "from meer Motives of Charity to a Prodigal," advised him to pursue land grants from the government for past service and sell them to pay debts. As a neutral who had sworn to take "no Part in the Great Controversy," Smith thought this might work.[4]

Rogers persuaded New York Governor William Tryon, a British appointee, to reissue some old land grants. He and Tryon spoke at length about colonial politics, with Rogers describing the atmosphere in Philadelphia and offering opinions on the ferment there. Tryon reported this conversation to Lord Dartmouth and, based on this and other conversations in late September and early October, went on to vouch for Rogers' "firmness and fidelity" to the Loyalist cause.[5]

The land grants Rogers sought from Tryon would have value only if England retained control of the colonies, giving Rogers a stake in a British victory. Two letters from this period confirm that Rogers, his overture to the Adamses notwithstanding, was solidly committed to England. On September 30, 1775, he wrote to General Gage, apologizing for their previous tensions and asking for a military appointment. Given his Philadelphia undertaking, he asked that the appointment and resulting service be located outside North America. On October 3, 1775, he wrote Board of Trade member John Pownall that "[s]ince my Arrival [in America] I have done all I can to undeceive these People, now laboring under an unhappy Delusion."[6]

Rogers left New York on October 10. His next verifiable location, almost five weeks later, was Hanover, New Hampshire, where he visited Eleazor Wheelock, the head of Dartmouth College.

Rogers' visit to Dartmouth perplexed Wheelock, who eventually reported the encounter to George Washington. Wheelock did not know Rogers, who had stopped at a tavern in the neighborhood for refreshment, and his stated purpose in calling on the academician made no sense to Wheelock. Rogers told him that in London Lord Dartmouth had spoken enthusiastically about Dartmouth College, and that Rogers had come to offer his services in helping to secure land grants to support the college. Wheelock noted that Rogers "was in but ordinary habit, for one of his character," suggesting his shabbily dressed visitor did not look the part of an effective fundraiser, and Wheelock "show[ed] some coldness in accepting" Rogers' proposal.[7]

Given Wheelock's lack of enthusiasm about his offer of assistance, Rogers left, saying "he was in haste to pursue his journey that evening." Instead Rogers spent the night at the tavern he had patronized earlier. The next morning, he told the landlord "he was out of money and could not pay the reckoning, but would pay him on his return." He never returned.[8]

This visit, while odd, likely would not have prompted a letter to Washington, but, more than two weeks after Rogers' departure, two army visitors from an American invasion force at Montreal told Wheelock a British prisoner had reported to them that Rogers had been to Montreal and was acting as second-in-command to Governor and Brigadier General Guy Carleton. Wheelock seems to have concluded that Rogers was in Hanover in connection with a visit to the British forces at Montreal. This news put Rogers in the enemy camp, prompting Wheelock to write to Washington. "If it shall prove of any service to detect such an enemy, I shall be glad."[9]

Wheelock's alert was almost certainly erroneous, but Rogers' reason for being in Hanover remains unclear. Hanover was far to the north of any place where Rogers seemed to have any business. He departed Hanover, directly or indirectly, for Portsmouth and what must have been an awkward reunion with Betsy. He wrote her shortly after leaving Portsmouth for Boston, apologizing, among other things, for having no money to give her.[10]

While Rogers was in New England, General William Howe had taken over from Gage as commander of British forces at Boston. Gage having departed for England, Howe inherited Rogers' request for a military appointment. Rogers made clear that the appointment he wanted had to take him somewhere other than North America, but Howe chose to interpret his appeal to Gage as an implicit offer to join the Loyalist cause. He reported to the Earl of Dartmouth in late November 1775, "I have given [Rogers] encouragement, by desiring him to make his proposals, and by giving an assurance that I am well inclined to do every thing in my power to afford him an opportunity of recommending himself to His Majesty's future favor." It is not clear how or when Howe contacted Rogers to give him this "encouragement." Lord Germain subsequently ratified Howe's attempt to recruit Rogers, telling him that the king approved "your attention to Major Rogers, of whose firmness and fidelity we have received further testimony from Governor Tryon."[11]

In mid-December, Rogers headed for Boston to seek an interview with Washington, then besieging that city. He wrote to the Continental Army commander-in-chief from a Boston suburb detailing his activities since arriving in America. He explained his long detour to the north as a visit to his brother James, who was "deeply concerned" regarding Rogers' efforts to settle his debts because James was "bound for me in several sums of money." He asked to meet with Washington, show him the certificates he had obtained from committees of safety, and obtain from Washington "a continuance of that permission for me to go unmolested where my private business may call me, as it will take some months from this time to settle with all my creditors." He told Washington that, as a retiree, he "never expect[ed] to be called into [British] service again." "I love North America," he assured Washington, "it is my native country and that of my family, and I intend to spend the evening of my days in it."[12]

By now Washington had read Wheelock's letter. He doubted Rogers' intentions. Was he hoping to get information about Continental Army dispositions outside Boston? Did he want the travel authorization to gain access to Patriot-controlled areas while spying for the British? Rather than agree to meet Rogers, Washington sent General John Sullivan to intercept and interrogate him. Sullivan had several meetings with Rogers, asking about Wheelock's report that he had been in Montreal. Rogers denied having been to Montreal and gave an account of his travels since leaving New York: he had gone from New York to Albany, where his progress was delayed by illness, then to the Mohawk Valley, then to western Massachusetts, then to visit his brother in south-central Vermont, all the while looking for parcels of land he might seek to have awarded to him. Rogers insisted witnesses would corroborate his presence at all these locations, but no one seems to have checked, and there is no record of anything that Rogers did during this period. Hanover, New Hampshire, was far to the north of the direct route from his brother's property in Vermont to his next declared stop, Portsmouth, New Hampshire, and Rogers did not explain the detour.[13] His presence in Hanover raises at least the possibility that he was on his way to or from Montreal.

Sullivan seemed satisfied that Rogers had not been to Canada, but he remained suspicious. Rogers already had a certificate from the Pennsylvania Committee of Safety recommending he be given free passage throughout the colonies, so Sullivan "asked him why he came to the camp, as he had no business with any particular persons, and had no inclination to offer his services to the American cause." Rogers responded that he was in the habit of seeking similar interviews with colonial authorities as "a piece of respect due to them," and was doing the same with Washington, from whom he sought a "license to travel unmolested," even if he did not strictly need it. Sullivan remained skeptical: "[w]hat may be his secret designs I am unable to say." He speculated that Rogers might have a mandate from the British to stir up the Indians against the colonial rebels.[14]

Washington declined to meet with Rogers or give him a certificate of safe passage. Rogers was able to have a brief reunion with old friend and fellow former Ranger officer John Stark, now a Continental Army colonel in Washington's camp outside Boston. Stark, a hero of Bunker Hill, subsequently a key player in the Saratoga campaign, was a committed Patriot who assured Rogers that "no proffers of rank or wealth could induce him to abandon the cause of his oppressed country." Rogers was much more ambivalent, telling Stark he had not decided which side to back and wanted "to make the best personal arrangement which circumstances would permit."[15]

Rogers headed to Albany. At Washington's request, General Philip Schuyler spoke with Rogers and further investigated Wheelock's report that Rogers had been in Montreal. Of the Wheelock report, Schuyler concluded "there is no truth in [it]": certain events reported to Wheelock had occurred before Rogers even arrived in America. Because of his valid travel passes from committees of safety, Schuyler allowed him to travel on to New York. Washington responded to Schuyler that he was "apt to believe the intelligence given Dr. Wheelock, respecting Major Rogers was not true, but being much suspected of unfriendly views to this Country, his conduct should be attended with some degree of Vigilance and Circumspection."[16]

In New York, Rogers mainly continued to seek land grants from Governor Tryon. Because of local Patriots' increased hostility, Tryon had decamped to a British ship, *Duchess of Gordon*, in New York harbor. Gradually, Patriot forces tightened restrictions on visits to the British governor, and Rogers' frequent calls on him drew attention. On February 19, 1776, Rogers wrote to the President of the New York Provincial Congress that "[b]usiness of a private nature, and such only as respects myself and my creditors, requires my attendance on board the Duchess of Gordon indispensably necessary." He said that in pursuing "several tracts of land within this Province, I shall be obliged frequently to attend the Governor and Council," and he asked for a blanket "permit to go on board the Governor's ship at any time when my business may require my attendance." Did Rogers really need frequent visits with Tryon for personal business, or was this merely a ruse to have regular contact with the governor? During this time, Rogers also met with British General Clinton about a military appointment outside North America. Clinton invited Rogers to join the Loyalist cause. Rogers said he would "if he could get rid of the oath" he had given when paroled by the Pennsylvania Committee of Safety. Clinton was the second senior British military officer to seek to recruit Rogers.[17]

Whether or not granted the permit he sought, Rogers kept visiting Tryon. Suspicion of Tryon continued to mount and at the end of February 1776, General Charles Lee, commander of colonial forces in New York, banned all visits to British ships in the harbor. Lee's replacement, General William Alexander, also known as Lord Stirling, reiterated the ban. On March 22, 1776, Rogers applied to Alexander for an exception, and for permission to send two men, including a surveyor named Joseph Blanchard, to visit Tryon with documents relating to Rogers' land grant requests. Alexander not only refused permission, he ordered Rogers to leave New York because of his suspicious contacts with Tryon. Rogers' explanation of his need for these visits cannot be disproved, but at the very least he was tone-deaf to the heated politics of the day. Among other things, he ignored the fact that seeking economic benefits from the British would be perceived as aligning with the enemy.[18]

Rogers then disappeared for a crucial two months, during which a major Loyalist conspiracy in New York, allegedly directed by Tryon and intending to assassinate Washington, Israel Putnam, and Nathanael Greene, was brewing. Rogers' whereabouts and activities during the development of this plot are unknown.[19] He next surfaced in Portsmouth, New Hampshire, in early June 1776, when he had a final meeting with Betsy.

Rogers came to Portsmouth in June primarily to solicit a letter from John Langdon, a prominent New Hampshire Patriot and member of the Continental Congress. Rogers asked Langdon to write to two other New Hampshire members of the Continental Congress then in Philadelphia, Joseph Bartlett and William Whipple, urging them to consider Rogers for a military appointment on the Patriot side. Langdon did so, stating that he found Rogers "well inclined and ready to Serve his Country in this Grand Struggle." He asked Bartlett to speak with Rogers and consider employing his "military abilities" if "anything should turn up for his advantage." Langdon gave the letter to Rogers to deliver personally. Langdon later realized his endorsement had been a mistake; he belatedly professed to having had misgivings about writing the letter considering Rogers' "Charectar and person, [which] was well known to most of the Members [of the Continental Congress]."[20]

Rogers' solicitation of the Langdon letter was odd and suspicious. His ostensible desire to serve the Patriot cause was inconsistent with the ambivalence he had declared to Stark, as well as those strong assurances of loyalty to England he had given Tryon, Pownall, and Clinton, among others. Rogers knew members of the Continental Congress and could easily and directly have offered his services, perhaps as a follow-up to his interactions with the Adamses. He had no need to travel to New Hampshire and back for a letter of introduction. But having a letter on his person from a member of the Continental Congress declaring his intent to join the Patriot cause and recommending consideration of this offer would be extremely useful should Patriot authorities detain Rogers. This motive seems a likelier explanation of the Langdon letter.

Letter in hand, Rogers left Portsmouth for points south. While he was in transit, the Loyalist plot in New York was uncovered. Following Howe's evacuation of Boston, Washington had come to New York and camped there with a large army since April. Howe's location was uncertain, but he was believed to be headed to New York by sea. The Loyalist plot was thwarted by its discovery, but it was said the conspirators planned to attack when Howe arrived in New York. A member of Washington's personal guard was implicated and executed. One of the first persons arrested was Joseph Blanchard, whom Rogers had sought in March to send to Governor Tryon on his behalf. This connection cre-

ated a strong suspicion that Rogers was involved in the plot. Tryon's papers from this period are missing, likely destroyed to obscure the conspirators' identities, and it is impossible to know what, if any, role Rogers
played in the plot.[21]

Washington, who had always been suspicious of Rogers, was taking
no chances. He had Rogers arrested on June 26, 1776, and brought to
New York for questioning. Washington and other Continental Army officers interrogated Rogers, and his answers did not satisfy Washington.
Rogers cited the letter he was carrying from Langdon and said he was
traveling to Philadelphia to offer his services to the Continental Congress. He had not declared his interest in joining the Patriot cause publicly, he said, because in the event his offer was declined, he wanted to
be free to seek a position with England but outside North America.
Washington thought it odd that Rogers did not take the most direct route
to Philadelphia, through New York, but instead crossed the Hudson well
north of New York and traveled south through New Jersey. Rogers did
not explain this, although he might have argued that, after his expulsion
from New York in March, he would have felt unwelcome there, and perhaps feared arrest.[22]

The most suspicious fact was that Rogers was found and arrested in
South Amboy, on the far side of Staten Island from New York, where
apparently he had been staying for some time. He told Washington that
he was there waiting for personal effects to be delivered from New York,
a rationale Washington described as a "pretence," and for repayment
of money he was owed by a person in New York, whom Washington
described as "of bad character." If Rogers really was waiting for lug-
gage and money from New York without having to enter the city himself, the logical place to do so would have been on the New Jersey shore
of the Hudson opposite lower Manhattan, not twenty miles south in
South Amboy. South Amboy was where Howe was expected to appear
imminently with his fleet and army, an appearance he in fact made
three days later. Rogers certainly looked as if he was waiting for Howe,
not waiting to offer his services to the Continental Congress in
Philadelphia.[23]

Because the Pennsylvania Committee of Safety had issued Rogers his
parole, Washington did not feel he could detain him indefinitely. He sent
Rogers to Philadelphia under guard, leaving it to Congress to determine
what to do with him. As to Rogers' supposed interest in joining the Patriots, Washington also left that for Congress to decide, although he made

his opinion clear: "I submit it to [Congress's] consideration, whether it would be dangerous to accept the offer of [Rogers'] services."[24]

Rogers arrived in Philadelphia on July 1, 1776, and was taken into custody. He contacted William Whipple, one of the intended recipients of the Langdon letter, telling him he had come on "important business with Congress" and asking Whipple to visit him. Whipple seems to have done so because he wrote to Langdon the same day, apparently aware of Langdon's letter, which Rogers presumably showed him. Whipple had strong misgivings about Rogers. Rogers had not formally made an application to Congress, Whipple noted, but "if he shod I think him a man of too infamous a Carrecter to be imploy'd in the Cause of Vertue."[25]

After holding Rogers for a week, Congress, having declared the United States of America an independent nation, decided to return Rogers to his home state of New Hampshire to be dealt with as authorities there thought appropriate. By this time, New Hampshire legislators had voted to have Rogers taken into custody as "inimical to the Rights and Liberties of Americans." Whether or not he knew this, Rogers undoubtedly suspected what awaited in his home state. He escaped from custody around July 9, 1776, made his way to General Howe on Staten Island, and joined the British forces about to attack New York.[26]

A POWERFUL argument can be made that Rogers intended from the outset to declare himself a Loyalist and that from his most recent arrival in America until June 1776 he was surreptitiously acting on behalf of the crown or at the least planning to declare for the Loyalist side as soon as he had concluded his personal business. His offer of services to the Adamses does not seem to have been serious, and he never followed up with them. His supposed intention of offering his services to the Patriot side in the spring of 1776 does not ring true. He was plainly comfortable confirming his allegiance to England to Tryon, Howe, Clinton, and Pownall. If he had reservations about actively opposing the Patriot cause because of the terms of his parole, this was not a restraint likely to deter him for long.

There are strong reasons to suspect that Rogers was actively working with the British long before his formal defection in July 1776. Tryon seems to have been trying to recruit him from as early as October 1775, Howe from that October or November, and Clinton in February 1776.

Rogers may well have responded to any of these overtures. This would explain his suspicious behavior at Wheelock's house in Hanover, New Hampshire. It would explain his pressing for an unnecessary meeting with Washington in December 1775 outside Boston. It would explain his frequent meetings with Tryon in New York in February and March, and his tarrying in South Amboy just when Howe was expected to arrive there for his assault on New York. Rogers had explanations of varying degrees of plausibility for each of these instances, and none of his explanations can be definitively disproven, but the fact that he had so many things to explain is itself suspicious. He actually could have been pursuing land grants, but that could have been a cover for his travels through the colonies. He was extremely anxious to protect himself from Patriot suspicions on these travels through such devices as the letter he sought from Washington and the letter he obtained from Langdon. He appears to have shown no such concern that the British, or Loyalist Americans, would question his intentions or attempt to interfere with him.

The evidence supports the conclusion that Rogers was always in the Loyalist camp and that, at some point before his detention in June 1776, he began actively to support the British cause against the movement for American independence. But the case is not airtight, and a case can also be made that Rogers was genuinely ambivalent about his loyalties and/or willing to sell his services to the highest bidder and desirous of keeping his options open as long as possible. He said so to John Stark outside Boston: he wanted "to make the best personal arrangement which circumstances would permit."

Even if this somewhat more benign interpretation of Rogers' activities in the ten months after his latest arrival in America were true, he would have wound up on the British side. As the opinions of Smith, Langdon, and Whipple make clear, Rogers had a terrible reputation in America, and when he returned from London in 1775 he had been gone a long six years. He had no friends in positions of power in the America of 1775. England, a rapidly expanding global empire, offered multiple opportunities for adventure and exploration. Rogers' land grants from Tryon would be worthless unless England defeated the colonies. England had a continuing interest in finding the Northwest Passage, which would slash sailing time between the British Isles and the Pacific. America was not likely to fund such an undertaking. Most of all, Rogers was in thrall of and hungry to join the British aristocracy. American Patriots, he believed, were "laboring under an unhappy Delusion." Whether Rogers was an undeclared Loyalist from the beginning or simply waiting to see which side had the better offer, England was sure to win his loyalties.

CHAPTER TWENTY-TWO

LOYALIST

W ILLIAM HOWE commissioned Rogers a lieutenant colonel and authorized him to recruit a battalion of Loyalists to be known as the Queen's American Rangers. Rogers inherited bits and pieces of earlier Loyalist units and began recruiting the remainder of his battalion on Staten Island. When Howe moved to Brooklyn toward the end of August, Rogers and the Queen's Rangers, still coalescing, followed. The unit does not appear to have participated in the Battle of Long Island, Howe's crushing defeat of Washington, but after that British victory, the Queen's Rangers deployed to the north shore of Long Island.[1]

Here occurred Rogers' principal contribution to the British cause. Washington, anxious for intelligence about Howe's plans in the wake of the Battle of Long Island, recruited Nathan Hale to go there and learn what he could. Posing as a Dutch schoolmaster, Hale landed close to the Rangers encampment on Long Island in mid-September. The Rangers were still recruiting, sometimes crossing Long Island Sound to Connecticut for that purpose. Among their duties was interrogating newcomers from Connecticut, both about developments there and to assess their utility as recruits. Rogers apparently immediately became suspicious of Hale.[2]

Rogers' full role in Nathan Hale's capture came to light only in 2000, when descendants of a Revolutionary War Loyalist, Consider Tiffany, donated his manuscript history of the Revolutionary War to the Library of Congress.[3] In Tiffany's account, Rogers decided to trick Hale, a recent Yale graduate with limited experience, none of it in spy craft. He invited Hale to a tavern and over drinks confided that he was uncomfortable on Long Island because "the inhabitants sided with the Britains against the American Colonies." Rogers' own sympathies, he said, were with the colonies. He intimated that he himself was on Long Island on behalf of the Continental Army to assess inhabitants' political leanings and British army movements. He proposed a toast to the Continental Congress. The gullible Hale "believe[d] that he had found a good friend, and one that could be trusted with the secrecy of the business he was ingaged in." He proceeded to "inform[ ] Rogers of [his] business and intent." Rogers invited Hale to dine with him the next day to meet likeminded friends, and after Hale repeated what he had told Rogers the night before, waiting troops arrested him and took him to New York.[4] Hale was hanged as a spy on September 22.[5]

By October, the British controlled the southern portion of Manhattan, the Americans the northern portion. Howe attempted to outflank the foe by landing in the Bronx, forcing Washington to retreat with the bulk of his forces north toward White Plains. The Queen's Rangers rowed across Long Island Sound to join in the pursuit. On October 21, 1776, they were in Mamaroneck, where a young resident writing in a later memoir described Rogers as "a very rough looking red eyed man." Evidently his appearance reflected his drinking.[6]

In Mamaroneck, Rogers fought his only battle of significance during his Revolutionary War service. A body of American troops slipped around behind Rogers' north-facing position on the night of October 22 and approached the Rangers from the more lightly guarded south. The American assault overran a company camped on the south side of the Rangers' position and sent those not killed or captured into retreat. Rogers rallied the main body of his troops and halted any further American advance. When the battle was over, the Americans had killed or captured fifty-five Rangers while suffering far fewer casualties, but in giving Rogers "a bloody nose" they had not scored a decisive victory.[7]

Because of Rogers' fame, Washington considered the destruction of the Queen's Rangers an important objective. The Continental Army made a second attempt to crush the unit in November 1776, but Rogers apparently was alerted about the impending attack and retreated out of the way. In January 1777, following American victories at Trenton and

Princeton, Washington ordered an advance on New York by colonial troops that had remained north of the city. This advance, which would have included the Queen's Rangers among its targets, fizzled without a major battle.[8]

Rogers was no longer the fearsome adversary Washington took him to be, and what the Continental Army could not accomplish, Rogers visited on himself. An audit of the Queen's Rangers by the Inspector-General of Britain's American Provincials concluded that they were hopelessly undisciplined and ineffective and recommended that the unit undergo a "thorough reformation." This was based on a finding that both officers and enlisted men were unqualified for their positions. The usual class and racial snobbery suffused the Inspector-General's findings. He complained that Rogers enlisted "Negroes, Indians, Mulattoes, Sailors and Rebel prisoners," and that many officers were "persons very improper to hold any commission," i.e., shopkeepers, mechanics, tavern owners, and others of the lower orders. Complaints about Ranger quality, discipline, and effectiveness had dogged Rogers throughout the French and Indian War, and the Queen's Rangers were a motley assortment mostly of city dwellers with little or no military experience. Howe, who had attempted to recruit Rogers in 1775 and who had without hesitation given him his command after his official defection in July 1776, readily accepted his Inspector-General's recommendation and required Rogers and most of his officers to resign. Howe would hardly have done so if he thought the Queen's Rangers were an effective fighting unit.[9]

Although Howe forced Rogers to retire from active duty, he allowed Rogers to continue recruiting. He likely believed that Rogers' name recognition would be helpful in this role. Rogers' recruiting efforts were desultory. There is some evidence that he engaged in recruiting during the spring of 1777, but he then largely disappeared for a year.[10]

In the spring of 1778, Rogers resurfaced with a new idea. Reasoning that the quality issues afflicting the Queen's Rangers stemmed from the men's urban backgrounds and lack of scouting or fighting experience, he proposed recruiting a Ranger force composed predominantly of frontiersmen from Canada and northern New England. He expected to find such men in Canada, which was both loyal to England and a refuge for expatriate American Loyalists. General Clinton, the British commander in New York, without approving or disapproving the proposal, gave Rogers permission to travel to Quebec and present the proposal to General Haldimand, the Governor there.[11]

During the French and Indian War, Haldimand had been one of the commanding officers at Fort Edward, where the Rangers had their base. Although he never developed the bitter antagonism toward Rogers that his predecessor Haviland did, Haldimand had had to mediate a dispute over rank between Rogers and a regular army officer, and, during a period when Rogers was away recuperating from frostbite, Haldimand had experienced an alarming series of incidents in which Rangers refused to go on scouting missions he had ordered. He undoubtedly shared the poor opinion of the Rangers that was widespread in the British regular army during the French and Indian War, a disdain likely reinforced by the news that Rogers had been forced to resign and his Queen's Rangers had had to be reorganized because of quality issues. In October 1778, Haldimand turned down Rogers' proposal, either because he doubted the effectiveness of the troops Rogers proposed to raise or because others were recruiting in Canada and Haldimand did not want too many recruiters competing for a limited pool of qualified candidates.[12]

Thwarted, Rogers decided to leave Quebec and sailed for London, seeking, as usual, to secure a perch somewhere in the empire. He got none, but he did obtain a fistful of testimonials to his talent and energy from supporters in London. He returned with these to New York, and in the spring of 1779, Clinton authorized him to raise two battalions of Rangers, each of over six hundred officers and men to be recruited in Canada and northern New England. Robert was to command one battalion, his older brother James the second.[13]

While in London, Rogers had renewed his acquaintance with Lord Amherst, who apparently encouraged him to write from America. Rogers sent a letter on June 16, 1779. He gave Amherst the good news about his orders to raise two Ranger battalions and provided an upbeat summary of the war, declaring, "[i]f Great Britain will persevere, America must soon be conquered." In a postscript, he got to the real point: "I flatter myself that my good Lord Amherst will not forget an old soldier, who has had the Honor to share in some of his glorious fateagues in America last War—but procure him some little addition to his present Rank in the British Army."[14]

Raising two battalions of qualified Rangers proved more easily said than done. In New York, recruiting was slow going. Rogers proposed sending recruiting officers to Quebec, both to recruit there and to receive and train recruits enlisted elsewhere and sent to muster in Quebec. He hoped that until the two battalions were operational, Governor

Haldimand would cover the pay and provisioning of recruits already signed up. James, who had previously commanded a body of Loyalists in Quebec and who had a good relationship with Haldimand, went to Quebec to oversee recruiting and training. Haldimand worried, as before, about too many recruiters competing for a limited supply of candidates. He prohibited James from recruiting in Canada, restricting him to the colonies. He also said he had no authority to pay recruits already enlisted and allowed them only half-pay as a stopgap. James's recruiting efforts stalled.[15]

While James was heading to Quebec, Rogers joined a British regular army expedition to reinforce Penobscot Bay, Maine, which British forces had recently seized from the colonies and which American forces were threatening to recapture. The British relief force destroyed an American naval force, and Rogers, landing after the battle, was able to sign up a few recruits for his Ranger battalions. In Nova Scotia he signed a few more. From Halifax, Rogers sent a second letter to Amherst. After describing the British victory at Penobscot Bay, he reported falsely that he had recruited an entire battalion of Rangers, now training in Canada. Neither he nor James had signed up more than a few dozen men. Rogers told Amherst that "in a short time I flatter myself your Lordship will hear of a spirited attack by my Indians & Rangers on the middle Frontier, to the great detriment of the Rebels." He followed with his usual pitch: he expected his attack to bring "such credit to myself as may entitle me to expect that [illegible] Generosity & Patronage I have ever received from Your Lordship." The British did unleash devastating attacks on the "middle frontier"—central New York—in 1779, 1780, and 1781, using Indian forces and apparently well-commanded Loyalist units, but Rogers had no role in these campaigns, nor is there any evidence that Haldimand contemplated giving him one.[16]

By the fall of 1779, Rogers had succeeded in recruiting at most forty men, not enough for a company, let alone a battalion. He decided to travel to Quebec to join James. He arrived to find that James had left for Montreal and then Fort St. Jean on the Richelieu River. In Quebec, Rogers disgraced himself, apparently because of drink. He pestered Haldimand to provide more money for pay and provisions for Rangers still "in training" in Quebec, falsely telling him that a letter was en route from the Halifax paymaster to the Quebec paymaster authorizing the payment. He lied to Haldimand that he had recruited a full seven hundred men, four hundred at Penobscot Bay, and three hundred closer to

Quebec. He presented a bill for £469 for the expenses of recruiting officers who had come to Quebec with James in mid-1779. The bill turned out to include sums Rogers needed to repay loans he had cadged from these officers. He lived on credit, and he borrowed money everywhere that he was unable to repay. Complaints about his debts and his drinking reached Haldimand. Without realizing the full scope of Rogers' misconduct, Haldimand gave him some of the expense money he requested but required him to return to Penobscot Bay, the primary post of his supposed Ranger battalion.[17]

Then came a bombshell. Haldimand suspected Rogers was exaggerating when he claimed to have enlisted seven hundred men; he was staggered to learn from the British commander at Penobscot Bay that the true number was "not above 40." Haldimand had his secretary write to James Rogers, who had not been in Quebec during the time his brother was there, detailing Robert's "extraordinary behavior," which had "injured and disgraced the service." James responded immediately and directly to Haldimand. "The conduct of my brother of late has almost unman'd me," he said. He explained that he had written to Robert repeatedly "in regard to his conduct and as often he promised to reform—I am sorry his good talents should so unguarded fall a prey to Intemperance."[18]

Rogers reached Halifax in April 1780. In May, he sent a final, odd letter to Amherst regarding his plans to recruit in Newfoundland, asking "your Lordship [to] give orders to the Military Officer Commanding in that Place to give me or my Officers all the Assistance he can which will much promote his Majesty's Service." Amherst, although a cabinet member and acting commander in chief in Great Britain, had no position in the military chain of command in North America. Even if he had, it would have been completely inappropriate for so senior an official to issue orders directly to a local officer about a minor operational matter. Rogers was simply hoping to showcase the support he thought he had from Amherst.[19]

Before this letter could reach its addressee, Rogers was again imprisoned, this time in Halifax for a debt approaching £600. The Halifax military commander said the debt was "due to [Rogers'] own mismanagement." Again a mound of debt had nothing to do with anything except Rogers' perpetually living beyond his means, aggravated by unauthorized spending of government funds and unsuccessful attempts to get the army to pay his personal expenses.[20]

Rogers was released from jail only after James guaranteed payment of the debt for which his brother had been imprisoned. James apparently also made good on Rogers' other Canadian debts. James had never recovered the £3,430 he had given Nathaniel Wheelwright to retire a loan Wheelwright had made to Robert. He had undoubtedly bailed Robert out on other occasions over the years. He had been thoroughly embarrassed by Robert's Quebec behavior, which threatened his own professional standing. Now he had had enough. After Robert's release from the Halifax jail, there is no evidence the two brothers ever communicated again.[21]

Rogers left Halifax for New York in December 1780. His ship was captured almost immediately by an American privateer. He was held as a prisoner of war for eight months or more, apparently released in a prisoner exchange in August or September 1781, shortly before Cornwallis' defeat at Yorktown. By this time, New Hampshire had barred him from returning to the colony for his support of the Loyalist cause. He was no longer on speaking terms with either his wife or his brother. He had nowhere to go in America. He returned to London sometime after being repatriated.[22]

THE FINAL YEARS

ROGERS lived another thirteen and a half years in almost complete obscurity, with none of the press attention of his French and Indian War years that reverberated after his first return. According to Robert J. Rogers, a descendant of his older brother James, Rogers "spent the last twelve years of his life living impoverished and improvidently in London," where his life "[drew] to an end in misery, partially brought on by an excessive use of alcohol."[1] Others echo this dismal assessment: Rogers led "a dissolute and improvident life" during his final years.[2] His "drinking continued" in his final years, periodically erupting in "drunken frenzies."[3] "The last thirteen years of Rogers' life were spent in drunken frenzies and the monotonous routine of debtors prison."[4] "Rogers ended his days a lonely exile, seeking blessed oblivion in the bottle."[5] During his last years, Rogers "spent much of his time in pubs and Debtors' prison."[6]

Rogers was not literally impoverished. His retired officer's half-pay of £280, equivalent to more than $50,000 in today's money, was, in an era before income taxes, "ample for the maintenance of life in comfort."[7] Rogers was not homeless or a derelict, but he lived recklessly beyond his means, constantly besieged by creditors. In May 1784, having been in

London for no more than two and a half years, he was imprisoned for six months for debts totaling £268, equivalent to a year's income. In late 1785, he was imprisoned for debt for three and a half years. He authorized the army to pay his retired officer's allowance directly to creditors in satisfaction of debts in 1781, 1788, 1793, and 1794.[8] He lived in Southwark, a poor, crowded, and unfashionable neighborhood south of the Thames and near the King's Bench debtors prison, where he spent more than three years between 1785 and 1789.[9]

A handful of anecdotes illustrate Rogers' life during these years, although their reliability is open to question. A Dublin newspaper reported Rogers having a drunken confrontation in a pub with a table of British army officers that almost turned violent in late 1784 or early 1785. An American newspaper reported him arriving in New York in September 1785 with an unidentified "Lady" and a menagerie "consisting of a female bear, two dogs, a bitch, a brace of quails, and a young robin." In July 1786, while in debtors prison, Rogers was charged with assault and breach of the peace. In 1787, he may have had a final confrontation with Benjamin Roberts in which he threw Roberts into a freshly dug grave and kicked dirt on him. Toward the end of his life, he is said to have bewildered his landlord by calling out names and places from the past while intoxicated.[10]

These anecdotes, together with the facts about Rogers' chronic problems with debt, support a grim assessment of his later years as a period dominated by drink, barely contained anger that sometimes exploded in violence, and financial irresponsibility. These traits were always part of Rogers' character. Whether alcohol abuse was a cause or a symptom, Rogers was always undisciplined, irresponsible, and insubordinate, with a quick temper and many enemies. For many years, press adulation papered over these flaws, and powerful patrons were prepared to overlook them. Over time, however, Rogers alienated the press and the patrons, and the sad life of his final years was all that remained.

Rogers died on May 18, 1795. He was 63. His death drew little attention in London, where his most frequently cited obituary was short. Seeming to confuse Rogers' service in the French and Indian War with his service in the Revolutionary War, the obituarist called him "a man of uncommon strength" who "performed prodigious feats of valor during the late war." The article concluded that "long confinement in the Rules of the King's Bench, had reduced him to the most miserable state of wretchedness."[11]

More remarkable than the limited coverage of Rogers' death in London was the complete absence of coverage in America. After the Revolutionary War, Rogers, a despised Loyalist, "vanished from the face of the Earth as far as the United States of America was concerned." His death was not reported in the United States, and no one in his family or circle of former friends and associates was aware of when and where he died. America would not learn until the twentieth century that Rogers died in London in 1795.[12]

CONCLUSION

ROBERT ROGERS was brave, strong, physically imposing, and capable of great feats of endurance. He was an outstanding scout and a capable small-unit raider. He had a charismatic personality. These qualities made him genuinely newsworthy, particularly during the early years of the French and Indian War, when the British and colonial war effort was otherwise generally lackluster and ineffective. To the colonial press, it was all the better that Rogers was a colonial, not a British, hero. Rogers eagerly embraced and then actively exploited his unexpected celebrity, and when he realized journalists were interested, he fed them stories, often embellished, about his exploits. Once the media narrative took root, it took on a life of its own, and once Rogers became a celebrity, he remained newsworthy for two decades.

Rogers' accomplishments, however, never matched his media image. He never became a truly effective military leader. His newsworthy adventures were mostly of a personal nature: acts of boldness or individual valor, and daring escapes in the face of impossible odds. With Rogers personally in command of smaller scouting and raiding parties, he achieved outstanding results, and he had an enviable, if not unblemished, record of keeping his men safe. Commanding larger bodies of troops, by contrast, Rogers' record was poor. Undisciplined himself, he was never able to forge, and then lead, a disciplined Ranger fighting force. Impulsive and cocky, he was prone to making avoidable mistakes.

He lacked the management and leadership skills to be an effective commander of any significant body of troops.

His best-known battles—the January 1757 ambush, the Battle on Snowshoes, the attack on St. Francis—were defeats. The loss after the St. Francis raid was self-inflicted, but a defeat nonetheless. The Battle on Snowshoes was catastrophic. All these setbacks were attributable, in whole or in part, to Rogers' deficiencies as a commander: his inability to control his troops, and his tactical or strategic errors.

Rogers never had a victory comparable in scale to any of these defeats.[1] The Battle of Fort Anne resulted in similarly large casualties, but with much greater numbers of fighters involved on both sides, and it cannot be considered a credit to Rogers' skills as a commander. The battle came about entirely because of Rogers' carelessness, participating in a target-shooting contest with a large enemy force nearby. As a result, it was not a battle fought according to plan. Instead, the fighting was chaotic and reactive. Rogers personally fought bravely, but the British regulars, who held their ground after the original ambush, preventing a rout and allowing the British and colonial force to bring their superior numbers to bear, were at least as responsible for the favorable outcome as Rogers and the Rangers. Although the British and colonial troops forced the French to retreat with heavy losses, they sustained heavy losses of their own.

The only battle that does Rogers any credit was the battle near Isle aux Noix in 1760. There, Rogers showed battlefield dexterity, picking an easily defended position for the Rangers, engaging in a skillful flanking maneuver that caught the numerically superior enemy by surprise, and forcing them to retreat. This victory achieved Rogers' immediate tactical objective, allowing him to get past Isle aux Noix for a raid further north. That raid, in turn, was highly successful, throwing the French off balance and netting dozens of prisoners without incurring significant additional casualties. The campaign, however, was neither decisive nor lopsided. In the initial battle, the Rangers sustained nearly as many casualties as they inflicted, and the positive results of the campaign were achieved against an enemy generally demoralized and in retreat.

Rogers was able to parlay this uninspiring record into fame and acclaim throughout the colonies and England through the simple expedient of exaggerating, and ultimately outright lying about, the outcomes of his most important battles and campaigns. Already a hero to the press and public, he transformed simple, obvious defeats into stunning, against-all-odds victories, secure in the knowledge that it would take years, even decades, for the truth to become widely known. His peers were not fooled, however, and their judgments about his military talents were consistent. For Gage, he was "not much addicted to Regularity" and his "schemes are very wild," i.e., he was not suited to a responsible position of command.[2] For Wolfe, he was "an excellent partisan for 2 or 300 men," i.e., an effective small-scale raider, not suited to more general command.[3] For Sir William Johnson, he was "a good Ranger," but "Nature [has not] calculated him for a large Command."[4] For an early biographer of John Stark, Rogers lacked "generalship," and "his force of character ran in minor adventures."[5]

The kind of fighting Rogers and the Rangers engaged in was not new. It consisted of the relatively straightforward hit-and-run raiding and defense against such raiding that have characterized frontier warfare for millennia. Rangering was well-entrenched in the frontier regions of all the American colonies long before Rogers. His Rules of Rangering were largely common-sense guidance, and they were of limited value to the British trainees to whom they were addressed. As one commentator put it, the Rules of Rangering "probably did not represent exactly the key to forest warfare sought by Loudoun."[6] These directives were too specific, in that they failed to express any broader of vision of irregular warfare, and at the same time they were too general, in that they failed to discuss the nuts and bolts of survival on the woodland frontier.[7] The training program for which Rogers wrote the Rules does not appear to have been repeated beyond a single session. The only truly unique operation in which Rogers engaged was the raid on St. Francis. That action arguably looks like something out of the U.S. Navy Seals playbook, but it was poorly thought out, poorly planned, and a costly mistake that Rogers never attempted to repeat. Special forces units like the Green Berets and the Seals have many antecedents, but Rogers was not a particularly important one and cannot be credited with being their spiritual father.[8]

Nor can Rogers be credited with formalizing informal irregular warfare practices of the frontier and using them to create an effective scouting and raiding force that could assist and supplement the regular army. The grudging admiration that many British officers had for Rogers' personal energy and boldness did not extend to the Rangers as a fighting force. The Rangers were notorious for poor discipline. Their companies were chronically under strength. There were constant complaints about the quality of Ranger recruits. And all this came despite their earning premium pay as a supposedly elite force.

The consistency of the negative British view of the Rangers is striking. Captain Abercrombie, following a scout with the Rangers, was beside himself with anger and frustration at their poor discipline and had a dozen of them cashiered.[9] His uncle Lord Abercromby conceded that, without Rogers, the Rangers were "good for nothing."[10] Wolfe called them "the worst soldiers in the universe."[11] Gage advised Amherst they were "not very alert in obeying orders."[12] Amherst, on his own, concluded they were the "most Careless, Negligent, Ignorant Corps I ever saw."[13] Several years later, turning down Rogers' proposal for a permanent, post-war Ranger force to patrol the frontier, with Rogers in command, Amherst bluntly told Rogers that, his personal regard for Rogers aside, Amherst had a "very Despicable [opinion] of the Rangers."[14] Dr. Huck, a British physician serving in Albany in 1759, pronounced the Rangers "not worth a Farthing."[15]

Not surprisingly, Canadian historians take a more skeptical view of the Rangers than do their American counterparts. One concludes, with understatement, that the Rangers were "probably not quite so formidable as they have been made out to be," while another says bluntly that they were "highly overrated."[16]

One last way of looking at Rogers' military record is to compare it to the record of his enemy counterparts, the Indians and the Canadian partisans fighting on the French side of the French and Indian War. While Rogers had a handful of modestly successful raids offset by multiple major defeats, his Canadian and Indian adversaries dominated irregular warfare on the frontier, seemingly able to strike at will, often devastatingly, behind British lines and in the no man's land between enemy lines. To take just the most noteworthy examples of Indian and Canadian partisan success on the Lake George front, their raiding parties killed or captured at least eighty-five British and colonial troops in a series of attacks in the spring and summer of 1756 between Albany and Lake George.[17] In the summer of 1757, a large Canadian partisan and Indian force ambushed and annihilated a large party of New Jersey Blues provincial regiment under Colonel Parker at Sabbath Point on Lake George, killing seventy and capturing 150.[18] In 1758, a Canadian and Indian irregular force attacked a huge supply train on the road between Fort Edward and the site of Fort William Henry, killing more than one hundred troops and civilians, taking dozens of prisoners, and ransacking almost forty wagonloads of supplies.[19] In 1759, Ranger Captain Burbank, with a force of thirty Rangers, was ambushed and wiped out to a man.[20] And, of course, the French and the Indians defeated Rogers in January 1757 and March 1758, inflicting heavy casualties. Rogers had nothing approaching this record of success.

In the irregular warfare competition, the Canadians and Indians clearly came in first. Despite a press and public reputation at odds with reality, Rogers could boast only a mixed and modest record at the end of the French and Indian War. And the French and Indian War was the high point of his career. From there it was all downhill.

O N a personal level, Rogers was outgoing, gregarious, an entertaining storyteller, and generally good company. He seems to have cared about the men who served under him, and they seem to have responded with loyalty and esteem. At the same time, Rogers had extremely troubling character flaws.

Foremost of these was dishonesty. By the mid-1760s, Rogers had acquired a general reputation for dishonesty that rested on a history of dishonest acts dating to his early adulthood. His participation in the distribution of counterfeit currency in 1754 was dishonest, and his plainly false testimony about the episode is striking for its audacity; one of the investigating justices facing him knew from personal experience that Rogers was lying. His scouting and battlefield reports, consistently exaggerated in his favor, were for a while within the range of what might be regarded as reasonable embellishments or honest mistakes, but his report of the St. Francis battle was utterly and deliberately false. Readers in the colonies or in England could not have known this, but his army colleagues certainly did. He filed inflated claims for expense reimbursement with Amherst, Gage, and his British superiors in Canada during the Revolutionary War. At the outset, these claims might have reflected good faith disagreements or mistakes, although Amherst's frustration with Rogers during the claims reconciliation process suggests otherwise. In claims submitted to Gage, Rogers was plainly just making things up. In private life, Rogers paid South Carolina creditors with counterfeit money; he gave worthless notes to Boyd; and he walked out on his lodging bill in Hanover, New Hampshire, to cite examples. At times, Rogers seemed to relish the game of cheating, or attempting to cheat, people he did business with.

Rogers was also chronically profligate. When it comes to spending and saving, the range of "normal" behavior is extremely broad, but Rogers' behavior was not within that range. His uncontrollable spending ruined his personal credit, then ruined his reputation, then led to a total of more than six years in debtors prison. And Rogers was not the only victim of his financial irresponsibility. Apart from arms-length creditors, Rogers constantly cadged money from friends, associates, and relatives that he never repaid, at times apparently using his position of authority to coerce subordinates to give him loans. Enormous debts for which his brother James wound up being responsible brought the final and complete break between the brothers. He never provided financial support for his wife and son.

Even allowing for the patriarchal view of the family that prevailed in the eighteenth century, Rogers was an abusive and irresponsible husband. He and Betsy appear to have been badly mis-matched, she the daughter of a city minister who took concepts of duty and ethical behavior seriously, he an unruly frontiersman given to drinking, gambling, womanizing, and extravagant living. His primary motive for the marriage appears to have been to improve his social status. Rogers' way of dealing with the incompatibility was to simply ignore Betsy. Professional obligations may have separated them for long periods, but even when he had no obligations, he invariably dawdled with friends or attended to business rather than spend time with her. As she learned from her Michilimackinac experience, this studied inattention was better than the alternative. Rogers' indifference to Betsy might have been forgivable if he had at least provided her with financial support, but he was consistently unable to support himself, much less any dependents. The marriage could not have been pleasant for him, but it must have been a nightmare for Betsy.

What role alcohol played in these failings is difficult to determine. This was an age when drinking water was generally unsafe, and many adults drank alcoholic beverages, albeit of generally low potency, throughout the day. As a result, chronic heavy drinking was not likely to be noticed or remarked upon, and alcoholism and its effect on behavior were not well understood. The best conclusion is that Rogers' alcoholism exacerbated pre-existing self-destructive traits—lack of discipline, irresponsibility, and disdain for social norms—and that this effect likely took hold far earlier in Rogers' life than is generally recognized. It seems highly probable that alcoholism explains some of Rogers' bizarre be-

havior at Michilimackinac. It seems likely that drink partly brought on
the crippling debts he had run up by the early 1760s and his indulgence
in the "unlawful pleasures and passions" that troubled the Reverend
Browne in 1764.

With respect to his political sympathies and leanings, there is a narrative about Rogers, rooted in his British army experience in the 1750s
and 1760s, that portrays him as a natural egalitarian democrat whose
native talent was stifled by a rigid, hierarchical British military and political system. This narrative is undermined by Rogers' emergence as an
aggressive Loyalist during the Revolutionary War. More importantly, it
misreads Rogers as a person. He may have been a product of the frontier, but he was always attracted to, and in awe of, the British aristocracy,
and he longed for nothing so much as to be an aristocrat in a hierarchical
society. The profound respect that Rogers shows in the *Journals* for Governor Shirley, Lord Loudoun, General Abercromby, Lord Howe, and
Lord Amherst is more than just playing to a London audience: he
revered the status these people enjoyed. He never stopped groveling before his aristocratic nemesis Thomas Gage as he sought appointments
commensurate with what he believed to be his worth. He relished his
audiences with King George III, and he relished hobnobbing with aristocrats like Amherst, Townshend, and Whitworth. He really wanted to
be a baronet.

It is probably most accurate to say that Rogers had no profound feelings about the American movement for independence; he was far too
preoccupied with personal concerns to delve deeply into politics. To the
extent that he had feelings, however, he had no sympathy for the colonial
sense of grievance against the mother country or his fellow Americans'
craving for independence. He regarded both as an "unhappy Delusion."[21]

Rogers' neighbor, friend, and fellow ranger John Stark was quieter,
steadier, and less flamboyant. He was a committed Patriot, and he
proved to be a highly successful colonial militia commander during the
Revolutionary War. He fought with distinction at Bunker Hill, and he
was the victor at the Battle of Bennington in the Saratoga campaign.
Overall, his military accomplishments were far more impressive than
his former comrade's. Stark is a better example of colonial achievement
than the much more famous Robert Rogers.

NOTES

AUTHOR'S NOTE

1. Eric W. Nye, "Pounds Sterling to Dollars: Historical Conversions of Currency," available online at https://www.uwyo.edu/nominate/currency.edu.

PREFACE

1. Ross, John F., *War on the Run: The Epic Story of Robert Rogers and the Conquest of America's First Frontier* (New York: Bantam Books, 2009) (hereafter "Ross"), 108.
2. Zaboly, Gary Stephen, *A True Ranger: The Life and Many Wars of Major Robert Rogers* (Garden City, New York: Royal Blockhouse LLC, 2004) (hereafter "Zaboly"), vi.
3. Todish, Timothy J., ed., *The Annotated and Illustrated Journals of Major Robert Rogers* (Fleischmann's, New York: Purple Mountain Press, 2002) (hereafter "*Journals*"), 49. This edition of Rogers' *Journals* includes editorial comments interspersed with Rogers' original text. Where the speaker is the editor rather than Rogers, I have so indicated with the notation "(editor)" following the cited page number.

CHAPTER ONE: THE EARLY YEARS

1. Zaboly, 17, 33, 52.
2. Zaboly, 12-13.
3. Zaboly, 32.
4. Zaboly, 34.
5. Zaboly, 32, 59-60.
6. Zaboly, 39-46.
7. Ibid.
8. Zaboly, 47.
9. Zaboly, 55.
10. Moore, Howard Parker, *John Stark of Rogers' Rangers* (United Kingdom: Leonaur Press, 2020) (hereafter "*John Stark*"), 118.
11. Eggleston, Michael A., *One Man's Traitor is Another's Patriot: George Washington & Robert Rogers* (CreateSpace, 2007) (hereafter "Eggleston"), 10.
12. Zaboly, 56.

13. *Journals*, 27.

14. Zaboly, 56-58.

15. Brumwell, Stephen, *White Devil: A True Story of War, Savagery, and Vengeance in Colonial America* (Cambridge, Massachusetts: Da Capo Press, 2004) (hereafter "Brumwell"), 49; Ross, 51.

16. Brumwell, 47.

17. Ross, 51-54.

18. Ross, 55-57.

19. Zaboly, 63-65.

20. Zaboly, 60; Rogers, Robert J., *Rising Above Circumstances: The Rogers Family in Colonial America* (Bedford, Quebec, Canada: Sheltus & Picard, 1998) (hereafter "*Rising Above Circumstances*"), 7-8. Robert J. Rogers is a direct descendant of James Rogers, Robert's older brother.

21. *Rising Above Circumstances*, 8. £1944 would have a present-day value of almost $400,000.

22. Zaboly, 64.

23. *Rising Above Circumstances*, 8.

CHAPTER TWO: THE COUNTERFEITER

1. Alld v. Rogers, New Hampshire Provincial Court Case No. 05066, New Hampshire State Archives, Concord, New Hampshire (hereafter "New Hampshire State Archives"); Zaboly, 67.

2. Ibid.

3. Counterfeiting Investigation Proceedings, New Hampshire Provincial Court Case No. 027267, New Hampshire State Archives (hereafter "Counterfeiting Investigation").

4. Zaboly, 72-73.

5. Examination of John McCurdy, Counterfeiting Investigation; Zaboly, 73.

6. Examination of Robert Rogers, Counterfeiting Investigation.

7. Examination of John McCurdy, Counterfeiting Investigation.

8. Examination of Robert Rogers, Counterfeiting Investigation.

9. Examination of John Stark, Counterfeiting Investigation.

10. Order Directing Counterfeiting Inquiry, February 5, 1755, Counterfeiting Investigation.

11. Examination of Robert Rogers, Counterfeiting Investigation.

12. Ibid. Rogers was not the only suspect to give implausible denials about participation in the counterfeiting ring. Ezekiel Greele testified that Sullivan boarded with him for a week, said he could make counterfeit money, and asked him to participate, but he declined. Like Rogers, Greele testified he had been cautioned strenuously by Joseph Blanchard, Jr., against any involvement. (Examination of Ezekiel Greele.) Similarly, James McNeil testified that Sullivan showed him plates for making counterfeit currency but that he refused to participate. (Examination of James McNeil.) Other witnesses, however, implicated both Greele and McNeil. (Counterfeiting Investigation.) William Alld, the seller of the Merrimack property that Rogers was unable to pay for, was called to testify but refused to answer any questions. (Examination of William Alld.)

13. Zaboly, 76.

14. Examination of Carty Gilman, New Hampshire Provincial Court Case No. 026954, New Hampshire State Archives. Because Gilman was examined some months later, by a different panel of investigators, his examination has a different case number.

15. Zaboly, 76 and fn. 29.

16. Examination of Carty Gilman, New Hampshire Provincial Court Case No. 026954.

17. Zaboly, 128.

18. Zaboly, 77-78.

19. Ibid.
20. Zaboly, 77-78, 127.

CHAPTER THREE: EARLY RANGERING

1. Zaboly, 89-90, 94-97.
2. O'Toole, Fintan, *White Savage: William Johnson and the Invention of America* (Albany, New York: State University of New York, 2005) (hereafter "*White Savage*"), 2-3, 68-69, 96-97, 102-104, 162-165, 169-177, 203-206, 211, 213, 282; Flexner, James Thomas, *Mohawk Baronet: A Biography of Sir William Johnson* (Syracuse, New York: Syracuse University Press, 1989, reprinting a manuscript originally published in 1959) (hereafter "*Mohawk Baronet*"), 65, 82, 152, 185-187, 201-208; Zaboly, 97, 103. A more southerly nation of Iroquois-speaking Indians, the Tuscarora, joined the federation in the early eighteenth century, making it the Six Nations.
3. Zaboly, 90, 98-100.
4. *White Savage*, 135-140; *Mohawk Baronet*, 142-146; Zaboly, 99.
5. Zaboly, 100.
6. *White Savage*, 153-154; Johnson, Sir William, *The Papers of Sir William Johnson* (Albany, New York: University of the State of New York, 1921-1965) (hereafter "Johnson Papers"), v. 2, 343-350. The Johnson Papers are cited hereafter as "Johnson Papers, [volume]:[page]." They are widely available online from multiple sources.
7. Zaboly, 103.
8. Shirley to Johnson, June 16, 1755, Hough, F.B., ed., *Journals of Major Robert Rogers* (Albany, New York: Joel Munsell's Sons, 1888) (hereafter "Hough Edition"), 206-209. This edition of Rogers' *Journals*, available online, contains an appendix of important documents following the Rogers text. All citations to the Hough Edition are to documents in this appendix. Johnson to Delancey, September 4, 1755, Johnson Papers, 2:6-9; Johnson to Cockcroft, September 15, 1755, ibid., 40-41; Johnson to Shirley, September 22, 1755, ibid., 73-78.
9. Johnson to Orem, September 18, 1755, ibid., 52; Johnson to Hardy, October 24, 1755, ibid., 238.
10. Ibid., 282-283.
11. Lake George flows north, emptying into Lake Champlain via the La Chute River. Lake Champlain also flows north, emptying into the Richelieu River, a tributary of the St. Lawrence. Traveling north on either lake is thus going "down" the lake, while traveling south is going "up."
12. *Journals*, 33-34; Zaboly, 104-106; Cuneo, John R., *Robert Rogers of the Rangers* (New York: Oxford University Press, 1959, reprinted by Richardson & Steirman, 1987) (hereafter "Cuneo"), 22-23; Ross, 83-87.
13. Wraxall to Johnson, October 3, 1755, Johnson Papers, 2:134.
14. *Journals*, 35; Cuneo, 24; Ross, 88-89; Zaboly, 107-108.
15. *Journals*, 35, 39; Ross, 89; Zaboly, 108; Cuneo, 24.
16. Minutes of Council of War, September 27, October 9, 1755, Johnson Papers, 2:107, 159; Johnson to Fitch, October 13, 1755, ibid., 186-188; Minutes of Council of War, October 20, 1755, Thompson-Pell Research Center, Ticonderoga, New York, Manuscript Collection Table of Contents No. 2030.
17. Shirley to Johnson, September 19, 24, 25, 1755, Johnson Papers, 2:57-62, 95-98, 100.
18. Shirley to Johnson, September 28, 1755, ibid., 111-112.
19. Wraxall to Johnson, October 3, 1755, ibid., 134.
20. Banyar to Johnson, ibid., 242; *see also* Zaboly, 109.

21. Minutes of Council of War, October 13, 1755, Johnson Papers, 2:187.

22. Johnson to Hardy, October 13, 1755, ibid., 190; Zaboly, 110.

23. Journals, 39; Ross, 92-93; Zaboly, 113.

24. Mohawk Baronet, 63.

25. Journals, 49, 47.

26. Journals, 99-10; Ross, 93-96; Zaboly, 115.

27. Journals, 40; Banyar to Johnson, November 11, 1755, Johnson Papers, 2:287.

28. Johnson to Shirley, November 11, 12, 1755, Johnson Papers, 2:290, 294; Johnson to Putnam, November 16, 1755, ibid., 302; Zaboly, 116.

29. Cuneo, 26; Johnson to Shirley, November 17, 1755, Johnson Papers, 2:307.

30. Bagley to Johnson, November 27, 1755, Johnson Papers, 9:324.

31. Zaboly, 117-118.

32. Zaboly, 334-335.

33. Journals, 41; Ross, 97-101; Zaboly, 119.

34. Journals, 42; Ross, 102, 105-107; Zaboly, 122.

35. Journals, 43-44 (editor); Zaboly, 125.

36. Zaboly, 123; Ross, 108.

37. Ross, 108; Zaboly, 123; Mary Cochrane Rogers Collection, Thompson-Pell Research Center, Ticonderoga, New York (hereafter "Mary Cochrane Rogers Collection"), Box 1, Folder 1.

38. Zaboly, 125.

39. Ross, 108.

40. Zaboly, 123.

41. Johnson to Hardy, October 24, 1755, Johnson Papers, 2:238; Johnson to Shirley, November 17, 22, 1755, ibid., 307, 324.

42. Johnson to Hardy, October 31, 1755, ibid., 258.

43. Johnson to Hardy, October 13, 1755, ibid., 190.

44. Johnson to Gage, January 25, 1766, Johnson Papers, 12:9.

45. Journals, 44; Cuneo, 32-35; Ross, 113-114; Zaboly, 125-126.

46. Zaboly, 127.

47. Zaboly, 130, 136-137, 143.

48. Journals, 46-48; Cuneo, 36-39; Ross, 115-119; Zaboly, 132-134.

49. Journals, 47; Cuneo, 37-38; Ross, 119; Zaboly, 133-134.

50. Ross, 120; Zaboly, 134.

51. Zaboly, 132, 133, and fns. 27, 43.

52. Journals, 47, 47 (editor); 48 (editor).

53. Journals, 48-49, 53-56.

54. Journals, 48-49; Zaboly, 137, 138.

55. Journals, 56; Zaboly, 147.

56. Zaboly, 142, 146, 147, 150.

57. Cuneo, 44; Brumwell, 82-83; Zaboly, 147-148, 150.

CHAPTER FOUR: THE 1757 CAMPAIGN

1. Zaboly, 153; Journals, 57.

2. In November 1755, Rogers engaged in an extended skirmish with French and Indian forces at the northern end of Lake George. Rogers had begun the expedition with a force of thirty, but, seeing an opportunity for an effective attack, he sent for and received an unspecified number of reinforcements. It is unclear how large the combined force was. Rogers

led that force for less than a day before withdrawing to Fort William Henry.

3. Zaboly, 154-156; *Journals*, 57.

4. Zaboly, 156; *Journals*, 57.

5. Ross, 125; *Journals*, 58 (editor); Zaboly, 156-157; *Rising Above Circumstances*, 193.

6. Zaboly, 47.

7. Zaboly, 156.

8. Zaboly, 156; *Journals*, 58 (editor). Of course, both sides would suffer equally from weapons malfunctioning because of dampness, and, in a continuing rain, the advantage of dry guns would diminish rapidly. Since the Rangers all had snowshoes, the advantage of traveling over an already broken track would appear to be limited.

9. *John Stark*, 39; Zaboly, 156.

10. *John Stark*, 40.

11. Ross, 128; *Journals*, 58; Zaboly, 157.

12. Zaboly, 157-158; *Journals*, 58.

13. Zaboly, ibid.; *Journals*, 59.

14. *Journals*, 58-59; Zaboly, 158-159.

15. *John Stark*, 39-43, 138.

16. *Journals*, 58.

17. *Journals*, 61-62 (editor); Zaboly, 159.

18. The quality of Speakman's and Hobbs' recruits was widely criticized, but Speakman and Hobbs themselves were seasoned frontier fighters, as was Lieutenant Kennedy, killed in the initial French volley. Zaboly, 147, 153.

19. *Journals*, 59; Zaboly, 162 fn. 62.

20. *Journals*, 59 (editor).

21. Zaboly, 157.

22. Zaboly, 160; Ross, 134.

23. *Journals*, 63.

24. *Journals*, 64; Zaboly, 164.

25. *Journals*, 64-65; Zaboly, 165-170.

26. Ross, 139; Zaboly, 172-173.

27. Ross, 139-140; Zaboly, 173-175.

28. Zaboly, 175, 178, 182; Ross, 141; Laramie, Michael G., *The Road to Ticonderoga: The Campaign of 1758 in the Champlain Valley* (Yardley, Pennsylvania: Westholme Publishing, LLC, 2023) (cited hereafter as "Laramie"), 32.

29. Zaboly, 178, 180; Ross, 141; Laramie, ibid.

30. Ross, 141-142; Zaboly, 180-181; Laramie, 43-44.

31. Ross, 142; Zaboly, 182.

32. *Journals*, 71-78; *Journals*, 71-78 (editor); Cuneo, 54-60; Zaboly, 185.

33. *Journals*, 79 (editor); Zaboly, 480.

34. *Journals*, 70; Cuneo, 71-72; Zaboly, 186-187.

35. Cuneo, 61-62; Ross, 152-154; Zaboly, 191.

36. Cuneo, 60-61; Ross, 162; Zaboly, 199.

37. Cuneo, 62-64; Ross, 149-152; Zaboly, 192-193.

38. Cuneo, 64-65; Ross, 155; Zaboly, 193-194.

39. Zaboly, 199, 206.

40. Zaboly, 199, 200; *Journals*, 86-87.

41. *Journals*, 86-88; Brumwell, 135.

42. Brumwell, 135; Zaboly, 334; Amherst to Rogers, December 26, 1762, War Offices Records, British National Archives, Kew Gardens, England (hereafter "WO"), series 34,

volume 93. War Office Records are cited hereafter as "WO [series number]/[volume number]:[document number]." These handwritten documents often lack document numbers and almost always lack individual page numbers, but they are generally maintained in chronological order and can be found easily from the series and volume numbers, together with the document's date. Where the document bears a document number, I have provided it. In some instances, an archivist has, at some unknown point in the past, given individual page numbers to an entire volume, and where this page number assists in identifying the material cited, I have provided it as well.

43. *Journals*, 85-86 (editor); Zaboly, 196-198; Ross, 160.

CHAPTER FIVE: THE BATTLE ON SNOWSHOES

1. Cuneo, 70; Ross, 162; Zaboly, 200-201.
2. Cuneo, 70-71; Zaboly, 201.
3. Cuneo, 72; Ross, 163; Zaboly, 203; Laramie, 58, 60.
4. Cuneo, 73-74; Zaboly, 206; Ross, 164-165.
5. Zaboly, 206.
6. *Journals*, 89.
7. Zaboly, 208.
8. *Journals*, 89-90.
9. *Journals*, 90-91; Laramie, 64-65.
10. *Journals*, 93 (editor).
11. *Journals*, 91-97; *Journals*, 91-97 (editor); Ross, 171-174; Zaboly, 210-211; Cuneo, 77; Laramie, 65.
12. *Journals*, 91; Ross, 173, 176-179; Cuneo, 77-78; Zaboly, 210-213; Laramie, 67.
13. *Journals*, 91, 94 (editor); Zaboly, 211-212; Ross, 178.
14. *Journals*, 98 (editor); Zaboly, 213-214.
15. *Journals*, 97-103 (editor); Zaboly, 213-214; Ross, 179-182.
16. *Journals*, 95; Zaboly, 213-214; Ross, 182.
17. Laramie, 68.
18. *Journals*, 88-89.
19. *Journals*, 95, 108 (editor), 112 (editor), 113; Zaboly, 210, 216 fn. 37; Ross, 176.
20. *Journals*, 91, 95; Zaboly, 213.
21. Zaboly, 215.
22. *Journals*, 89 (emphasis in original).
23. *Journals*, 89-90; Zaboly, 209-210; Laramie, 62-64.
24. *Journals*, 95.
25. Zaboly, 218; *Journals*, 113-114.
26. *Journals*, 115-117; Zaboly, 219-222.
27. *Journals*, 118-119; Zaboly, 222-223; Ross, 187-190, 193-195; Cuneo, 83-84.
28. *Journals*, 119; Zaboly, 223-224; Ross, 195-197; Cuneo, 83-86; Laramie, 116.
29. *Journals*, 119, 123; Zaboly, 225, 228; Cuneo, 86-87; Ross, 197.
30. *Journals*, 123 (editor); Zaboly, 225.
31. *Journals*, 126-127 (editor); Zaboly, 228; Laramie, 129.
32. *Journals*, 128-129; Zaboly, 229-232; Ross, 201-205; Laramie, 145, 149-150.
33. Zaboly, 233; Ross, 205-206.

CHAPTER SIX: FORT ANNE, TICONDEROGA, AND CROWN POINT

1. *Journals*, 130; Zaboly, 234; Ross, 207.

2. *Journals*, 130; Zaboly, 234-235; Ross, 207.

3. *Journals*, 130, 138 (editor); Zaboly, 238-240.

4. Zaboly, 240-242; *Journals*, 134, 139 (editor); Ross, 209-210; Laramie, 168 and fn. 18. There are conflicting reports about who shot the Indian leader, but all accounts place him in the center of the French and Indian line, opposite Dalyell's regulars, while Rogers and the Rangers were stationed further to the right.

5. *Journals*, 130, 134, 135 (editor), 138 (editor), 141 (editor), 142 (editor), 144 (editor), 145 (editor); Zaboly, 240, 241, 242, 243; Ross, 209, 211.

6. *Journals*, 134; Zaboly, 248.

7. *Journals*, 134 (editor), 135 (editor), 141 (editor), 142 (editor), 145 (editor), 146 (editor); Zaboly, 240, 241; Ross, 209; Laramie, 167.

8. *Journals*, 135 (editor), 141 (editor); Zaboly, 242-243; Ross, 211-212.

9. *Journals*, 146-147; Zaboly, 246.

10. *Journals*, 147; Cuneo, 90-91.

11. *Journals*, 150-151; Zaboly, 248-249; Ross, 216.

12. Amherst to Rogers, February 13, 1759, WO 34/54:121; Gage to Amherst, February 18, 1759, WO 34/46A:11; Amherst to Rogers, April 1, 1759, WO 34/54:122.

13. Amherst to Rogers, April 1, 1759, WO 34/54:122; Gage to Amherst, February 18, 1759, WO 34/46A:11; Gage to Amherst, April 2, 1759, Thomas Gage Papers, William L. Clements Library, University of Michigan (hereafter "Gage Papers"), Letter Books and Account Books, Box 1, January 20-April 27, 1759 (Winter Quarters 1759); *Journals*, 150; Ross, 216; Brumwell, 135; Amherst to Delancey, June 23, 1759, WO 34/30:52.

14. Amherst to Rogers, November 24, 1759, WO 34/81:185; Amherst to Rogers, December 24, 1759, WO 34/81:202; Rogers to Amherst, April 24, 1760, WO 34/39:126.

15. Gage to Amherst, February 18, 1759, WO 34/46A:11; Cuneo, 92.

16. Zaboly, 255; Gage to Amherst, April 9, 1759, Gage Papers, Letter Books and Account Books, Box 1, January 20-April 27, 1759 (Winter Quarters 1759). Zaboly cites Gage's April 9, 1759, letter to Amherst for both of these quotations, *see* Zaboly, 255 and fn. 85, but only the second quotation, that Rogers' "schemes are very wild," appears in that letter. I have been unable to find the correct citation for the "true Ranger" quotation.

17. Zaboly, 250, 292.

18. Zaboly, 258, 260-261; *Journals*, 155, 159, 164 (editor).

19. Zaboly, 260.

20. Zaboly, 262-263; *Journals*, 166-167.

21. Zaboly, 263-265; *Journals*, 167-168.

22. Zaboly, 265.

23. Zaboly, 207.

24. Zaboly, 268; *Mohawk Baronet*, 201-210; *White Savage*, 203-208.

CHAPTER SEVEN: THE ST. FRANCIS RAID

1. Cuneo, 100; Brumwell, 146, 148-149; Ross, 235-236.

2. *Journals*, 170-171; *Journals*, 170-171 (editor); Brumwell, 158-159; Zaboly, 270; Rogers to Amherst, December 12, 1759, WO 34/78:182.

3. *Journals*, 171; Brumwell, 159.

4. *Journals*, 171.

5. Brumwell, 161-165; Zaboly, 270-271.

6. *Journals*, 179; Brumwell, 170-171; Zaboly, 272-273.

7. *Journals*, 179; Brumwell, 171-172, 173-174; Ross, 233-235; Zaboly, 272-273.

8. *Journals*, 179; Brumwell, 179; Ross, 239; Zaboly, 273.

9. *Journals*, 179; Brumwell, 181-182; Ross, 240-241; Zaboly, 274.

10. *Journals*, 179.

11. *Journals*, 179; Zaboly, 275; Brumwell, 184-185; Ross, 242.

12. *Journals*, 179; Brumwell, 187-188.

13. *Journals*, 180, Zaboly, 276; Ross, 246-247; Brumwell, 188-189.

14. *Journals*, 172 (editor). Todish notes that Rogers' account would put the attack on St. Francis on October 6 but makes clear that October 4 is the correct date, putting the approach to St. Francis on October 3.

15. *Journals*, 172; Brumwell, 191-193; Ross, 247-249; Zaboly, 279-280.

16. *Journals*, 173 (editor); Brumwell, 193-195; Ross, 249; Zaboly, 279-280.

17. The Stockbridge Indians were largely of the Mahican tribe, and the Abenaki oral tradition suggests that the Indian who warned the village may have identified himself as a Mahican and may have said he was part of the force about to attack the village. This story is not improbable; although they fought on opposite sides of the war, the Mahicans and the Abenaki historically had close ties. *Journals*, 173 (editor); Brumwell, 193, 195. Rogers had sent most of the Indians who originally accompanied his expedition back to Crown Point because of illness, and one source concludes that the Stockbridge Indian Rogers reported killed in the attack was the very one who had warned the village the night before. *Journals*, 173-174 (editor). It would be a curious coincidence if the attackers' only fatality was the Indian who had warned the village, raising the interesting possibility that this Indian may have been killed by the Rangers, who may have learned of the warning from prisoners or freed captives and killed the informer in retaliation.

18. *Journals*, 174; Brumwell, 196-197.

19. *Journals*, 175; Brumwell, 204-205; Ross, 252; Zaboly, 283.

20. *Journals*, 173; Brumwell, 203; Ross, 252.

21. *Journals*, 173, 174-175; Brumwell, 203; Ross, 254, 255; Zaboly, 282.

22. *Journals*, 175; Zaboly, 285.

23. *Journals*, 175, 186-187 (editor); Zaboly, 284-286; Brumwell, 213-214.

24. *Journals*, 186-187 (editor); Brumwell, 228-230, 233-235; Zaboly, 286-287.

25. Brumwell, 228-230, 233-235; Zaboly, 286-287, 291 fn. 105; *Journals*, 173-174 (editor), 186-187 (editor).

26. *Journals*, 180; Brumwell, 227-228; Zaboly, 287-288.

27. Amherst to Stevens, October 4, 1759, WO 34/81:52; Ross, 264-269; *Journals*, 189 (editor); Zaboly, 287-288; Brumwell, 186-187, 227-228.

28. Brumwell, 224, 231; *Journals*, 180-181; Zaboly, 286, 288; Ross, 265-266.

29. *Journals*, 180-181; Zaboly, 288; Brumwell, 231-232; Ross, 266-267.

30. Zaboly, 282, 286; Brumwell, 212-213; Ross, 253-254; Amherst to Delancey, November 13, 1759, WO 34/30:93.

31. Amherst to Delancey, November 2, 1759, WO 34/30:91; Amherst to Delancey, November 13, 1759, WO 34/30:93; *Journals*, 181; Ross, 268.

32. *Journals*, 186 (editor), 193; Zaboly, 293, Brumwell, 242-243; Ross, 268.

33. Brumwell, 195; *Journals*, 191 (editor); Cuneo, 108.

34. *Journals*, 173 (editor).

35. Zaboly, 282, 283; Ross, 253-254.

36. *Journals*, 191 (editor).

37. Brumwell, 202, 242.

38. *Journals*, 173 (editor).

39. Brumwell, 202.

40. *Journals*, 173 (editor); Zaboly, 282-283.

41. Brumwell, 214.

42. *Journals*, 172-173.

43. Zaboly, 292.

44. Brumwell, 240-241, 317-319.

45. Zaboly, 293; Brumwell, 212, 246.

46. Rogers to Amherst, December 12, 1759, WO 34/78:182.

47. Amherst to Rogers, December 24, 1759, WO 34/81:201.

48. Rogers to Amherst, January 1, 1760, WO 34/82:2; Amherst to Delancey, November 13, 1759, WO 34/30:93.

49. Brumwell, 240-241, 248; Zaboly, 288-289.

50. Brumwell, 248, 307 fn.

51. Amherst to Rogers, December 24, 1759, WO 34/81:202; *Journals*, 181, 194 (editor); Zaboly, 293.

52. Brumwell, 247-248; Zaboly, 295.

53. Brumwell, 244; Zaboly, 283.

54. Brumwell, 244; Zaboly, 283; Ross, 269-270.

55. Brumwell, 256.

56. The Sullivan campaign against the Seneca in 1779, launched in retaliation for devastating Indian raids on the New York and Pennsylvania frontier during the Revolutionary War, is a good example. The campaign destroyed forty towns, several larger than St. Francis. It was nonetheless generally considered a failure because it did not inflict significant casualties or force the Seneca into a decisive battle. Berleth, Richard, *Bloody Mohawk: The French and Indian War & American Revolution on New York's Frontier* (Catskill, New York: Black Dome Press, 2009), 281-282, 286.

CHAPTER EIGHT: THE 1760 CAMPAIGN

1. Cuneo, 118-119; Zaboly, 294; Ross, 275.

2. Rogers' Account for St. Francis Equipment, WO 197/2:464; Rogers' Account for Costs of St. Francis Rescue Party, Clothes for Survivors, WO 197/2:466; Amherst to Rogers, December 24, 1759, WO 34/81:201; Gage to Amherst, December 30, 1759, WO 34/46A:69; Zaboly, 301 fn. 13; Ross, 268.

3. Rogers to Amherst, December 14, 1759, WO 34/78:187; Amherst to Rogers, December 24, 1759, WO 34/81:201; Gage to Amherst, December 30, 1759, WO 34/46A:69.

4. *Journals*, 196.

5. Cuneo, 119; Rogers to Amherst, May 23, 1760, WO 34/82:219; Amherst Order re: Rogers Accounts, May 18, 1761, WO 34/199:213.

6. *Journals*, 194-195; Zaboly, 294-295; Ross, 272-274.

7. *Journals*, 194-195; Brumwell, 250-251; Ross, 272-274; Zaboly, 294-295.

8. *Journals*, 197-199; Zaboly, 295-296.

9. *Journals*, 199-200; Zaboly, 296; Ross, 277-278; Cuneo, 121; Brumwell, 253.

10. Brumwell, 253-255; *Journals*, 200-203; Zaboly, 296-298; Cuneo, 121-124; Ross, 280-285.

11. Ibid.

12. *Rising Above Circumstances*, 139; *Journals*, 201-202; Zaboly, 297.

13. Haviland to Amherst, June 6, 1760, WO 34/51:38; Amherst to Haviland, June 10, 1760, WO 34/52:46; Amherst to Haviland, June 26, 1760, WO 34/52:68; Amherst to Haviland, July 11, 1760, WO 34/52:69; Amherst to Rogers, July 11, 1760, WO 34/52:72.

14. *Journals*, 206; Zaboly, 298; Ross, 286.

15. *Journals*, 206; Zaboly, 299; Ross, 286.
16. *Journals*, 206-207; Zaboly, 300; Ross, 287.
17. *Journals*, 207; Zaboly, 300; Ross, 287.

CHAPTER NINE: DETROIT

1. Cuneo, 129; Zaboly, 304, 305.
2. Burbeen to Douw, September 22, 1760, Papers Concerning Robert Rogers, New York Public Library (hereafter "Rogers Papers"), Folder 3.
3. Zaboly, 311.
4. Cuneo, 132; Zaboly, 307; Inventory of Merchandise Shipped at Niagara for Detroit, October 1760, Rogers Papers, Folder 4; Mayer, Josephine Janes, "Major Robert Rogers, Trader," *New York History*, v. 15, no. 4 (October 1934) (hereafter "Mayer") (available online at jstor.org), p. 390; Ross, 296-297.
5. *Journals*, 211-212; Zaboly, 308-309; Croghan to Johnson, November 1, 1760, Johnson Papers, 3:276.
6. *Journals*, 210, 214, 217 (editor); Rogers, Major Robert, *A Concise Account of North America* (New York: Heritage Books, 2007, a reprint of the 1765 original) (hereafter "Concise Account"), 172-174.
7. *Journals*, 219-221.
8. Mayer, ibid.; Zaboly, 311; Croghan to Johnson, January 13, 1761, Johnson Papers, 3:302; Johnson to Amherst, February 12, 1761, Johnson Papers, 3:331-332; Amherst to Johnson, February 22, 1761, Johnson Papers, 3:345.
9. *Journals*, 222-224; Zaboly, 312.
10. Deeds to Robert Rogers and Others, December 23, 1760, Burton Historical Collection, Detroit Public Library; Zaboly, 313.
11. Croghan to Johnson, January 13, 1761, Johnson Papers, 3:302.
12. Ibid., 303.
13. Zaboly, 312.
14. Ross, 308-309; Zaboly, 314.
15. Ross, 309-311; Zaboly, 317-318.
16. Ross, 311; Zaboly, 318; Rogers Power of Attorney to Askin, March 17, 1761, Rogers Papers, Folder 5.
17. Mayer, 393; "Reminiscences of James Gordon," *New York History*, v. 17, no. 4 (October 1936) (hereafter "Gordon") (available online at jstor.org), p. 429; Rogers & Co. Final Settlement, March 11, 1763, Rogers Papers, Folder 4; Zaboly, 336.
18. Mayer, 393, 394, 397; Gordon, 430.
19. Zaboly, 318, 332; Johnson to Colden, June 18, 1761, Johnson Papers, 3:409-410.

CHAPTER TEN: SETTLING ACCOUNTS

1. Cuneo, 143, 149; Ross, 312; Zaboly, 294, 319.
2. Zaboly, 293.
3. Mary Cochrane Rogers Collection, Box 1, Folder 12, pp. 5-9. The documents in Folder 12 appear to be Mary Cochrane Rogers' handwritten transcriptions of original documents, not the originals themselves. The citation she provides throughout Folder 12 is "Treasury Papers 64/21," presumably a reference to Treasury documents maintained at the British National Archives in Kew Gardens. Treasury Papers 64/21 contains various army records of reimbursement for claims during the French and Indian War, but I was unable to find anything relating to Rogers' 1761 claim in this volume. The most important document re-

garding the disposition of Rogers' claim, the detailed Warrant issued by Amherst in final resolution of the claim, appears at WO 34/193:213-214, but I have been unable to locate the originals for much of the back and forth among Rogers, Appy, Amherst, and the three-officer panel regarding claims that appear in Folder 12. The Folder 12 documents are nonetheless plainly transcriptions of original records, and, except for possible scrivener's errors, appear completely trustworthy.

4. See generally Mary Cochrane Rogers Collection, Box 1, Folder 12.

5. Cuneo, 143; Ross, 312. Zaboly may understand this point at least in part: Zaboly, 318.

6. Gordon, 430; Zaboly, 319.

7. Cuneo, 146-147; Ross, 313.

8. Mary Cochrane Rogers Collection, *id.*, pp. 20-23, 26-29.

9. Warrant for Expenses of Detroit Expedition, March 3, 1761, WO 34/199:73; Amherst Order re: Rogers Accounts, May 18, 1761, WO 34/199:213-214; Mary Cochrane Rogers Collection, ibid., 1-2.

10. Rogers to Appy, May 17, 1761, Mary Cochrane Rogers Collection, idid., pp. 26-29. None of Rogers' biographers appears to be aware of this significant concession by Rogers concerning the amount he was owed.

11. Report of Three-Officer Panel, May 16, 1761, Mary Cochrane Rogers Collection, ibid., 20-23.

12. Amherst Order, ibid.; Rogers to Appy, May 17, 1761, Mary Cochrane Rogers Collection, Box 1, Folder 12, 25.

13. Mary Cochrane Rogers Collection, ibid.; Amherst Order, ibid.

14. Amherst Order, ibid.; Mary Cochrane Rogers Collection, ibid., 5-9, 20-23.

15. Amherst Order, ibid.; Mary Cochrane Rogers Collection, ibid.

16. Rogers-Roche Collection, William L. Clements Library, University of Michigan (hereafter "Rogers-Roche Collection"), Folder 1; Zaboly, 320-321.

17. Rogers to Amherst, May 23, 1760, WO 34/82:219; Zaboly, 334-335.

18. Amherst Order, ibid.; Mary Cochrane Rogers Collection, ibid., 5-9, 18-19; Amherst to Rogers, May 18, 1761, WO 34/88:248; Zaboly, 319-320, 334-335.

19. Amherst Order, ibid.; Mary Cochrane Rogers Collection, ibid., 5-9, 20-23, 30.

20. See, e.g., *Journals*, 44, 63-64, 86, 196.

21. Rogers to Amherst, May 11, 1761, Mary Cochrane Rogers Collection, ibid., 10-17; Appy to Amherst, undated, Mary Cochrane Rogers Collection, ibid., 30.

22. Mary Cochrane Rogers Collection, ibid., 5-9, 20-23.

23. Amherst Order, ibid.; Zaboly, 319.

24. Amherst Order, ibid.

25. Mary Cochrane Rogers Collection, ibid., 10-17; Rogers to Amherst, April 24, 1760, WO 34/39:126; Zaboly, 305; Appy to Amherst, undated, Mary Cochrane Rogers Collection, ibid., 30.

26. Amherst to Rogers, May 8, 1761, Mary Cochrane Rogers Collection, ibid., 5-9; Appy to Amherst, May 17, 1761, Mary Cochrane Rogers Collection, ibid., 26-28.

27. Amherst Order, ibid.; Barrington to Gage, August 9, 1766, Gage Papers, English Series (hereafter "ES"), v. 7.

28. Zaboly, 337; James Rogers v. Robert Rogers, New Hampshire Court Case No. 7863, New Hampshire State Archives. The precise date of the loan is also not recorded, but Rogers was on the Detroit expedition until mid-February 1761, and en route to, or in, South Carolina after early July. There is no record of his being in Boston before his British army settlement, but there is evidence of his being there immediately after, and this is the most likely time of the loan.

CHAPTER ELEVEN: MARRIAGE

1. Zaboly, 319-323.

2. Petition of Elizabeth Rogers to the Honorable Council of House of Representatives, January 26, 1778, New Hampshire State Archives, Petitions (hereafter "Elizabeth Rogers' Divorce Petition"); Zaboly, 323.

3. Zaboly, 321; Cuneo, 142.

4. Cuneo, 151, 169, 233; Zaboly, 323.

5. Rogers to Betsy, July 19, 1761, Rogers-Roche Collection, Folder 2; Rogers to Betsy, November 9, 1761, May 17, 1762, Rogers-Roche Collection, Folder 3; Rogers to Amherst, April 29, 1762, WO 34/90:100. Zaboly believes Betsy retained "all of Robert's letters." Zaboly, 323. There is no way of knowing if this is literally true, but from the context of the letters that are preserved, there do not appear to be many missing.

6. Zaboly, 332.

7. Rockingham County Deed Books, New Hampshire State Archives (hereafter "Deed Books"), v. 69, 58.

8. Browne v. Rogers, New Hampshire Provincial Court Case N. 5883, New Hampshire State Archives.

9. Zaboly, 337.

10. Ibid.

11. Zaboly, 337-338.

12. Zaboly, 338.

13. Rogers to Betsy, June 21, 1763, Rogers-Roche Collection, Folder 5; Rogers to Betsy, June 30, July 16, 1763, Rogers-Roche Collection, Folder 4; Zaboly, 339-340.

14. Zaboly, 349.

15. Elizabeth Rogers' Divorce Petition.

16. Rogers to Betsy, February [?], 1765, Rogers-Roche Collection, Folder 5; Zaboly, 355.

17. Elizabeth Rogers' Divorce Petition.

18. Armour, David A., *Treason? At Michilimackinac* (Mackinac Island, Michigan: Mackinac Island State Park Commission, 1967) (hereafter "*Treason?*"), 25-26.

19. Elizabeth Rogers' Divorce Petition; Winwood Serjeant to Betsy, May 21, 1774, Serjeant Family Letters, History Cambridge (formerly Cambridge Historical Society), Cambridge, Massachusetts (hereafter "Serjeant Letters") (accessible online).

20. Zaboly, 403, 411-412; *Treason?*, 94-95; Cuneo, 231.

21. Zaboly, 403.

22. Zaboly, 414.

23. Rogers to Betsy, January 26, 1770, Rogers-Roche Collection, Folder 8; Zaboly, 415; Rogers to Betsy, February 20, 1770, Rogers-Roche Collection, Folder 9.

24. Rogers to Betsy, June [?], 1770, July 20, 1766 [*sic*—should be 1770], Rogers-Roche Collection, Folder 10; Zaboly, 414, 419, 421.

25. Rogers to Betsy, March 18, 1774, Rogers-Roche Collection, Folder 11; Serjeant to Betsy, May 21, 1774, June 15, 1774, Serjeant Letters.

26. Zaboly, 430, 436, 437, 439; Rogers to Betsy, December 17, 1775, Rogers-Roche Collection, Folder 12.

27. Elizabeth Rogers' Divorce Petition (emphasis in original).

28. Zaboly, 462-463.

29. Zaboly, 337.

30. Nevins, Allan, *Introduction to Rogers's "Ponteach"*, University of Illinois Master's Thesis,

1913, reprinted by Forgotten Books, 2018 (hereafter "Nevins"), 80-81. Nevins' work, a Master's Thesis for the University of Illinois in 1913, contains no citations for anything. The work as a whole appears well-researched and generally accurate.

CHAPTER TWELVE: THE SOUTH, THE NORTHEAST, AND DETROIT AGAIN

1. Zaboly, 325-328, 330-331.

2. Rogers to Betsy, June 21 [?], 1763, Rogers-Roche Collection, Folder 5; Rogers to Betsy, June 30, 1763, Rogers-Roche Collection, Folder 4; Zaboly, 339.

3. Rogers to Amherst, March 20, 1762, WO 34/90:64; Rogers to Amherst, April 29, 1762, WO 34/90:100; Zaboly, 331; Rogers to Amherst, July 10, 1762, WO 34/91:32; Amherst to Rogers, August 23, 1762, WO 34/93:89.

4. Amherst August 23, 1762 letter to Rogers, WO 34/93:89.

5. Zaboly, 332; Gordon, 429-430; Mayer, 393; Estate of Volkert Douw v. Rogers, New Hampshire Court Case No. 24599, New Hampshire State Archives.

6. Amherst to Rogers, December 26, 1762, WO 34/93:272.

7. Zaboly, 334; Ross, 333.

8. Zaboly, 334-335, 337; James Rogers v. Robert Rogers, New Hampshire Court Case No. 7863, New Hampshire State Archives.

9. Pearson v. Rogers, New Hampshire Provincial Court Case No. 28218, Karr v. Rogers, New Hampshire Court Case No. 718, Brinkerhoff v. Rogers, New Hampshire Court Case No. 561, New Hampshire State Archives.

10. Amherst's correspondence is arranged chronologically at the National Archives in Kew Gardens, with separate volumes for letters from Amherst and letters to Amherst. Amherst's reply to Rogers is in the correct place in the "from Amherst" volume, but the letter it responds to, "of Yesterday's Date," is not in the "to Amherst" volume.

11. Amherst to Rogers, May 3, 1763, WO 34/96:125.

12. Ibid.

13. Amherst to Winepress, May 8, 1763, WO 34/96:137.

14. WO 34/94:108-110; Zaboly, 338.

15. Zaboly, 338.

16. Zaboly, 348.

17. Zaboly, 339; Nevins, 75; Ross, 346.

18. Zaboly, 338-340.

19. Zaboly, 339-341; Gordon, 430; Amherst to Johnson, November 21, 1762, Johnson Papers, 3:941-942.

20. Gordon, 430-431; Carroll, Justin M., The Merchant John Askin (East Lansing, Michigan: Michigan State University Press, 2017) (hereafter "Carroll"), 24-25, 30, 66, 77, 82-83; Zaboly, 349, 380.

21. Zaboly, 341-343.

22. Zaboly, 343.

23. Zaboly, 344-345, 348-349.

24. Nevins, 79-80.

CHAPTER THIRTEEN: THE LOST YEAR

1. Rogers to Gage, March 4, 1764, Gage Papers, American Series (hereafter "AS"), v. 15.

2. Zaboly, 350.

3. Zaboly, 4, 350; Cuneo, 170-171; Ross, 353-354.

4. Zaboly, 350-351.
5. Ibid.
6. Rogers to Gage, March 4, 1764, Gage Papers, AS, v. 15.
7. Ibid.
8. Rogers to Gage, March 3, 1764, Gage Papers, AS, v.15.
9. Gage to Rogers, March 19, 1764, Gage Papers, AS, v. 15; Zaboly, 351-352.
10. Gage to Johnson, January 13, 1766, Johnson Papers, 13:380-381.
11. Zaboly, 349, 351, 352.
12. Boyd v. Rogers, New Hampshire Court Case No. 535, New Hampshire State Archives.
13. *Treason?*, 74; Nevins, 81, 92; Clements, William L., "Journal of Major Robert Rogers," *Proceedings of the American Antiquarian Society*, October 1918, reprinted by the Library of Congress and available online (hereafter "Clements"), 10, 5. Clements was the donor who created the William L. Clements Library at the University of Michigan. This article discusses, and includes the text of, Rogers' Michilimackinac Journal.
14. Zaboly, 353; Deed Books v. 70, p. 492.
15. Deed Books v. 71, 488, 491; v. 72, 119, 406-407, 412, 425, 441, 486; v. 75, 154; v. 104, 135.
16. Rogers to Betsy, February 27 [?], 1765, Rogers-Roche Collection, Folder 5; Zaboly, 355, 357; Nevins, 81; Cuneo, 173.
17. James Rogers v. Robert Rogers, New Hampshire Court Case No. 7863, New Hampshire State Archives.
18. Zaboly, 7, 434; Gage to Johnson, January 13, 1766, Johnson Papers, 13:380-381; *Treason?*, 74; Roberts to Gage, March 30, 1769, Gage Papers, AS, v. 84.

CHAPTER FOURTEEN; A NEW LEASE ON LIFE

1. Zaboly, 354-355, 357; Butterfield, L.H., ed., *The Adams Papers: Diary of John Adams* (Cambridge, Massachusetts: Harvard University Press, 1962) (hereafter "Diary of John Adams"), v. 1, 278, entry of December 27, 1765.
2. Ross, 353-354; Zaboly, 358.
3. Zaboly, 357-358, 360.
4. Zaboly, 358.
5. Zaboly, 358, 361; Nevins, 90.
6. *Journals*, 44, 63, 86.
7. *Journals*, 70, 113, 114.
8. *Journals*, 59, 91, 95, 173.
9. *Journals*, 86-88; cf. Mary Cochrane Rogers Collection, Box 1, Folders 10, 11.
10. *Journals*, 64.
11. *Journals*, 195 fn.
12. Concise Account, 22, 39, 41, 43, 51, 52, 63, 64, 87, 100.
13. Concise Account, 118, 122, 125, 132.
14. Concise Account, 153-156, 167.
15. Concise Account, 173.
16. Zaboly, 365-366, 422.
17. Zaboly, 360.
18. "A Proposal By Robert Rogers, Esq.," Colonial Office Records (hereafter "CO"), British National Archives, series 323, volume 18, document number 134, p. 327. Colonial Office Records are cited hereafter as "CO [series number]/[volume number]: [document number], [page number, if any]".

19. Ibid., 327-328.

20. Ibid., 327.

21. Ibid., 328.

22. Ibid.

23. Ibid.

24. CO 323/18:134, p. 329.

25. CO 323/27:70; Zaboly, 360.

26. Zaboly, 360, 362-363; Widder, Keith R., "The 1767 Maps of Robert Rogers and Jonathan Carver: A Proposal for the Establishment of the Colony of Michilimackinac," *Michigan Historical Review* 30:2 (Fall 2004) (hereafter "Widder"), 57.

27. Zaboly, 362.

28. Barrington to Gage, September 16, September 17, 1765, Gage Papers, ES, v. 4; Conway to Gage, October 12, 1765, Gage Papers, ES, v. 5.

29. Zaboly, 362; Cuneo, 179-180.

30. Zaboly, 365.

CHAPTER FIFTEEN: RETURN TO AMERICA

1. Zaboly, 365, 367; Rogers to Johnson, February 14, 1766, Hough Edition, 220.

2. Nevins, 92; Gage to Barrington, January 15, 1766, Gage to Conway, January 16, 1766, Gage Papers, ES, v. 5.

3. Johnson Papers, 13:380-381.

4. Johnson to Gage, January 25, 1766, Johnson Papers, 12:8-11, Hough Edition, 215-216.

5. Ibid.

6. Ibid.

7. Nevins, 92-93.

8. Johnson to Gage, January 30, 1766, Hough Edition, 218-219.

9. Gage to Johnson, February 3, 1766, Johnson Papers, 5:30.

10. Gage's Instructions to Rogers, Johnson Papers, 12:1-2, Hough Edition, 217-218; *Treason?*, 10-13. These instructions are dated January 10, 1766, but although this is possible (Rogers arrived in New York on January 6), it is more likely that this is a dating error and should be February 10. Gage wanted to consult with Johnson before giving Rogers his orders; his correspondence with Johnson runs into early February, and his letters to Barrington and Conway in mid-January indicate that he "will" give Rogers the requested appointment.

11. Instructions to Major Rogers, June 3, 1766, *Treason?*, 13-14; Johnson to Cramahe, July 23, 1768, Johnson Papers, 6:288-289.

12. Croghan to Johnson, January 13, 1761, Johnson Papers, 3:303; *see also* Johnson Papers, 3:331, 345.

13. Johnson to Gage, August 14, 1765, Johnson Papers, 4:833-834.

14. Gage to Conway, June 24, 1766, Gage Papers, ES, v. 7.

15. Johnson to Gage, August 14, 1765; Gage to Conway, June 24, 1766.

16. Johnson to Gage, November 14, 1765, Johnson Papers, 4:870-872.

17. Gage to Conway, June 24, 1766, Gage Papers, ES, v. 7.

18. Gage to Barrington, January 15, 1766, Gage Papers, ES, v. 5; Zaboly, 369.

19. Zaboly, 369; Cuneo, 185, 186-187; Ross, 375.

20. Cuneo, 186.

21. Barrington to Gage, September 17, 1765, Gage Papers, ES, v. 4; Barrington to Gage, August 9, 1766, Gage Papers, ES, v.7. Apart from Cuneo, who mentions it only in passing, none of Rogers' biographers appears to be aware of this letter.

22. Ibid.

23. Rogers to Gage, July 9, 1767, Gage Papers, AS, v. 67.

24. Zaboly, 368-369; Elizabeth Rogers' Divorce Petition.

25. Elizabeth Rogers' Divorce Petition; Nevins, 97.

26. Zaboly, 369.

27. Zaboly, 369; *Treason?*, 47-48.

28. Zaboly, 369-370.

29. Zaboly, 370-371.

30. Zaboly, 371-372.

31. Hopkins Letter, *Treason?*, 44-46.

32. Ibid.

33. Ibid.

34. Gage to Johnson, June 2, 1766, Johnson to Gage, June 12, 1766, Gage Papers, AS, v. 52; Zaboly, 372.

35. Gage to Johnson, June 22, 1766, Gage Papers, AS, v. 53.

36. Johnson to Gage, November 20, 1766, Gage Papers, AS, v. 59.

CHAPTER SIXTEEN: MICHILIMACKINAC

1. Zaboly, 375.

2. Gage's Instructions to Rogers, *Treason?*, 10-11; Johnson Papers, 12:1-2; Hough Edition, 217-218; Claus to Johnson, October 16, 1766, Hough Edition, 228 fn. Rogers' biographers generally agree that his action, whether or not a good idea, was insubordinate: Zaboly, 377 (Rogers acted "despite the decrees from Johnson Hall"); Eggleston, 189 (Rogers acted "in violation of instructions given to him"); Widder, 37 (Rogers guilty of "insubordination").

3. Zaboly, 376; Ross, 383.

4. Claus to Johnson, October 16, 1766, Hough Edition, 228 fn.; Zaboly, 381.

5. Zaboly, 382.

6. Widder, 36 ff.

7. *Treason?*, 47-49; Zaboly, 377.

8. *Treason?*, 50-51.

9. *Treason?*, 51-52; Widder, 49.

10. *Treason?*, 52.

11. *Treason?*, 49, 52-53.

12. Discovery of North-West Passage Act of 1744, 18 Geo. 2. C. 17.

13. Widder, 43, 44; Roberts to Johnson, September 31 [*sic*], 1767, Johnson Papers, 5:711.

14. "A Proposal By Robert Rogers, Esq.," CO 323/18:134.

15. *Treason?*, 51-52.

16. Ibid., 53.

17. *Treason?*, 52, 54; Zaboly, 377, 385, 392.

18. *Treason?*, 54-55.

19. Zaboly, 392.

20. Zaboly, 378-383, 386.

21. Zaboly, 383; Cuneo, 202.

22. Bernard dit Jolicoeur Testimony, *Treason?*, 78-79; Zaboly, 386; Cuneo, 203-205; Ross, 390-392.

23. Widder, 54.

24. Gage to Johnson, May 11, 1767, Johnson Papers, 5:547-549; Gage to Johnson, April 13, 1767, Johnson Papers, 5:536.

25. Johnson to Gage, September 11, 1767, Hough Edition, 222; Johnson to Cramahe, July 23, 1768, Johnson Papers, 6:288-289.

26. Zaboly, 388.

27. Johnson to Gage, September 11, 1767, Hough Edition, 222; Johnson to Gage, August 24, 1768, Johnson Papers, 6:332.

28. Johnson to Hillsborough, August 17, 1768, Hough Edition, 251; Zaboly, 386.

CHAPTER SEVENTEEN: THE MICHILIMACKINAC PROPOSAL

1. Clements 37-58; "Major Rogers Memorial to the Board of Trade" (hereafter "Rogers Memorial"), CO 5/85:171-195.

2. Ross, 388.

3. Widder, 37, 49.

4. Rogers Memorial, CO 5/85:178-182.

5. CO 5/85:183-185.

6. CO 5/85:186.

7. CO 5/85:186-188.

8. CO 5/85:189-190.

9. CO 5/85:190-193.

10. Widder, 66.

11. Widder, 74; Ross, 390; Cuneo, 206.

12. Clements, 9.

13. Johnson to the Earl of Shelburne, December 3, 1767, Hough Edition, 242-247.

14. Ibid.

15. Clements, 41.

16. Carroll, 2.

17. *Journals*, 44, 86-87.

18. Carroll, 2.

19. Rogers Memorial, CO 5/85:173.

20. Zaboly, 387-389; *Treason?*, 47, 49, 50.

21. Roberts to Johnson, August 12, 1767, Johnson Papers, 5:614; Carroll, 67, 107-108.

22. Zaboly, 391, 393.

23. Ibid.; Testimony of Benjamin Roberts, *Treason?*, 16-20; Rogers to Gage, September 22, 1767, Gage Papers, AS, v. 70.

24. Potter Deposition, *Treason?*, 20-23; Zaboly, 389-390; Rogers to Gage, September 22, 1767, Gage Papers, AS, v. 70.

25. Gage to Johnson, September 21, 1767, Hough Edition, 223.

CHAPTER EIGHTEEN: ARRESTED FOR TREASON

1. Roberts Testimony, *Treason?*, 16-20.

2. Ibid.; Spiesmaker Testimony, *Treason?*, 24-26; Zaboly, 391, 393.

3. Potter Deposition, *Treason?*, 20-23.

4. Ibid.

5. Ibid.

6. Ibid.

7. Ibid.

8. Shelburne to Gage, December 19, 1767 (enclosing Carleton to Shelburne, October 9, 1767), Gage Papers, ES, v. 10; Carleton to Gage, October 13, 1767, Gage Papers, AS, v. 71.

9. Johnson to Gage, October 22, 1767, Hough Edition, 224; Johnson to the Earl of Shelburne, October 22, 1767, Hough Edition, 225-230; Zaboly, 397.

10. Shelburne to Gage, December 19, 1767, Gage Papers, ES, v. 10; Zaboly, 397; Bostwick Testimony, *Treason?*, 66-68.

11. Spiesmaker Testimony, *Treason?*, 24-27; Rogers to Gage, December 11, 1767, Gage Papers, AS, v. 72.

12. Spiesmaker Testimony, ibid.

13. Spiesmaker Testimony, ibid., 27-28.

14. Ibid., 28.

15. Ibid.; Broomhead Testimony, *Treason?*, 73-74; Dowden Testimony, Ibid., 79-80.

16. Zaboly, 404.

17. Zaboly, 404-405.

CHAPTER NINETEEN: THE TRIAL

1. *Treason?*, 9-10.

2. Rogers' Opening, *Treason?*, 61; Johnston Testimony, *Treason?*, 68; MacCarty Testimony, *Treason?*, 74.

3. Potter Deposition, *Treason?*, 20-23.

4. Roberts Testimony, *Treason?*, 16-20; Broomhead Testimony, ibid., 74.

5. Fullerton Testimony, *Treason?*, 34-36.

6. Ibid.

7. Spiesmaker Testimony, *Treason?*, 26-32; Frobisher Testimony, ibid., 32-33.

8. Ainsse Testimony, *Treason?*, 37-43.

9. Ibid.; Spiesmaker Testimony, *Treason?*, 26-32; Rogers' Opening, ibid., 65.

10. Bostwick Testimony, *Treason?*, 66-68; Gosenor Testimony, ibid., 71-73.

11. Rogers' Opening, *Treason?*, 60, 64.

12. Ibid., 62.

13. Ibid.; Levy Testimony, *Treason?*, 97-98; Johnston Testimony, ibid., 44.

14. Rogers' Opening, ibid., 63.

15. Rogers' Closing, *Treason?*, 95; Johnson to Cramahe, July 23, 1768, Johnson Papers, 6:288-289.

16. *Treason?*, 13-14; Des Rivières Testimony, ibid., 70-71; Solomon Testimony, ibid., 75-78; *Treason?*, 87.

17. Fleurimond Testimony, *Treason?*, 75; Widder, 54.

18. Johnson to Gage, August 24, 1768, Johnson Papers, 6:332; *Treason?*, 98.

19. Roberts to Johnson, May 11, 1769, Johnson Papers, 6:753; Zaboly, 412-413.

20. *Treason?*, 99-100.

21. Zaboly, 413.

22. Zaboly, 413-414; Estate of Volkert Douw v. Rogers, New Hampshire Court Case No. 24597, New Hampshire State Archives.

CHAPTER TWENTY: LONDON, 1769–1775

1. Zaboly, 414.

2. Zaboly, 414; Roberts to Johnson, February 19, 1770, Johnson Papers, 7:399.

3. Johnson to Gage, March 15, 1766, Johnson Papers, 5:78-81; Johnson to Roberts, March 24, 1769, Johnson Papers, 6:669.

4. Roberts to Johnson, February 19, 1770, Johnson Papers, 7:399; Rogers to Betsy, January 26, 1770, Rogers-Roche Collection, Folder 8; Zaboly, 415.

5. Rogers to Betsy, February 20, 1770, Rogers-Roche Collection, Folder 9; Zaboly, 417.

6. Zaboly, 418, 420.

7. Rogers to Betsy, June 4, 1770, July 20, 1770, Rogers-Roche Collection, Folder 10.

8. Rogers to Betsy, July 20, 1770, ibid.

9. Zaboly, 420; Claus to Johnson, August 3, 1771, Johnson Papers, 8:209.

10. Zaboly, 420.

11. Petition of Major Robert Rogers, June 14, 1771, Treasury Papers, British National Archives, series 29, volume 41, document 111, p. 218.

12. Rogers Petition to Hillsborough, November 11, 1771, CO 5/54:29.

13. Zaboly, 421 and fn. 45.

14. Rogers to Johnson, August 10, 1772, Johnson Papers, 8:567.

15. "Proposal to the King's most Excellent Majesty in Council," February 11, 1772, CO 323/27:70.

16. Ibid.

17. Ibid.

18. Ibid.

19. Ibid.

20. Ibid.

21. Zaboly, 422; *Rising Above Circumstances*, 169.

22. *Rising Above Circumstances*, 169, 210-211.

23. Zaboly, 424-425.

24. Zaboly, 424; Rogers to Betsy, March 18, 1774, Rogers-Roche Collection, Folder 11.

25. Zaboly, 425.

26. Petition of Captain Jonathan Carver, undated (apparently 1769), CO 323/28:77; Zaboly, 417, 425-426.

27. Zaboly, 425-426.

28. Zaboly, 427.

CHAPTER TWENTY-ONE: AMERICA AGAIN, 1775-1776

1. Major Rogers before the Pennsylvania Committee of Safety, Hough Edition, 258-261.

2. Diary of John Adams, v. 2, p. 177, entry of September 21, 1775.

3. Rogers to Whitworth, September 29, 1775, *The American Magazine*, v. 2, no. 1 (Spring-Summer 1986), 24, quoted in Eggleston, 205-206.

4. Zaboly, 433-434.

5. Tryon to Dartmouth, October 10, 1775, CO 5/1106; Germain to Howe, January 5, 1776, Hough Edition, 267.

6. Zaboly, 433, 434; Rogers to Gage, September 30, 1775, Rogers to Pownall, October 3, 1775, CO 5/1106.

7. Wheelock to Washington, December 2, 1775, Hough Edition, 261-263.

8. Ibid.

9. Ibid.

10. Zaboly, 435; Rogers to Betsy, December 17, 1775, Rogers-Roche Collection, Folder 12.

11. Howe to Dartmouth, November 26, 1775, Hough Edition, 261; Germain to Howe, January 5, 1776, Hough Edition, 267.

12. Rogers to Washington, December 19, 1775, Hough Edition, 263-264.

13. Sullivan to Washington, December 17, 1775, Hough Edition, 264-266.

14. Ibid. Rogers' letter to Washington would seem to precede Sullivan's letter to Washington, so one or the other is likely misdated in the Hough Edition.

15. Zaboly, 436.

16. Schuyler to Washington, January 5, 1776, Washington to Schuyler, January 16, 1776, Hough Edition, 266-267.
17. Rogers to Woodhull, February 19, 1776, Hough Edition, 267-268; Eggleston, 219-220.
18. Zaboly, 438-439.
19. Zaboly asserts that Rogers was in Philadelphia for at least part of this time, Zaboly, 439, but he cites no authority for this proposition and gives no account of what Rogers was doing.
20. Zaboly, 439-440.
21. Zaboly, 440; Eggleston, 223-226.
22. Washington to Congress, June 27, 1776, Hough Edition, 272-273.
23. Ibid.; Zaboly, 440.
24. Washington to Congress, June 27, 1776, ibid.
25. Zaboly, 443-444.
26. Zaboly, 444; Journal of the New Hampshire House, July 2, 1776, Hough Edition, 269-272.

CHAPTER TWENTY-TWO: LOYALIST

1. Zaboly, 445-447.
2. Zaboly, 447-448.
3. Zaboly, 448 and fn. 53.
4. Hutson, James, "Nathan Hale Revisited: A Tory's Account of the Arrest of the First American Spy," *Library of Congress Information Bulletin*, v. 62, no. 7/8 (July/August 2003) (available online on the Library of Congress website).
5. Zaboly, 448.
6. Zaboly, 449-450.
7. Ross, 444-445.
8. Zaboly, 452, 454.
9. Zaboly, 445, 460.
10. Zaboly, 461-462.
11. Zaboly, 463.
12. Zaboly, 252, 254, 463.
13. Zaboly, 463-464.
14. Rogers to Amherst, June 16, 1779, WO 34/115:71.
15. Zaboly, 464-465.
16. Rogers to Amherst, September 11, 1779, WO 34/155:181.
17. Zaboly, 465-466.
18. Zaboly, 466.
19. Rogers to Amherst, May 8, 1780, WO 34/163:129; Zaboly, 463.
20. Zaboly, 466-467.
21. *Rising Above Circumstances*, 58, 61. The book puts the date of Rogers' imprisonment for debt in Halifax as May 1781, but it was in fact May 1780.
22. Zaboly, 467-468.

CHAPTER TWENTY-THREE: THE FINAL YEARS

1. *Rising Above Circumstances*, 185.
2. Nevins, 153.
3. Cuneo, 278.
4. *Treason?*, 101-102.
5. Brumwell, 281.

6. Eggleston, 266.

7. Nevins, 153.

8. Zaboly, 468,469; Cuneo, 278; *Rising Above Circumstances,* 185.

9. *Rising Above Circumstances,* 185; Brumwell, 281; Cuneo, 278; Zaboly, 469.

10. Zaboly, 468-469; *Rising Above Circumstances,* 185; Cuneo, 278.

11. *Rising Above Circumstances,* 185.

12. Zaboly, 474-475.

CONCLUSION

1. Some commentators have credited Rogers with a major victory over the French and Canadian force that blundered into the advancing British and colonial force during the 1758 Ticonderoga campaign and was almost completely wiped out. Zaboly, 224-225; Ross, 196. This was the battle in which Lord Howe was killed. Rogers' own account of the battle, however, makes clear that he and the Rangers were only minor participants, acting under the orders of a superior colonial officer. *Journals,* 119.

2. Zaboly, 255; Gage to Amherst, April 9, 1759, Gage Papers, Letter Books and Account Books, Box 1, January 20-April 27, 1759 (Winter Quarters 1759).

3. Zaboly, 228; Ross, 223. Wolfe arrived in Canada only in early 1758, while Rogers returned from an earlier Louisbourg campaign to the Lake George region in September 1757. Wolfe and Rogers may never have met at all, and certainly had no substantial professional interaction, so this opinion presumably reflects the consensus among British senior officers.

4. Johnson to Gage, January 25, 1766, Johnson Papers, 12:9.

5. *John Stark,* 66.

6. Cuneo, 59.

7. *Journals,* 78 (editor); Cuneo, 59-60.

8. Zaboly, 479-480; Brumwell, 17.

9. Cuneo, 61-62; Ross, 152-154; Zaboly, 191.

10. Zaboly, 199.

11. Brumwell, 135.

12. Gage to Amherst, February 18, 1759, April 9, 1759, Gage Papers, Letter Books and Account Books, Box 1, January 20-April 27, 1759 (Winter Quarters 1759).

13. Amherst to Delancey, June 23, 1759, WO 34/30:52.

14. Amherst to Rogers, December 26, 1762, WO 34/93:272.

15. Brumwell, 135.

16. Brumwell, 17, citing C.P. Stacey, "The British Forces in North America during the Seven Years' War," *Dictionary of Canadian Biography,* III, xxix, and W.J. Eccles, review of Douglas Edward Leach, *Arms for Empire: A Military History of the British Colonies in North America, 1607-1763,* in *William and Mary Quarterly* (3rd Series), XXXVI (1974), 502.

17. Zaboly, 130, 136-137, 143.

18. Ross, 139-140; Zaboly, 174-175.

19. *Journals,* 130; Zaboly, 234-235; Ross, 207-208.

20. Zaboly, 258; *Journals,* 159; Ross, 223.

21. Rogers to Pownall, October 3, 1775, CO 5/1106.

BIBLIOGRAPHY

PRIMARY SOURCES

Armour, David A. *Treason? At Michilimackinac.* Mackinac Island, MI: Mackinac Island State Park Commission, 1967.

Butterfield, L.H., ed. *The Adams Papers: Diary of John Adams.* Cambridge, MA: Harvard University Press, 1962.

Colonial Office Records. British National Archives, Kew Gardens, England.

Gage, Thomas. Thomas Gage Papers. William L. Clements Library, University of Michigan, Ann Arbor, Michigan.

Gordon, James. "Reminiscences of James Gordon." *New York History*, v. 17, no. 4 (October 1936).

Hough, F.B., ed. *Journals of Major Robert Rogers.* Albany, NY: Joel Munsell's Sons, 1888.

Johnson, Sir William. *The Papers of Sir William Johnson.* Albany, NY: University of the State of New York, 1921-1965.

New Hampshire Court Cases and Provincial Court Cases. New Hampshire State Archives, Concord, New Hampshire.

Papers Concerning Robert Rogers. New York Public Library, New York, New York.

Rockingham County Deed Books. New Hampshire State Archives, Concord, New Hampshire.

Rogers, Elizabeth. *Petition of Elizabeth Rogers to the Honorable Council of House of Representatives*, January 26, 1778. Petitions, New Hampshire State Archives, Concord, New Hampshire.

Rogers, Elizabeth. Rogers-Roche Collection. William L. Clements Library, University of Michigan, Ann Arbor, Michigan.

Rogers, Mary Cochrane. Mary Cochrane Rogers Collection. Thompson-Pell Research Center, Ticonderoga, New York.

Rogers, Major Robert. *A Concise Account of North America.* New York: Heritage Books, 2007 (reprint of the 1765 original).

Serjeant Family Letters. History Cambridge, formerly Cambridge Historical Society, Cambridge, Massachusetts.

Todish, Timothy J., ed. *The Annotated and Illustrated Journals of Major Robert Rogers.* Fleischmann's, NY: Purple Mountain Press, 2002.

Treasury Papers. British National Archives, Kew Gardens, England.

War Office Records. British National Archives, Kew Gardens, England.

SECONDARY SOURCES

Berleth, Richard. *Bloody Mohawk: The French and Indian War & American Revolution on New York's Frontier.* Catskill, NY: Black Dome Press, 2009.

Brumwell, Stephen. *White Devil: A True Story of War, Savagery, and Vengeance in Colonial America.* Cambridge, MA: Da Capo Press, 2004.

Carroll, Justin M. *The Merchant John Askin.* East Lansing, MI: Michigan State University Press, 2017.

Clements, William L. "Journal of Major Robert Rogers." *Proceedings of the American Antiquarian Society*, October 1918. Reprinted by the Library of Congress.

Cuneo, John R. *Robert Rogers of the Rangers.* New York: Oxford University Press, 1959. (Reprinted by Richardson & Steirman, 1987.)

Eggleston, Michael A. *One Man's Traitor Is Another's Patriot: George Washington & Robert Rogers.* CreateSpace 2017.

Flexner, James Thomas. *Mohawk Baronet: A Biography of Sir William Johnson.* Syracuse, NY: Syracuse University Press, 1989.

Gara, Donald J. *The Queen's American Rangers.* Yardley, PA: Westholme Publishing, 2015.

Hughes, Ben. *The Siege of Fort Henry: A Year on the Northeastern Frontier.* Yardley, PA: Westholme Publishing, 2011.

Hutson, James. "Nathan Hale Revisited: A Tory's Account of the Arrest of the First American Spy." *Library of Congress Information Bulletin*, v. 62, no. 7/8 (July/August 2003).

Laramie, Michael G. *The Road to Ticonderoga: The Campaign of 1758 in the Champlain Valley.* Yardley, PA: Westholme Publishing, 2023.

Loescher, Burt Garfield. *The History of Rogers Rangers*. 4 volumes. Bowie, MD: Heritage Books, 2001.

Mayer, Joshephine Janes. "Major Robert Rogers, Trader." *New York History*, v. 15, no. 4 (October 1934).

Moore, Howard Parker. *John Stark of Rogers' Rangers*. United Kingdom: Leonaur Press, 2020.

Nevins, Allan, *Introduction to Rogers's "Ponteach."* University of Illinois Master's Thesis, 1913. Reprinted by Forgotten Books, 2018.

O'Toole, Fintan. *White Savage: William Johnson and the Invention of America*. Albany, NY: State University of New York Press, 2005.

Rogers, Robert J. *Rising Above Circumstances: The Rogers Family in Colonial America*. Bedford, Quebec, Canada: Sheltus & Picard, 1998.

Ross, John F. *War on the Run: The Epic Story of Robert Rogers and the Conquest of America*. New York: Bantam Books, 2009.

Todish, Timothy J. *To Distress the French and Their Allies: Rogers' Rangers, 1755-1763*. Catskill, NY: Black Dome Press, 2023.

Widder, Keith R. "The 1767 Maps of Robert Rogers and Jonathan Carver: A Proposal for the Establishment of the Colony of Michilimackinac." *Michigan Historical Review* 30:2 (Fall 2004).

Zaboly, Gary Stephen. *A True Ranger: The Life and Many Wars of Major Robert Rogers*. Garden City Park, NY: Royal Blockhouse, 2004.

ACKNOWLEDGMENTS

M Y GREATEST DEBT in writing this book is to Gary Zaboly, author of the 2004 biography *A True Ranger: The Life and Many Wars of Major Robert Rogers*. Exhaustively researched and documented, meticulously detailed in presentation, *A True Ranger* provides an indispensable chronology of every phase of Rogers' life. I have disagreed with several conclusions Zaboly draws about Rogers, and I have independently reviewed the original source documents relevant to my analysis, but this book would have been much more difficult without Zaboly's assembly and discussion of the basic facts.

Librarians and archivists must be among the nicest people on the planet. Everywhere I went to conduct original research, I was assisted by staff who were uniformly knowledgeable, friendly, patient, and generous with their time, concerned, above all else, to help me find the materials I was looking for. Terese Murphy at the William L. Clements Library at the University of Michigan in Ann Arbor, Gary Gilmore and Ashley Miller at the New Hampshire State Archives in Concord, and Matthew Keagle at the Thompson-Pell Research Center in Ticonderoga, New York, were particularly helpful.

My former law partner John Oller, who has published multiple works of non-fiction of his own, gave me invaluable advice about the process of writing and publishing a book. He kindly agreed to review and comment on my book proposal, and he offered numerous helpful suggestions on issues it had not even occurred to me to think about. I greatly appreciate his assistance.

INDEX

Note: The abbreviation RR is used to
refer to Robert Rogers.

in RR's *Journals*, 137–138

and RR's pay advance for new recruits, 82

RR's proposal to, for attack on St. Francis, 28–29

and RR's reimbursement claim, 105

RR's respect for, 236

Louisbourg campaign, 34–35

Lower Coos, 7, 66–68, 70–71, 72, 139

Loyalists

Clinton's invitation for RR to join, 214

Rogers (James) as member of, 3

RR as member of, 116, 210, 212, 217–219, 220–226

Washington assassination plot of, 214–216

Lyman, Colonel, 49

Mamaroneck, Battle of, 221

Marin, Joseph, 54–56, 61, 91

marriage. *See* Rogers, Betsy Browne

Masonic Lodge, 24, 109

Massachusetts recruitment, 11–12

McCormick (Rogers & Co. partner), 92, 96, 97

McCurdy, John, 9, 10, 12

McDaniel, John. *See* Sullivan, John

McMullen, Andrew, 66, 71

Merrimack, Massachusetts, 4, 8

Michilimackinac

Askin in, 123

Betsy Rogers in, 113–114, 116, 154, 181

command at, 142, 145–146

failure to reach, in December 1760, 93

fur trade policy at, 151–152, 159–160, 162

Gage/Johnson correspondence on, 147–150

reimbursement for expenses at, 198, 201, 202

request for retroactive appointment at, 204

RR's arrest and confinement at, 186–187

RR's behavior at, 235–236

Michilimackinac Indian council, 151, 168–171, 179–180, 196–197

Michilimackinac proposal

discussion of, with Potter, 184

flaws in, 176, 178

goal of, 162, 165, 171

and the Hopkins letter, 157–158

Johnson's reaction to, 175–176

overview of, 173–175

preface to, 178–179

Roberts and, 202

See also Hopkins letter

militia, Canadian, 30, 35, 54

militia, colonial, 14–15, 17, 20–21, 24, 36, 236

Millan (publisher), 140, 206

Missisquoi Bay, 64–65, 84

Mohawk Indians

in Battle of Lake George, 15

in capture of Fort Niagara, 61, 202

Johnson's relations with, 13–14

reinforcements of, at Fort Edward, 36

RR's attempt to buy land from, 97

RR's trade with, 124

scouting reports by, 18, 20

Monckton, Robert, 92

money problems. *See* financial issues

Monongahela, Battle of the, 14, 59

Monro, Colonel, 35–36

Montcalm, Louis-Joseph de, 35–37, 49, 50, 52, 59–60

Montreal

British capture of, 87

and the fur trade, 91–92

and reimbursement for time in, 202

reports of RR's visit to, 211, 212–213

Roberts on RR's behavior in, 130

treason trial in, 189–198

New Burnett Township land, 129

New Hampshire

Congress' decision to return RR to, 217

counterfeiting scheme in, 8–11

funds for troop pay, 21, 103–104, 120, 138

land grants, 129

recruitment in, 11–12

RR's ban from, 116, 226

See also specific locations in

New Jersey Blues regiment, 35, 64, 233